THE
LOST
SAMURAI

JAPANESE MERCENARIES IN
SOUTH EAST ASIA
1593–1688

This book is dedicated to Francis Turnbull:
my grandson and fellow historian.

THE
LOST
SAMURAI

JAPANESE MERCENARIES IN
SOUTH EAST ASIA
1593–1688

STEPHEN TURNBULL

FRONTLINE
BOOKS

THE LOST SAMURAI

First published in Great Britain in 2021 by

Frontline Books
An imprint of
Pen & Sword Books Ltd
Yorkshire - Philadelphia

ISBN 978 1 52675 898 9

Typeset in 10.5 / 13 pt Palatino
by SJmagic DESIGN SERVICES, India.

Printed and bound in the UK by TJ Books Ltd.

Pen & Sword Books Ltd incorporates the Imprints of Aviation, Atlas,
Family History, Fiction, Maritime, Military, Discovery, Politics, History,
Archaeology, Select, Wharncliffe Local History, Wharncliffe True Crime,
Military Classics, Wharncliffe Transport, Leo Cooper, The Praetorian Press,
Remember When, Seaforth Publishing and Frontline Publishing.

For a complete list of Pen & Sword titles please contact

PEN & SWORD BOOKS LTD
47 Church Street, Barnsley, South Yorkshire, S70 2AS, England
E-mail: enquiries@pen-and-sword.co.uk
Website: www.pen-and-sword.co.uk

Or

PEN AND SWORD BOOKS
1950 Lawrence Rd, Havertown, PA 19083, USA
E-mail: Uspen-and-sword@casematepublishers.com
Website: www.penandswordbooks.com

MIX
Paper from
responsible sources
FSC
www.fsc.org   FSC® C013056

Contents

Preface

Conventional understanding has it that almost all the wars fought by Japan prior to modern times were civil wars. The invasion of Korea in 1592 is usually cited as the only exception, but this book will show that some samurai, as Japan's warriors are conventionally known, fought overseas on an individual basis for almost a century. Their operations may have been conducted on a much smaller scale than the Korea expedition, but through these campaigns the samurai of Japan wrote their own little-known chapter in the history of East Asia.

This book about the Japanese mercenaries began life following a suggestion in 2008 from David Karunanithy that I should write about them. I became immediately interested in the topic, and the project took on its initial shape in the form of a lecture I was privileged to present to the World History Association Conference held at Panasastra University, Siem Reap, Cambodia in January 2011. The comments made at the time and the helpful critical reactions to the paper's contents, which were circulated as an unpublished manuscript, directed further research. This I undertook with the kind cooperation of the Siam Society in Bangkok among others. Information for the Japanese side came largely from Nagasaki Prefectural Library, whose staff were more than helpful.

I soon realised that the story had to be told within the wider context of Japan's relations with places like Siam, Cambodia and the Philippines, and the impact placed upon those exchanges by the arrival of European colonial powers. The comparative dimension also developed into a key factor in my research. For example, the little-known story of the Japanese plans to invade the Philippines during the seventeenth century provided fascinating parallels to the Second World War, a topic I was able to place under the scholarly scrutiny of the officers of the US Naval War College in Newport RI, whom I addressed in 2013.

Much useful feedback was also provided following my lectures on the topic in Fort Worth, Kennesaw State University in Atlanta and the University of Boston. I am most grateful for those invitations to speak: nothing concentrates a scholar's mind better than to have his ideas bounced back from a learned audience!

I would also like to thank Michael Charney of SOAS for suggestions regarding south-east Asian warfare, while Jonathan Clements kindly provided me with translations from Chinese for the chapter on Koxinga, and drew my attention to certain rare Japanese sources. In particular I warmly acknowledge the scholarship and friendly cooperation of Adam Clulow, whose outstanding work on the Dutch presence in south-east Asia is key to understanding so much of the background to what follows.

In terms of style, when using quotations from the diaries of servants of the East India Company I have modified the original spelling for the benefit of readers whose first language is not English. Japanese names are given in the conventional style of family name/clan name first, personal name second, e.g. Toyotomi Hideyoshi not Hideyoshi Toyotomi. Note, however, that the personal name is normally used as the identifier in a textual narrative. So, for example, 'Hideyoshi ordered an attack', not 'Toyotomi ordered an attack'.

Chapter 1

The Japanese 'Wild Geese'

In 1639 a Portuguese missionary and traveller called Sebastien Manrique (1590–1669) visited the kingdom of Arakan in Burma, and wrote as follows:

> as the news of my arrival had already spread, the Japanese Christians came with their Captain. They had accompanied the King, in whose guard they were serving. As soon as they had learned where I was they had come to see me. Their Captain, called Leon Donno, came forward and knelt to me.[1]

Manrique's discovery – that certain members of the Japanese Christian community in Arakan were serving as its king's bodyguard – is the sole reference ever made to this particular instance of a phenomenon to be found throughout south-east Asia during the seventeenth century: the Japanese overseas mercenary.

As soldiers fighting for a foreign employer the followers of Leon Donno (the suffix *dono* 殿 was used to indicate a leader in Japanese) fitted the first element of the usual definition of a mercenary, which is that of a paid fighter who comes from outside the society for which he fights, is not part of its regular forces, and is motivated primarily by the desire for private gain. An individual mercenary may also possess a romantic tinge as a soldier of fortune journeying far from home to seek adventure, although sympathy tends to replace admiration for those mercenaries who experience by choice or coercion the life of 'The Wild Geese': the mournful expression first used for the Irish Catholic soldiers who fled to continental Europe after the Treaty of Limerick in 1691.[2] Many of the Japanese Wild Geese we will encounter in the pages which follow shared with their Irish counterparts that same factor of religious

1

exile, because the persecution of Christians prevented them from ever returning to Japan, whose rulers were ignorant of their very existence. Those men were indeed the lost samurai.

The elusive samurai

Throughout my long writing career I have always had a fatal weakness for a snappy title, and this book is no exception. Its lead title *The Lost Samurai* is an obvious play on the name of a well-known film, but together with the subtitle it introduces three expressions which need to be clarified at this stage. They are the use of 'samurai' to identify the Japanese fighting men, 'mercenary' for their conditions of service and 'south-east Asia' for their area of operation.

Beginning with the word 'samurai', it will become obvious from the pages that follow that Japan's overseas mercenaries do not fit into the popular stereotype of a samurai, which is that of a brave aristocratic warrior who knows his way round a tea bowl and never gets his hands dirty in a paddy field. That archetypal samurai was a superlative swordsman, loyal to the point of death, who would leave a battlefield holding a severed head and then reach for a brush and an ink stone to compose a poem about the beauties of the autumn moon. Few of the men who became Japan's overseas mercenaries are likely to have been noble warriors or romantic poets. Many had past experience not of lordly service, but of mercantile activity or piracy, and far from having their loyalty assumed and their service valued by their employers, they were often treated as disposable commodities.

A samurai may, however, be more simply understood by his practice of bearing arms rather than any social status or aesthetic sensibilities. The word therefore becomes a generic term for any pre-modern Japanese fighting man, and there is something to be said for such a pragmatic view, because the official definition of the word samurai changed considerably over the centuries. For much of Japanese history (if contemporary writings are to be believed) everyone with something to defend – a landowner, a villager, a priest or a pirate – was armed to the teeth and was therefore a warrior (*bushi* 武士 or *musha* 武者) of some sort at some time. Yet back in the tenth century AD no fighter of any reputation would have wished to be called a samurai, because that expression still had connotations of menial rather than military service. By the thirteenth century the word had acquired the exclusively military meaning it enjoys today, although to be a samurai still involved the notion of subservience to someone else. The samurai's superiors were leaders called *gokenin* 御家人 ('honourable houseman'), whose élite status derived not only from their skills at warfare, but also from the ownership of the patches of land from which they took their surnames. *Gokenin* expected loyalty from the non-landowning samurai who followed them into battle. Their samurai followers (the European notion of a squire is a good parallel) were able to rise in society because of good service and the rewards that followed.

And rise they did, until the expression 'samurai' acquired an élite connotation that allowed it to encompass the entirety of Japan's military aristocracy. The samurai's upward social mobility found its greatest expression during the Sengoku Period, Japan's 'Age of War', which is conventionally dated from 1467 to 1603. The long conflicts of the Sengoku Period sucked into their whirlpool a huge number of élite mounted warriors, lowly fighting samurai, armed monks, village communities and an intermediate class of *jizamurai* ('local samurai'), who owned some land and were both farmers and fighters at the same time.

The Sengoku Period had begun with a succession dispute within the family of the shogun, the institution that had ruled Japan for almost four centuries by commission from the sacred emperor. When Japan's court and capital dissolved into chaos both land and status were up for grabs, and the local warlords who had once governed provinces only on the shogun's behalf saw the opportunity to create petty kingdoms of their own that were independent of any central control. These daimyo 大名 (literally 'great names') – the *gokenin* of their age but on a much larger scale – controlled samurai armies and fought each other for land and prestige until Japan was reunified in 1591 under a brilliant general called Toyotomi Hideyoshi (1537–98), a samurai who had begun his own military career as a simple foot soldier. In 1588 Hideyoshi set in motion the *katana gari* (sword hunt), a nationwide pacification process whereby local militias, temples and villagers were forcibly disarmed. Hideyoshi's agents confiscated all weapons from anyone except the followers of daimyo, most of whom were by then Hideyoshi's appointees chosen from his most loyal generals. A thorough land survey was already under way and rapid progress was also being made towards the total separation of the warrior and farmer classes, so that the samurai – now much more closely defined as men who fought and did little else – were removed from the land and became stipendiary warriors in the new castle towns.

Unfortunately for Hideyoshi, he did not enjoy his triumph for long, because his dynasty passed away within one generation in favour of the family of Tokugawa Ieyasu (1542–1616), whose descendants were to rule Japan until 1868. Hideyoshi's new class system was retained and flourished, so the precise definition of a samurai now took its final form within the social stratification of the ensuing Tokugawa Period, which would be a time when samurai and farmers were two separate social classes divided by an unbridgeable gulf. Only the samurai now enjoyed the right to wear swords, although subsequent events would show that the attempts at disarming the non-samurai classes had been far from complete. Yet even though a few minor revolts shook the confidence of the Tokugawa, they would ultimately be no more than an insult to the pride of the all-powerful samurai élite.

Because the overseas service of the Japanese mercenaries happened precisely during this time of great social change, it is difficult to use the term 'samurai' for them in anything but the broadest terms, and the situation is further complicated when we examine the mercenaries' sources of supply. The first trawl, which happened while the Sengoku Period was at its height, came from within the ranks of the *wakō* 倭寇, a term that is usually translated as 'Japanese pirates', even though the word does not appear in medieval Japanese texts and derives from the Chinese word *wokou* (literally 'dwarf bandits'), a pejorative term that was meant to indicate a distinctive Japanese origin for the raiders.[3] There are records of the employment by China of Japanese pirates as mercenaries from the fourteenth century onwards, but by the mid-sixteenth century these savage marauding bands had acquired a strong international dimension. Many now had Chinese rather than Japanese leaders, and combined seaborne raids on places like the Philippines with organised crime at home, operating out of small defensible harbours on the Chinese coast as illegal yet highly efficient trading organisations. As Jonathan Clements drily observes, 'It was helpful to blame China's new coastal problems on foreigners', rather than accepting that some of them were Chinese fishermen driven to desperation by their own rulers' policies.[4]

The first instance of China enlisting mercenaries from within the *wakō* ranks came when Hu Weiyong, the Grand Councillor of and rebel against the Ming, requested military assistance for a planned coup in 1378 against the Ming leader Zhu Yuanzhang. A Japanese warrior called Joyō (who is supposed to have been a Zen monk) headed for China with 400 soldiers in the guise of an embassy paying tribute. Their plot involved the assassination of Zhu Yuanzhang using smuggled gunpowder and swords concealed among large candles, but when the coup failed the ringleaders were executed.[5] Recruitment of *wakō*

4

as mercenaries by neighbouring Korea began in about 1400 when the Yi dynasty took some of them into its employment as part of its own programme to curb the pirates. In the words of one commentator, 'some surrendered to Korea, accepted government positions, and received grants of food, clothing and shelter', although the nature of the tasks they performed is not clear.[6] Recruitment of *wakō* by powerful *wakō* leaders might also be classed as mercenary activity. For example, in 1578 a noted Chinese *wakō* leader called Lin Daoqian 林道乾 (known as 'Vintoquián' in the Spanish records) is noted as having used Japanese *wakō* for an unsuccessful attack on Siam.[7]

To the Chinese who suffered their raids *wakō* were simply pirates, but on the outlying islands of southern Japan where many of the gangs were based the distinction between *wakō* and legitimate overseas traders was a very loose one. Some very influential Japanese daimyo of the Sengoku Period even boasted of having *wakō* among their ancestors, and when Hideyoshi began to curtail their piratical activities several erstwhile *wakō* leaders found a legitimate outlet for their skills by acting as his admirals of the fleet for the invasion of Korea in 1592. Not surprisingly, to the Koreans that savage operation was little more than a huge *wakō* raid that was being conducted with official approval.

The Matsuura family of Hirado Island, whose name will appear frequently in the pages which follow, were a very prominent example of a daimyo lineage that could trace its forebears back to a pirate band. The Matsuura were keen to establish links with the European traders who started arriving in the late 1540s, and that trade consisted of much more than cloth and other goods because successive Matsuura daimyo made samurai available as well. In particular, Hirado would become an important source of supply for the Japanese mercenaries who served the Dutch East India Company, which established a base on the island in 1609. For almost a decade the Hirado soldier trade was carried on with the full support of the shogun, and unlike all their other employers the Dutch hired inside Japan itself. The company's 'soldiers from Japan' (*soldaten van Japon*) tended to be unemployed and masterless *rōnin* 浪人 ('men of the waves') who had been thrown on to the scrap heap by the death or disgrace of their former leaders during the wars of the Sengoku Period. They were experienced samurai and were often desperate for employment, and some were also refugees from Christian persecution.

In addition to pirates and local recruits a third source of supply for mercenaries came from the well-established emigrant Japanese communities in places like Siam, Cambodia and the Philippines. Dilao, an enclave of Manila, had an estimated population of about 3,000 Japanese residents in 1600, compared to 1,500 for Siam and 350 for Cambodia, and all of them supplied troops to their indigenous masters from time to time.[8] As contemporary diplomatic correspondence reveals, some of the inhabitants of the *nihonmachi* ('Japan towns') had a reputation for violence and unruliness.[9] That trait may well have been related to a previous life as *wakō*, but it was one that could be put to positive use through military service. Others were no doubt refugee *rōnin* who owed their immigrant status to unemployment or religious persecution, but the majority of the settlers were just merchants with military skills who had migrated on a voluntary basis, so many of the Japanese who served overseas juggled two careers as palace guards and hard-working overseas traders. The best examples of these are the Japanese auxiliaries who served the Siamese kings, whose dual roles as merchants and warriors meant that the closest parallel to them within Japan itself would be the part-time farmer/warriors called *jizamurai* of the Sengoku Period.

With so many variations in origins and conditions of service I therefore suggest that the word 'samurai' is an appropriate title for a Japanese mercenary only when it is used in the colloquial sense of the term as a casual expression that indicates a Japanese warrior of any class and at anytime. This will be the implicit understanding when the word is used in this book.

Samurai as mercenaries

The word 'mercenary' is almost as controversial as the expression 'samurai'. As suggested by the definition cited earlier, the typical mercenary soldier encountered throughout world history is a remunerated temporary outsider, but the precise make-up of any band of mercenaries and the circumstances of their employment varies tremendously across a wide spectrum that includes the mechanism of recruitment and the individual soldier's personal motivation for becoming a mercenary in the first place. That motivation need not be a completely economic one, and Janice Thomson, in her excellent study of the subject, suggests that the financial aspect can easily be excluded from the notion of a mercenary. Examples of service that are not primarily for monetary gain include mercenaries who suffer exile because of religious beliefs. The volunteers who fought in the International Brigades of the Spanish Civil War were paid soldiers motivated instead by political ideals, so Thomson suggests that the concept of a mercenary can be fully understood merely through 'the practices of enlisting in and recruiting for a foreign army'.[10]

6

Thomson's straightforward notion fits the Japanese situation very well. As to the mercenary's personal motivation, in his own study of mercenaries Anthony Mockler has identified in some a peculiar need for fighting, suggesting thereby that the essence of a mercenary is 'a devotion to war for its own sake', involving 'the mercenary's casting aside of a moral attitude to war'. This, says Mockler, 'is often hypocritical, at best uneasy, [and] both fascinates and repels'.[11] Mockler's concept also implies an inherently violent streak in certain people that finds easy expression in mercenary service, so it is not surprising to find many writers throughout history being contemptuous of mercenaries. One early critic was Niccolò Machiavelli (1469–1527), who was scornful of mercenaries and even more condemnatory towards the rulers who employed them. 'Mercenaries and auxiliaries are useless and dangerous', he wrote. 'If a prince bases the defence of his state on mercenaries he will never achieve stability or security. For mercenaries are disunited, thirsty for power, undisciplined, and disloyal'.[12]

Machiavelli, of course, had in mind the notorious Italian mercenary bands of his day who would fight for a particular city one month and for its rivals the next. Their interests lay in prolonging war, not ending it.[13] Matters were not much different a few decades later, and in a brilliant evocation of the cynical use of mercenaries in Europe during the sixteenth century, J.R. Hale notes that a Venetian diarist called them 'Noah's Ark armies', who operated in a world where 'national wars' were fought by 'internationalist, mongrel armies'.[14] Two centuries later German mercenaries were supplied and hired on a vast scale in the so-called 'German Soldier Trade', a system described during one British parliamentary debate of the time as 'the common market for supplying the slaughter houses of human nature'.[15] Such high-minded condemnation did not, however, prevent the same parliament from making use of them, because the state of Hesse-Kassel provided 30,000 troops to Great Britain in an attempt to suppress the American Revolution.[16]

Official disapproval of the mere existence of mercenaries could also go hand-in-hand with the callous way in which they were treated, both by their suppliers and their employers. The rulers of Hesse-Cassell did not appear to be at all concerned that their soldiers might end up on opposing sides during the same conflict, as would happen during the War of the Austrian Succession (1740–48).[17] Mockler also produces some statistics from an earlier age which show how perilous a mercenary's life could be, because they were 'amateurs in treachery when compared with their employers'. Out of eleven noted Italian mercenary captains

7

named by Mockler three were beheaded, four were strangled, two were poisoned, one was murdered by other means and one was executed, and all by their own employers, not their enemies![18]

The Japanese 'Wild Geese' shared some of these stereotypes, but not all of them. For example, Japanese mercenaries did indeed fight for opposing sides, but never at the same time. Everything depended upon who their hirers were and in which theatre of operations the mercenaries were deployed. It is also important to appreciate that the use of the Japanese for military service in south-east Asia was carried out in places where mercenary use was already well established and completely acceptable. The local rulers had long sought troops from a wide range of nationalities. Some of those recruits came from Europe, perhaps bringing with them a welcome knowledge of up-to-date firearms technology; others were adventurers seeking quick fortunes or looking for an escape from justice. A few unfortunate mercenaries had been press-ganged into service after they had been captured from ships or following the fall of coastal towns, although for those who had served in the cramped and often deadly confines of ships the comparative freedom of military service on land might have seemed like waking from a nightmare.

For examples of the common use of mercenaries in East Asia during the sixteenth century we may note the King of Sunda (located on the west of Java) who had a personal bodyguard of forty Portuguese mercenaries, while his neighbour the ruler of Demak (on the north coast of Java) had serving under him a mixed bag of adventurers including Acehnese, Dutch, Turkish and Malabari fighters. There appears to have been no shortage of supply of such troops. Indeed, there was often something of a competition for employment, with rival contingents denouncing the competence of others to gain personal advantage. In Arakan the king's Muslim mercenaries sowed seeds of doubt in the royal mind over the capabilities of his Portuguese mercenaries.[19]

The mercenaries' 'outsider' status, which reduced the risk of a palace coup, was no doubt an appealing factor to any monarch, but it also encouraged the hired soldiers to seek more than a meagre court stipend for their services. This boldness in negotiating terms no doubt derived from an absence of the cultural restraints that would have intimidated someone from the indigenous population making such demands. It was however a characteristic shared by all mercenaries and was coupled with no little pride. For example, the Dutch mercenaries who served the rulers of Demak boasted that, 'We are… much feared here and there is no Javanese who would be so brave as to dare arouse our anger.

They say we are not men but devils'.[20] On occasions this self-confidence encouraged some mercenaries to set to one side all accepted notions of deference and loyalty. In 1686 for example, mercenaries in Makassar attempted a coup against their employer.[21]

The Japanese who found long-lasting and honourable service with the king of Siam, for example, would therefore have rubbed shoulders with men from many different origins. In 1534 King Chairacha of Siam had hired 120 Portuguese soldiers, and men from the Netherlands would have been found in service there during the seventeenth century. In between these two dates the rulers of Siam and Cambodia courted mercenary service from the Japanese diaspora from the *nihonmachi* in the capital Ayutthaya with an enthusiasm that would later be paralleled by the European colonial powers, although the mercenaries' respective roles developed in very distinct ways. The Spanish in the Philippines employed local Japanese on a temporary basis for specific campaigns, while the Dutch sought troops from Japan itself on longer-term contracts. In contrast, the south-east Asian kings tended to use them in a manner somewhere between the two; so those who served the kings of Siam were always able to switch back easily to their other lives as merchants and traders.

Parallel to the above distinction between European and Asian employers in the mercenaries' modes of employment, we may also discern a profound difference in attitude towards them, because the south-east Asian monarchs tended to place long-lasting trust in their Japanese troops, while the Europeans showed little expectation of continuing loyalty. This may have been because mercenaries in contemporary Europe were notoriously fickle, but their experience of the Japanese variety would have given them no grounds for thinking that they would behave any differently, and words like 'rashness' and 'indiscipline' crop up time and again in descriptions of them. Worse still, the European commanders who had charge of Japanese mercenaries often had additional suspicions that these reckless warriors might even rise up against their masters, and the fact that the Wild Geese were indeed very difficult to control in certain situations would have added to the worries about revolt. In short, the Europeans admired the mercenaries but also feared them, so that in every case a shift in attitude may be discerned from an initial enthusiasm to great suspicion that the Japanese might one day turn against them, either from within the expatriate communities or even by invasion from Japan with the help of a local fifth column of experienced warriors. This led to a progressively negative attitude of mistrust that was largely absent from the south-east Asian kingdoms.

9

East Asia and European trade

Last on our list of inappropriate titles, 'south-east Asia' is clearly an inadequate expression to define an area of the world encompassing Japan, China, Taiwan, the Philippines, Burma, Cambodia, Siam, the Spice Islands of the Indonesian archipelago and even (in one obscure case) India. It is therefore used here merely as a convenient shorthand for an extensive theatre of operations in a tumultuous century when widely separated cultures met for the first time. To a large extent this meeting of cultures was a result of a worldwide development of trade, although one particularly decisive stimulus came about from the curtailment of trade, not its expansion. This was the series of attempts by the Ming dynasty of China to control overseas commerce. The trigger had been the early *wakō* raids, hence the first *haijin* (sea ban) of 1341, a policy that would be continued until 1567, although the ultimate result would be not to control piracy, but to shift much of China's international trade into the sphere of illegality represented by the pirate bases run by warlords of the sea. At the same time the Chinese responded to genuinely Japanese sea raids by the establishment of coastal defence works and the recruitment of former *wakō* to help with the building of them, just as they had done during the fourteenth century.[22] One example of a role in China for former *wakō* clearly identifiable as that of the mercenary soldier is recorded for 1574, when a Japanese ship was suddenly fired upon by Chinese coastguards off Fujian Province. To the crew's astonishment they found that the Chinese guards were in fact Japanese.[23]

Into this turbulent mix sailed the fleets of Europe, led by the great ships of Portugal and Spain and followed a few decades later by the Dutch and the English. At first trade went hand-in-hand with Christian missionary work, a two-pronged incursion that Ronald Toby calls the 'Xavierian moment, the mid-sixteenth century era of Iberian irruption into East Asia'.[24] Toby's expression of course evokes the name of the Church's most successful evangelist: St Francis Xavier (1506–52), the tireless 'Apostle to the Indies'. Xavier was a member of the missionary order called the Society of Jesus, commonly known as the Jesuits. His travels led him to many of the places mentioned in this book including Japan itself, which Xavier visited as its first Christian missionary in 1549.

The most cursory glance at European missionary work in East Asia reveals how much its spread depended upon successful trade links and how those links had to be backed up by the creation of overseas bases defended by military force. This often imperialistic process was regarded by an earlier generation of historians as being virtually unstoppable, the inevitable product of the triumph of superior Western technology in the form of firearms and ocean-going sailing ships. If one confines the study of Iberian expansion to the Spanish conquest of the Americas and the rapid elimination of Inca and Aztec power by a handful of conquistadors, the process does indeed look overwhelming, but the situation in Asia would be very different.[25] The Asian mode of contact and development was not that of the arrival of a steely-eyed European adventurer raising his flag on a beach and conducting an *ad hoc* ceremony of possession on behalf of his own monarch. The East Asian rulers were already used to dealing with foreigners, so diplomacy became the norm, even if the situation sometimes deteriorated into violence. The western dominance that had carried everything with it in the Americas could therefore be controlled in East Asia to some extent, and even when international diplomatic relations were not sufficiently developed to provide a cordial partnership, military conflict could be contained and European power could be counterbalanced.[26] As Adam Clulow puts it so well, the East Asian pattern was one of adjustment and accommodation, with the Europeans making concessions to Asian rulers that would have been undreamed of in South America.[27]

The first European arrivals in the general area covered by this book were the Portuguese, who captured Malacca in 1511 and made it their point of entry for south-east Asia and the valuable trade in spices. Further voyages took them as far as Japan when, in a famous incident in 1543, Portuguese traders arrived on the island of Tanegashima as a result of a shipwreck, an accident that both nations were to turn to their mutual advantage. The Portuguese quickly realised that the absence of official trading links between Japan and China gave them the opportunity to act as reliable middlemen for a lucrative clandestine trade that consisted above all else in the exchange of Chinese silk for Japanese silver. Smuggling of the products had gone on for decades in the face of the Ming ban, but sometime around the year 1550 the Portuguese reached an understanding with the Chinese for an annual fair for the legitimate exchange of silk. This was followed within a few years by the founding of Macao (modern Macau) as the Chinese end of what soon became a thriving trade route operated by Portugal's self-styled honest brokers.[28]

The annual Portuguese *naó*, the large ship called a carrack in English and Dutch sources, would leave Macao laden with silk to catch the southwestern monsoon for the voyage to Japan, returning with huge quantities of silver. The profits derived from the system were among the largest the Portuguese ever realised in Asia, and whoever was chosen as Captain-Major for the voyage would be set up for life. Similarly, the benefits accrued to the rulers of Japan encouraged them to tolerate the foreigners' presence and their alien religion.[29]

For the Portuguese, economic success in the venture depended upon obtaining a friendly Japanese harbour in which to disembark and trade, a factor for which the disunited state of Japan during the Sengoku Period provided certain advantages. The daimyo of Kyushu (Japan's southern main island), whose ports were the nearest stopping places for the annual ship, vied with one another for the privilege of welcoming it into their domains, although factors other than trade greatly influenced the choice of host. Conflict between the daimyo – a fact of life everywhere in the Sengoku Period – together with sporadic persecution of Christians and the current attitude of the local ruler towards foreigners all played their part in the delicate selection process. In some instances the Portuguese became directly involved in inter-daimyo rivalry; otherwise careful diplomacy and the creation of alliances, especially with those daimyo who had converted to Christianity, became the hallmark of the Portuguese presence in Japan. As a result, over the period of a few decades the annual ship docked at different ports depending upon the welcome it would receive or the dangers it might face from local warfare.

Until the 1590s Portugal's Spanish rivals operated in a totally different sphere of influence, an arrangement that had been formalised by the Pope in 1494 through the Treaty of Tordesillas which had divided the world between them. Having established a firm foothold in the Americas the Spanish approached East Asia from the opposite direction to the Portuguese. They were eager to establish a presence in the general area of south-east Asia, but because the fabled and much-coveted Spice Islands had already fallen under Portuguese control, the Spanish settled for the Philippines as an alternative, arriving on the islands in 1564 as a result of an expedition from the Americas under Miguel López de Legazpi. They made Manila their headquarters in 1570, although the intricate and diverse nature of the archipelago meant that the Spanish were far from being conquistadors in spite of fighting numerous battles against native uprisings and incursive *wakō*. To the peaceful Chinese and Japanese traders who also frequented the islands the Philippines would never be a Spanish colony. Instead the archipelago was neutral territory where different cultures could meet and trade in an environment free from the Ming prohibitions, a situation Birgit Tremml-Werner calls 'Asian co-colonialism'.[30]

Yet even if East Asia was no pushover compared to the Americas, violence and warfare were always available to back up the careful diplomacy that was needed to arrange treaties and establish trading posts. Unlike the diplomacy, violence was usually manifested at a local level. To give but one example among many, the first Dutch expedition to south-east Asia, which arrived in the port of Bantam (modern Banten) on the island of Java in 1596, was initially welcomed by local officials eager to trade with the newcomers, but when a dispute occurred over the supply of goods relations rapidly deteriorated. Having, as the Dutch put it, 'fallen into disgrace with the inhabitants', the leaders of the expedition decided to bombard the harbour in order to force the ruler to accept their terms of trade. The violence then escalated, and 'we discredited ourselves even further when we captured and imprisoned some inhabitants and even arrogantly attacked the town, blockading the harbour and firing some ordnance, defying the town with as much spitefulness and rude behaviour as we could muster'.[31]

English merchants arriving in the Indian Ocean in the early seventeenth century were equally prepared to use violence. Indeed, some of their earliest ventures were little more than thinly disguised pirate expeditions designed to seize as much plunder as possible under the cover of legitimate trade. In 1612 Henry Middleton of the East India Company explained his own plans very clearly. Because 'they would not deal with us at their own doors we, having come so far with commodities fitting their country... I thought we should do ourselves some right... to cause them to barter with us'.[32] His ships then attacked fifteen merchant vessels in just two weeks and only ceased the assault when Middleton reported jubilantly that he had captured as many ships as he knew what to do with.[33]

For a period of almost a century this heady mix of warfare, trade, piracy and evangelism saw colonial outposts being established, defended and lost throughout East Asia, with merchants, immigrants and refugees travelling from Japan to the islands and kingdoms of south-east Asia to become traders and mercenaries. During this time war was never long absent within Japan or China, while in their own heavily defended outposts the Spanish and Portuguese would become locked in a desperate struggle with heretical foes when the area was contested by the Dutch and the English from the early seventeenth century onwards.[34] This was the turbulent world that took samurai exiles and adventurers far from their homes to become the Japanese Wild Geese.

Notes

1. Manrique, Sebastien *Travels of Fray Sebastien Manrique Vol. 1: Arakan* The Hakluyt Society, 2nd Series No. LIX (1926) pp. 128-129.
2. Murphy, James H. 'The Wild Geese' *The Irish Review* 16, (1994), p. 23. The use of the expression 'Wild Geese' to denote mercenaries was given wider publicity in 1978 as the title of a film about a group of modern mercenaries serving in Africa.
3. Shapinsky, Peter D. *Lords of the Sea: Pirates, Violence and Commerce in Late Medieval Japan* (Ann Arbor: University of Michigan, 2014), p. 9.
4. Clements, Jonathan *A Brief History of China* (Tokyo, Tuttle, 2019), p. 197.
5. Wang Yong 'Realistic and Fantastic Images of "Dwarf Pirates": The Evolution of Ming Dynasty Perceptions of the Japanese' in Fogel, Joshua A (ed.) Sagacious Monks and Bloodthirsty Warriors: Chinese views of Japan in the Ming-Qing period (New York 2002) pp. 21 & 27.
6. Tanaka, Takeo 'Japan's Relations with Overseas Countries' in Hall, John Whitney and Toyoda, Takeshi (eds.) *Japan in the Muromachi Age* (Berkeley, 1977) p. 162.
7. González de Mendoza, Juan *The history of the great and mighty kingdom of China and the situation thereof* Vol. 2 Translated by Parke, Robert (1588), edited by Staunton, Sir George Thomas (London, Hakluyt Society 1853-54), p. 7; Wolters, O.W. 'Ayudhyā and the Rearward Part of the World' *The Journal of the Royal Asiatic Society of Great Britain and Ireland* No. 3/4 (Oct., 1968), p. 171. For Lin Daoqian's later career (in which Japanese are not specifically mentioned) see Igawa, Kenji 'At the Crossroads: Limahon and wakō in Sixteenth Century Philippines' in Anthony, Robert J. (Ed.) *Elusive Pirates, Pervasive Smugglers: Violence and Clandestine Trade in the Greater China Seas* (Hong Kong, Hong Kong University Press, 2010), p. 80.
8. Clulow, Adam 'Like Lambs in Japan and Devils outside Their Land: Diplomacy, Violence and Japanese Merchants in south-east Asia' *Journal of World History* 24, 2 (2013), p. 343.
9. Clulow, Adam 'Like Lambs in Japan and Devils outside Their Land: Diplomacy, Violence and Japanese Merchants in south-east Asia' *Journal of World History* 24, 2 (2013), pp. 335-358.
10. Thomson, Janice *Mercenaries, Pirates, and Sovereigns: State Building and Extraterritorial Violence in Early Modern Europe* (Princeton University Press, 1996), pp. 26-27.

11. Mockler, Anthony *Mercenaries* (London: Macdonald 1970) p. 21.

12. Macchiavelli, Niccolò *The Prince* (Translated with an introduction by George Bull) (London: Penguin Books, 1961), p. 77.

13. Dodenhoff, George H. 'A Historical Perspective of Mercenaries' *Naval War College Review* 21, 7 (1969), p. 93.

14. Hale, J.R. *War and Society in Renaissance Europe 1450-1620* (London: Fontana 1985), p. 70.

15. Wilson, Peter H. 'The German 'Soldier Trade' of the Seventeenth and Eighteenth Centuries: A Reassessment' *The International History Review* 18, 4 (1996), p. 764.

16. Wilson, Peter H. 'The German 'Soldier Trade' of the Seventeenth and Eighteenth Centuries: A Reassessment' *The International History Review* 18, 4 (1996), p. 759.

17. Wilson, Peter H. 'The German 'Soldier Trade' of the Seventeenth and Eighteenth Centuries: A Reassessment' *The International History Review* 18, 4 (1996), p. 759.

18. Mockler, Anthony *Mercenaries* (London: Macdonald 1970) pp. 48-49.

19. Charney, Michael *south-east Asian Warfare, 1300-1900* (Leiden, 2004), pp. 224-227.

20. Charney, Michael *south-east Asian Warfare, 1300-1900* (Leiden, 2004), p. 225.

21. Charney, Michael *south-east Asian Warfare, 1300-1900* (Leiden, 2004), pp. 225-226

22. Takegoshi, Yosaburo *The Story of the Wako: Japanese Pioneers in the Southern Regions* (translated by Hideo Watanabe) (Tokyo, 1940), p. 103.

23. Takegoshi, Yosaburo *The Story of the Wako: Japanese Pioneers in the Southern Regions* (translated by Hideo Watanabe) (Tokyo, 1940), pp. 103-104.

24. Toby, Ronald P. 'The "Indianness" of Iberia and Changing Japanese Iconographies of Other' in Schwartz, Stuart B. (ed.) *Implicit Understandings: Observing, Reporting and Reflecting on the Encounters between Europeans and Other Peoples in the Early Modern Era* (Cambridge: Cambridge University Press, 1995), p. 341.

25. Marshall, P.J. 'Western Arms in Maritime Asia in the Early Phases of Expansion' *Modern Asian Studies* 14. 1 (1989), pp. 13-28.

26. Subrahmanyam, Sanjay. *The Political Economy of Commerce: Southern India, 1500-1650.* (New York: Oxford University Press, 2011), p. 297.

27. Clulow, Adam. *The Company and the Shogun: the Dutch encounter with Tokugawa Japan* (New York: Columbia University Press, 2014).

28. Boxer, C.R. *Fidalgos in the Far East 1550-1770* (Hong Kong: Oxford University Press, 1968). p.3.
29. Cooper, Michael 'The Mechanics of the Macao-Nagasaki Silk Trade' *Monumenta Nipponica* Vol. 27, 4, pp. 423-433.
30. Tremml-Werner, Birgit 'Friend or Foe? Intercultural Diplomacy between Momoyama Japan and the Spanish Philippines in the 1590s' in Andrade, Tonio (Ed.) *Sea Rovers, Silver, and Samurai: Maritime East Asia in Global History, 1550-1700* (Honolulu: University of Hawai'i Press, 2016), p. 69.
31. Clulow, Adam 'Like Lambs in Japan and Devils outside Their Land: Diplomacy, Violence and Japanese Merchants in south-east Asia' *Journal of World History* 24, 2 (2013), p. 344.
32. Samuel Purchas, *Hakluytus posthumus, or, Purchas his Pilgrimes: contayning a history of the world in sea voyages and lande travells by Englishmen and others* (Glasgow, J. MacLehose and Sons, 1905-7), 1: 272.
33. Jourdain, John, *Journal of John Jourdain, 1608-17: His Experiences in Arabia, India and the Malay Archipelago* (Cambridge: Printed for the Hakluyt Society, 1905), p. 210.
34. Boxer, C.R. 'Portuguese and Spanish Projects for the Conquest of south-east Asia 1580-1600' *Journal of Asian History* III (1969), p. 119.

Chapter 2

'The Spaniards of Asia': imaging the Japanese warrior

Japanese warriors were first hired as mercenaries by the European colonial powers during the last quarter of the sixteenth century, but long before that decision was made an image had been growing in Western minds of their character, fighting abilities and weaponry.[1] The picture thereby constructed would have a profound influence on the mercenaries' first major employers: the Spanish in the Philippines, whose impression of the Japanese was almost always highly positive, even though much of it derived from sorry experiences at the hands of *wakō* raiders. Later observations of friendly Japanese fighting as loyal troops on the Spaniards' behalf did nothing but enhance the initial image of ferocity and efficiency, and in the years to come the notion of the Japanese warrior as a breed apart would be enriched still further by accounts of them serving other European and south-east Asian masters.

This long process of image creation began in around 1561 and culminated in 1653 in what was (from its author's point of view at least) the greatest compliment that could ever be paid to the Japanese people. It consisted of a brief remark in the widely read novel *El criticón* by the Spanish Jesuit Baltasar Gracián (1601–58). Gracián had never visited Japan and had almost certainly never met a Japanese person, but great learning achieved at second hand through Jesuit circles led him to describe the Japanese as '*los españoles del Asia*' ('the Spaniards of Asia').[2] Gracián's 'learned remark', as it was dubbed in 1725 by fellow admirer Gaspar de San Agustin,[3] soon acquired a life of its own, and together with numerous earlier comments, such as those made in 1580 by the Jesuit Alessandro Valignano that the Japanese were 'white, courteous and highly civilised', had a considerable influence on public

17

opinion in the Spanish colonies.[4] Valignano's early statement is also typical of an overall trend whereby most of the positive comments about the Japanese would be juxtaposed in jarring contrast to negative ones about 'Indians' or 'natives', whose very humanity was sometimes up for discussion.

These authors were of course describing what they saw as the personal qualities of the Japanese people, not their fighting abilities, but opinions on the latter had always tended towards a similarly singular and admiring tone, and over the course of about fifty years descriptions would be made of such matters as the Japanese warriors' readiness to undertake death-defying charges and their need to preserve their sense of honour by suicide or revenge. There are also several mentions of their weapons, including the famous Japanese sword, and a frequent acknowledgement of their bravery. To give one example among many, in the account noted above Valignano goes on to say that the Japanese are 'the most warlike and bellicose race yet discovered on the earth… They think nothing more of killing a man than they do an animal… many men kill themselves by cutting their intestines with a dagger'.[5]

The writers quoted above would have been wholly unaware of earlier references to Japanese fighting abilities that had followed a very similar line. These dated from the thirteenth and fourteenth centuries and came from Chinese and Korean writers whose impressions of Japan veered between admiration for its scholars and horror at the depredations of the *wakō*. Reference was made earlier to the international make-up of the *wakō* gangs, and whereas this is undeniably true, there are enough descriptions of genuinely Japanese *wakō* in action for a specifically Japanese warrior image to have emerged. Good examples come from the brush of Zheng Sixiao (1241–1318), who wrote that they were 'fierce and do not fear death… A group of ten Japanese soldiers will fight, even if it is against an enemy unit of one hundred. They will forfeit their lives in battle, even if they are unable to win'. In a chilling metaphor Huang Zhencheng (1287–1362) described the sword-wielding Japanese as 'a multitude of dancing butcher knives that randomly appear and disappear and as monsters that appear to be flying when they walk'.[6]

The first European description of Japanese warriors in action is much less eloquent in tone. It concerns a mundane yet deadly street brawl on the island of Hirado in 1561 between Portuguese traders and followers of the local daimyo Matsuura Takanobu I 松浦 隆信 (1529–99), the current lord of the family noted above who had a long-standing *wakō* tradition. The Hirado dispute, known in Japan simply as the Miyanomae jiken 宮ノ前事件 ('the incident in front of the shrine') arose

18

over the price of a piece of cloth and ended with the death of fourteen Portuguese including the current Captain-Major Fernão de Sousa.[7] The Jesuit missionary and historian Luis Fróis noted that Matsuura Takanobu treated the affair as a trifling incident and failed to punish the offenders.[8] That was the limit of Fróis's opinion on Japanese attitudes to violence, although John Huyghen van Linschoten, commenting on the affair thirty years later as part of his description of Hirado, mentioned that three decades earlier 'in this haven fourteen Portugales were slain', and put it down to their 'pride and presumptuousness' in the face of 'a stubborn and obstinate people'.[9]

Matsuura Takanobu's sporadic antagonism towards his Portuguese visitors accounts for the next recorded instance of international conflict between Europe and Japan, because the Hirado incident persuaded the Portuguese traders to seek an alternative port for the annual *naó* within the domain of a much more promising host: the sympathetic Christian convert and therefore *'kirishitan daimyo'* (Christian lord) Ōmura Sumitada 大村純忠 (1533–87). Sumitada first welcomed the Portuguese to his harbour of Yokoseura, only for the place to be burned down in an attack by his rivals in 1563, so in 1565 he put forward the port of Fukuda as an alternative.[10] At this point Matsuura Takanobu seems to have realised what he was missing now that Hirado was no longer the destination for the richly laden vessel, so he sent a fleet of eighty ships to attack the *naó* in good old *wakō* style as it lay at anchor in Fukuda Bay.[11] In command of the Portuguese fleet was that year's Captain-Major João Pereira. The Japanese opened fire with harquebuses and a bullet struck Pereira on his helmet. Fortunately for him the iron helmet proved to be bulletproof, but when he was carried below to recuperate the Japanese forced their way on board his ship, 'fighting audaciously', as Fróis describes it. They broke into Pereira's cabin and would have killed him had he not been rescued by the crew, who overcame the raiders and drove them overboard into the sea.[12]

The Japanese attack on Fukuda Bay – the first armed encounter in history between Europeans and organised Japanese warriors – no doubt made an impression on the Portuguese, although Fróis's brief mention of the Japanese showing 'audacity' is merely a footnote to his telling of the story. More importantly, even though the Japanese musketeers had been skilled enough to put a bullet into the captain's helmet, the Portuguese turned their interpretation of the action on its head. The Battle of Fukuda Bay was therefore hailed as proof of Western military superiority, particularly through the Europeans' own deployment of firearms at close range. The Portuguese merchants thus happily convinced themselves that Fukuda Bay had shown the extent to which their mercantile and evangelistic cause was backed up by a military capacity that had to be reckoned with, and this point would be used in the future as a propaganda tool on their behalf. So firmly would this be believed that the Portuguese appreciation of Japanese military prowess developed but little in spite of a number of similar attacks over the following decades.

The next written contributions to the Japanese warrior image were made by Spanish observers on the Philippines. Their appreciation of Japanese fighting skills would be much more realistic, although the first Spanish description of the Japanese settlers on the islands notes only their peaceful side. On 23 July 1567, in a letter to King Philip II, Miguel López de Legazpi, his 'very humble and faithful servant who kisses your hands and feet', writes that Chinese and Japanese come to trade on the larger islands, bringing with them 'silks, woollens, bells, porcelains, perfumes, iron, tin, coloured cotton cloths, and other small wares'.[13] The idea that the friendly Japanese could be in any way dangerous is never hinted at until 1573 when an officer called Diego de Artieda makes what is probably the first reference in Spanish to military matters concerning Japan. Artieda had never visited 'Xipon', but he had heard about the quality of Japanese swords, 'which they call leques (*tachi*). These have single or double hilts, are very sharp, and are curved like Turkish cutlasses. On the side without any edge, they are about half as thick as the finger, but the edge is very sharp'.[14]

As with so many other observations that would follow over the next twenty years, Artieda was trying to interpret information about a remote population 'through lenses of culturally constructed iconographies'.[15] For this reason his description and those that followed tended to be based on comparisons with familiar European examples, although it would be little more than a year before Artieda and his fellow colonists experienced the sharp edges of Japanese swords for themselves. In 1574 and again in 1582 the Spanish fought against marauding bands of *wakō*, and it is in the accounts of these two major raids that we find the earliest detailed descriptions in any European language of Japanese weapons and tactics.

The first *wakō* attack on the Philippines occurred on St Andrew's Day (30 November) 1574, when the raiders were driven off after two fierce assaults on Manila in a Spanish victory that was still being celebrated up to fifty years later.[16] The invaders' leader was a famous Chinese *wakō* called Lin Feng 林鳳 (known as Limahon or Limahong in European accounts), whose second-in-command was a Japanese referred to as

Sioco, the first Japanese warrior to be named in the Spanish sources.[17] Lin Feng was an ambitious *wakō* leader, whose grandiose motive was assumed to be to the seizure of the Philippines as a base for his piratical activities. According to Juan González de Mendoza's account, written only ten years after the event, 'This rover Limahon determining to go and to take the Ilands Philippinas, and to make himself lord and king over them all, but first to kill the Spaniards, which he thought easily to be done, for that there was so few'.[18]

A detailed (and perhaps exaggerated) account of the operation was produced in 1698 by Gaspar de San Agustin in his *Conquistas de las Islas Philipinas*, which tells how on 29 November 1574 Lin Feng arrived off Corregidor Island at the entrance to Manila Bay with a fleet of 72 ships and 2,000 warriors armed with personal weapons and artillery. They also had with them 3,500 women, most of whom had probably been captured in raids and forced into slavery. Lin Feng entrusted Sioco with the following day's surprise assault, but Sioco's approach was observed by the Spanish. A warning was sent to the local commander Martín de Goiti, who dismissed the news as a false alarm until Sioco's men actually attacked his headquarters. Thinking the raid was being conducted only by local natives, Goiti's wife screamed at them to go away. Her remarks were translated for the benefit of Sioco, who took great offence and destroyed Goiti's house and killed him. Goiti's ears and nose were cut off to be presented to Lin Feng as a samurai-style trophy; his wife was badly injured but somehow survived. The Spanish then brought up two artillery pieces and opened up their ranks in the shape of a half-moon to envelop Sioco's men and bombard them. At this other Spanish troops stationed nearby arrived, but instead of attacking them Sioco prudently withdrew to plan a second assault. The miraculous deliverance of the Spanish was ascribed to the 'prayers and tears' of the religious community.[19]

Wishing to avoid any loss of face at his reversal, Sioco ordered his men to bury their dead and commanded the wounded to stay hidden from sight. His master Lin Feng was nevertheless satisfied that Sioco's move had been a prudent tactical withdrawal, and was so confident of victory that he ordered his army to take a three-day rest. It was a fatal mistake, because the delay gave the Spanish time to regroup their forces to withstand an attack on Manila itself, where trenches were dug and artillery positions established. Reinforcements also arrived.

The following morning Lin Feng made Sioco swear that he would either die in battle or sleep that night in the house of the governor of the Philippines.[20] Sioco then took charge of a dawn attack at the head of 1,500 men, but the determined and well-prepared Spanish lured the *wakō* into Manila to ambush them there. Sioco led the charge, but when they converged on the main street the Spaniards opened fire on them with muskets and cannon. The Japanese rushed at the Spanish trenches, hurling fire bombs, but a Spanish counter-attack followed during which Sioco appears to have been killed.[21] San Agustin's narrative is light on other detail, but a parallel description of the action by Francisco de Sande describes the armour and weapons of the *wakō*, and we may presume that the account refers to Sioco's Japanese contingent because it mentions them making the first attack:

> in the boats there were seven hundred men, among whom were a few arquebusiers, and many pikemen, besides men armed with battle axes. They were clad in corselets which are coats lined with exceedingly thick cotton. They had durable bamboo hats, which served as helmets; they carried cutlasses, and several daggers in their belts; and all were barefoot. Their manner of warfare or of fighting, was to form a squadron composed of men with battle axes, among whom were placed some arquebusiers, a few of the latter going ahead as skirmishers. One of every ten men carried a banner, fastened to his shoulders and reaching two palms above his head. There were other and larger banners also, so that it appeared as if some important personage was coming who served in the capacity of master-of-camp. These, then, were the people who made the first attack.[22]

The above description tallies very well with contemporary Japanese accounts of the armour and weapons that would have been employed by lower-ranking samurai of the time. The banners fastened to the shoulders are the *sashimono*, the small flags worn on the back of a suit of armour, while the word 'cutlasses' identifies the curved-bladed Japanese sword called a *katana*. There is however one error of translation. The original Spanish expression translated into English by Blair and Robertson as 'battle axes' is *armas enastadas*, which literally means 'weapons fastened to handles'. As battle axes are almost unknown in the Japanese context and there are Spanish references elsewhere to the use of 'lances' – i.e. straight-bladed pole arms or *yari* – we must conclude that these weapons are curved-bladed halberds, either the broad-bladed Chinese variety or more likely the Japanese glaive or *naginata*.

A further type of edged weapon is noted later by San Agustin in his account of the second *wakō* raid described below, because he contrasts certain large Japanese swords to their smaller 'scimitars of sharp steel' and describes the former as being 'handled with both hands, like broadswords, against which there was no weapon to match'.[23] They would have been the extra-long Japanese swords called *nodachi* or perhaps *nagamaki*, a sword that had a blade and handle of equal length. The fire bombs are an interesting addition, and could have been the large grenades called *hōrokubiya*, which consisted of two iron hemispheres fastened tightly together, filled with gunpowder, and wrapped in a layer of paper. They were hurled on the end of a rope sling and were primarily anti-personnel weapons. Lighter versions intended for incendiary purposes were made from layers of paper rather than iron and were more portable.

Japanese armour would be further noted in a letter of 16 June 1582 to the King of Spain from the Governor of the Philippines, Gonzalo Ronquillo de Peñialosa. He begins by referring to the Japanese as 'the most warlike people in this part of the world', and adds that they 'have artillery and many arquebuses and lances. They use defensive armour for the body, made of iron, which they have owing to the subtlety of the Portuguese, who have displayed that trait to the injury of their own souls'.[24] Peñialosa's comment is an obvious expression of disgust at his Iberian rivals, who had clearly been supplying the Japanese with bulletproof European breastplates.

To conclude this descriptive section we may note a later reference to Japanese weapons from 1589 when a cache of arms including more than 500 arquebuses, many swords and some 'battle axes' (*sic*) was discovered on board a Japanese ship in Manila. The find caused some concern because of unrest among the native inhabitants of the Philippines, but when it was explained that the weapons were intended for Siam the crew were released and the ship continued its voyage.[25]

Japanese battle tactics

Further important information relating to weapon deployment and Japanese battle tactics may be gleaned from the accounts by Gaspar de San Agustin and others of a second engagement between a named Japanese *wakō* leader and the Spanish that occurred in 1582. This well-recorded operation took place in Cagayan Province (modern Vigan City) and was conducted by a *wakō* leader called Taifusa (Tayfusa or Tay Zufu), whose romanised name may derive from the suffix *tayū* or *daibu* 大夫 that was used in official Japanese titles.[26] The life and career of Taifusa, who is described in a strangely romantic fashion by

Gregorio Zaide as 'an audacious sea-hawk and swashbuckling pirate',[27] is sometimes conflated with that of a merchant from Sakai called Naya Sukezaemon 納屋助左衛門, known as 'Sukezaemon of Luzón' (Ruson Sukezaemon 呂宋助左衛門), who operated in Cambodia around the year 1600.[28] A statue of Sukezaemon/Taifusa now gazes defiantly out to sea from Sakai's modern harbour. Whatever his real identity, Taifusa's raid in 1582 was anything but peaceful, and he was eventually defeated by the use of the two resources in which the Spanish had the upper hand: artillery and fortifications.

Like Lin Feng, Taifusa, 'who does not know any superior in Europe' wished to establish a base for himself in the Philippines and chose Cagayan because of its proximity to Japan.[29] Juan Baptisto Roman, who was an eyewitness to the attack by 'Tay Zufu', concludes that the Japanese were 'a race at once valorous and skilful'[30] and 'a warlike people'[31] after relating how the Spanish first engaged Taifusa in a sea battle and used their artillery to good effect:

> The Japanese put out grappling-irons and poured two hundred men aboard the galley, armed with pikes and breastplates. There remained sixty arquebusiers firing at our men. Finally, the enemy conquered the galley as far as the mainmast. There our people also made a stand in their extreme necessity, and made the Japanese retreat to their ship …and with the artillery and forces of the ship overcame the Japanese; the latter fought valiantly until only eighteen remained, who gave themselves up, exhausted.[32]

The story is continued in an anonymous document called *Relation of the Philipinas Islands,* which relates how Pablo de Carrión, the Spanish commander at the scene, then headed up the Cagayan River and built a makeshift fort in which he mounted his artillery. Faced by these defences Taifusa tried to negotiate a settlement, making direct contact with Carrión and suggesting that because the Spanish 'were robbers like himself, but that he was there first, and had come at his king's command', then Carrión should bribe him with gold to go away. Not surprisingly, Carrión declined, and when the Japanese realised that no bribe was forthcoming they attacked the fort at dawn. The Spanish fired back from behind their defences, losing only one man in the operation. Taifusa suffered many casualties and then withdrew.[33]

An alternative description of the attack was written by Fray Diego de Aduarte, one of the leading Dominicans in the Philippines, and echoes Francisco de Sande's account of Sioco's assault on Manila in 1574.

According to Aduarte the rudimentary Spanish fortifications on the Cagayan River were built from turf and fascines held between wooden stakes and were attacked by the Japanese in a fierce and reckless charge with swords in hand. It was a tactic designed to terrify and disorder an enemy, and Aduarte mirrors the other accounts about what appeared to be the only means of resistance to it. That was to fire volleys of bullets and cannonballs at the oncoming waves of men from within the protection of the earthwork:

> they made a very spirited and courageous assault, but were beaten back with even greater courage once, twice, and three times. After a short rest, they attacked again with wonderful spirit, although the arquebuses and muskets brought many to the ground. Finally, the whole force of Japanese attacked our fort on the side where the cannon were, without knowing what awaited them there. The cannon were filled to the muzzle with ammunition, and were fired so seasonably that they did great execution among the Japanese. Those who were left alive, seeing what had happened, retreated, leaving their camp full of dead and mangled men.[34]

This demonstration of the faith the Spanish put into the application of overwhelming firepower has echoes of the claims made by the Portuguese after the battle of Fukuda Bay, and it is interesting to compare both these instances with a fight at sea between *wakō* and an English vessel in 1605 where concentrated fire also proved decisive. Sir Edward Michelborne was in command of the *Tiger*, and encountered a Japanese ship as it was heading back to Japan having raided China, Cambodia and Borneo, 'and to enter into the country of Borneo they durst not, for the Japons are not suffered to land in any port in India with weapons; being accounted a people so desperate and daring, that they are feared in all places where they come'. The meeting initially involved an exchange of courtesies, and Sir Edward, who was as much of a pirate as the Japanese were, was invited on board. He sent a party to make a full reconnaissance of the strange vessel with a view towards capturing it. As good manners between strange crews were something of a rarity, the Englishmen completely misunderstood the polite Japanese behaviour and after their own survey they allowed a group of *wakō* to board the *Tiger* without being disarmed. When sufficient *wakō* were on board the Japanese struck out with their swords against the English crew. On reaching the gun room they found Captain John Davis, who soon became the first Englishman ever to be killed

25

by a Japanese person. Sir Edward saved the day by handing pikes to his men. With these they were able to keep the sharp Japanese blades at a distance, and slowly the Englishmen drove them down into the interior of the ship. The desperate *wakō* then confined themselves in a cabin that no one dared approach, and were finally disposed of by firing cannon loaded with case shot and bullets into the side of the cabin at point blank range. All but one of the twenty-two *wakō* were killed. The English cannon were then turned on the *wakō* ship, and once again European firepower triumphed over a reckless charge.[35]

Returning to the Philippines incident, both Aduarte and San Agustin include a description of a different and very unusual Japanese tactic that Taifusa's *wakō* had learned to employ against the renowned Spanish pikemen. It was a death-defying technique never encountered in Europe or South America, whereby the Japanese recipient of a pike-thrust ignored the wound it had inflicted and then used that same pike to his own advantage. This was done by seizing the pike that had cut or even impaled him and using it to drag the pikeman off his feet; the man could then be finished off with a sword stroke. The Spanish must have been familiar with the trick by 1582, because Aduarte's description of its deployment refers explicitly to the accepted way of countering it:

> Since they had learned by experience that Japanese who are wounded by pikes grasp hold of the pikes in order to kill those who have wounded them, the captain had the pikes greased on the upper half, in order that our men might be able to draw them from the bodies and the hands of the Japanese, if the latter should pull by the pikes; and this device was of great use in the conflict which ensued.[36]

Interestingly, several years later Aduarte refers to the employment of the same pike-grasping technique in a battle of 1598, but this time he is describing its use by Japanese mercenaries fighting hostile Filipino natives on the Spaniards' behalf. The native spears were 'like a pike, with iron points', and their users had clearly not heard of the technique of greasing the shafts. The attackers killed one Japanese mercenary and badly wounded another, who 'came back with his arm pierced, and with a wound a span long above the pit of his stomach, but not entering it; but he was very well satisfied because, by throwing himself forward by the pike, he had killed the Indian who had wounded him – so proud is that race'.[37]

By this time the Spanish had been employing Japanese mercenaries for over ten years, and in a letter of 1587 to Philip II the then Governor of the Philippines Santiago de Vera describes the Japanese as, 'an energetic race, skilled in the use of our weapons. All the other nations lack that spirit, and are cowardly, dastardly, and abject'.[38] Later in the same letter he writes that the Japanese are indeed 'a warlike race, feared among all the natives, and most by the Chinese, who tremble at their very name, because of the many damages they have inflicted'.[39]

For the next half century that superior image continued to develop and drew even more admiration, even though, according to Aduarte, the Japanese were 'too much given to rashness in war'.[40] Similar sentiments were expressed in 1609 by Antonio de Morga, who described the Japanese mercenaries as 'a spirited race, of good disposition, and brave... They employ many ceremonies and courtesies, and attach much importance to honour and social standing'.[41] The latter point was to be illustrated in no uncertain fashion in 1599 when a confrontation developed between a Spanish soldier and a Japanese mercenary in Cambodia, recorded as follows by Gabriel Quiroga de San Antonio:

> It is the custom in these Eastern Kingdoms that when two people meet on a road, the inferior stands aside to make way for the superior. A Japanese and a Castila met and had to decide who was the superior and most worthy of respect. After they had had a long argument with each other, they came to blows and the Castila kicked the Japanese and slapped his face so much that he left him in a very bad condition. ...The Japanese, who were numerous, were outraged and fought for their nation's dignity and honour.[42]

It is no wonder that Baltasar Gracián, looking back on almost a century of contact with these proud and fierce warriors, would dub them, 'the Spaniards of Asia'!

Notes

1. For a wide-ranging selection of early European observations see Cooper, Michael *They Came to Japan: An Anthology of European Reports on Japan, 1543-1640* (London: Thames and Hudson, 1965).
2. Gracián y Morales, Baltasar *El criticón Part II* Clásicos castellanos 166 (Madrid: Espace-Calpe 1971), p. 180.

3. Gracian's 'learned remark' was quoted in 1725 in the 'Letter from Fray Gaspar de San Agustin to a friend in Espana who asked him as to the nature and characteristics [genio] of the Indian natives of these Philipinas Islands'; in Blair, Emma Helen and Robertson, James Alexander (eds.) *The Philippine Islands, 1493-1803.* (Cleveland: Oxford Univ. Press on behalf of the American Historical Association, 1903–09), vol. 40, p. 192.

4. Sanabrais, Sofia '"The Spaniards of Asia": the Japanese presence in colonial Mexico' *Bulletin of Portuguese-Japanese Studies* 18, 2009 pp. 223-251. The quotation from Valignano is taken from his *Sumario de las cosas de Japón* of 1583, as translated in Boxer, C.R. *The Christian Century in Japan: 1549-1650* (Berkeley, 1951), p. 74.

5. Valignano, Alessandro *Sumario de las cosas de Japón* of 1583, as translated in Boxer, C.R. *The Christian Century in Japan: 1549-1650* (Berkeley, 1951), p. 74.

6. Wang Yong 'Realistic and Fantastic Images of "Dwarf Pirates": The Evolution of Ming Dynasty Perceptions of the Japanese' in Fogel, Joshua A (ed.) *Sagacious Monks and Bloodthirsty Warriors: Chinese views of Japan in the Ming-Qing period* (New York 2002) p. 24.

7. Yamashita, Noboru 'The Jesuit Mission in Hirado and the Vanished Christians of Takushima - A Historical and Anthropological Research' (Nagasaki University Academic Output Site, 2015), p. 44: http://hdl.handle.net/10069/35761 (Accessed 29 January 2019).

8. Fróis Part 1, Chapter 40 in Matsuda, Kiichi and Kawasaki, Momota (Trans.) *Kanyaku Furoisu Nihon shi Vol. 6:* (Tokyo: Chuokoron-Shinsha, 2000), pp. 267-268.

9. Van Linschoten, John Huighen; Philip, William (trans.) *His Discours of Voyages Into Ye Easte [and] West Indies: Deuided Into Four Bookes* (London: John Wolfe, 1598), p 383. Another Portuguese fatality in Satsuma Province in that same year of 1561 was attributed to an accident. See Boxer, C.R. *Fidalgos in the Far East 1550-1770* (Hong Kong: Oxford University Press, 1968), p. 33.

10. Fróis Part 1, Chapter 48 in Matsuda, Kiichi and Kawasaki, Momota (Trans.) *Kanyaku Furoisu Nihon shi Vol. 9:* (Tokyo: Chuokoron-Shinsha, 2000), pp. 94-96.

11. Boxer, C.R. *Fidlagos in the Far East 1550-1770* (Hong Kong: Oxford University Press, 1968), pp. 36-37.

12. Fróis Part 1, Chapter 63 in Matsuda, Kiichi and Kawasaki, Momota (Trans.) *Kanyaku Furoisu Nihon shi Vol. 9:* (Tokyo: Chuokoron-Shinsha, 2000), pp. 179-180.

13. Miguel López de Legazpi to Philip II, 23 July 1567, in Blair and Robertson 1903-09, vol. 2, p. 238.

14. *Relation of the Western Islands called Filipinas* by Diego de Artieda [1573], in Blair and Robertson, 1903-09, vol. 3, p. 204.

15. Toby, Ronald P. 'The "Indianness" of Iberia and Changing Japanese Iconographies of Other' in Schwartz, Stuart B. (ed.) *Implicit Understandings: Observing, Reporting and Reflecting on the Encounters between Europeans and Other Peoples in the Early Modern Era* (Cambridge: Cambridge University Press, 1995), p. 329.

16. Wolters, O.W. 'Ayudhyā and the Rearward Part of the World' *The Journal of the Royal Asiatic Society of Great Britain and Ireland* No. 3/4 (Oct., 1968), p. 171.

17. The action is summarised briefly in Paske-Smith, ".R. 'Japanese Trade and Residence in the Philippines' *Transaction* of the Asiatic Society of Japan XLII (2) (1914), p. 690. Sioco's name does not appear in the two earliest accounts of the battle, which are González de Mendoza, Juan *The history of the great and mighty kingdom of China and the situation thereof* Vol. 2 Translated by Parke, Robert (1588), edited by Staunton, Sir George Thomas (London, Hakluyt Society 1853-54). pp. 10-18, and *Relation of the Filipinas Islands* by Francisco de Sande; Manila, 7 June 1576 in Blair and Robertson 1903-09, vol. 4, pp. 24-35. The main source for Sioco is San Agustin, Gaspar de; Mañeru, Luis Antonio (Trans.) *Conquistas de las Islas Filipinas: Conquest of the Philippine Islands 1565-1615* (Manila: San Agustin Museum, 1998), pp. 655-663.

18. González de Mendoza, Juan *The history of the great and mighty kingdom of China and the situation thereof* Vol. 2 Translated by Parke, Robert (1588), edited by Staunton, Sir George Thomas (London, Hakluyt Society 1853-54). p. 10.

19. San Agustin, Gaspar de; Mañeru, Luis Antonio (Trans.) *Conquistas de las Islas Filipinas: Conquest of the Philippine Islands 1565-1615* (Manila: San Agustin Museum, 1998), pp. 657.

20. San Agustin, Gaspar de; Mañeru, Luis Antonio (Trans.) *Conquistas de las Islas Filipinas: Conquest of the Philippine Islands 1565-1615* (Manila: San Agustin Museum, 1998), pp. 661.

21. San Agustin, Gaspar de; Mañeru, Luis Antonio (Trans.) *Conquistas de las Islas Filipinas: Conquest of the Philippine Islands 1565-1615* (Manila: San Agustin Museum, 1998), pp. 663.

22. *Relation of the Filipinas Islands* by Francisco de Sande; Manila, 7 June 1576 in Blair and Robertson 1903-09, vol. 4, p. 27.

23. San Agustin, Gaspar de; Mañeru, Luis Antonio (Trans.) *Conquistas de las Islas Filipinas: Conquest of the Philippine Islands 1565-1615* (Manila: San Agustin Museum, 1998), p. 847.
24. Letter to Philip II by Gonzalo Ronquillo de Peñialosa; Manila, 16 June 1582 in Blair and Robertson 1903-09, vol. 5 p. 27.
25. Letter from Gaspar de Ayala to Philip II 15 July 1589 in Blair and Robertson 1903-09, vol. 7, p. 126.
26. Koop, Albert J. and Inada, Hogitarō *Japanese names and how to read them: a manual for art-collectors and students* (London: Routledge, 1923), p. 72.
27. Zaide, Gregorio F. *Philippine Political and Cultural History* (Manila: Philippine Education Co., 1957), vol. 1, p. 288.
28. Miyamoto, Kazuo *Vikings of the Far East* (New York, Vantage Press, 1975), pp. 88-89.
29. San Agustin, Gaspar de; Mañeru, Luis Antonio (Trans.) *Conquistas de las Islas Filipinas: Conquest of the Philippine Islands 1565-1615* (Manila: San Agustin Museum, 1998), p. 845.
30. Letter from Juan Baptisto Roman to the Viceroy, 25 June 1582 in Blair and Robertson 1903-09, vol. 5, p. 194.
31. Letter from Juan Baptisto Roman to the Viceroy, 25 June 1582 in Blair and Robertson 1903-09, vol. 5, p. 195.
32. Letter from Juan Baptisto Roman to the Viceroy, 25 June 1582 in Blair and Robertson 1903-09, vol. 5, p. 193.
33. *Relation of the Philipinas Islands.* [Unsigned and undated; 1586?] in Blair and Robertson 1903-09, vol. 34, pp. 384-385.
34. *Historia de la provincia del Sancto Rosario de la Orden de Predicadores* by Diego Aduarte, O.P.; Manila, 1640 in Blair and Robertson 1903-09, vol. 30, pp. 274-5.
35. As recounted with gusto in many works, including Milton, Giles. *Nathaniel's Nutmeg: how one man's courage changed the course of history* (London, Hodder and Stoughton 1999), pp. 114-120.
36. *Historia de la provincia del Sancto Rosario de la Orden de Predicadores* by Diego Aduarte, O.P.; Manila, 1640 in Blair and Robertson 1903-09, vol. 30, p. 274; San Agustin, Gaspar de; Mañeru, Luis Antonio (Trans.) *Conquistas de las Islas Filipinas: Conquest of the Philippine Islands 1565-1615* (Manila: San Agustin Museum, 1998), p. 847.
37. *Historia de la provincia del Sancto Rosario de la Orden de Predicadores* by Diego Aduarte, O.P.; Manila, 1640 in Blair and Robertson 1903-09, vol. 31, pp. 114-115.
38. Letter to Philip II by Santiago de Vera; Manila, 26 June 1587 in Blair and Robertson 1903-09, vol. 6, pp. 304-305.

39. Letter to Philip II by Santiago de Vera; Manila, 26 June 1587 in Blair and Robertson 1903-09, vol. 6, p. 310.

40. *Historia de la provincia del Sancto Rosario de la Orden de Predicadores* by Diego Aduarte, O.P.; Manila, 1640 in Blair and Robertson 1903-09, vol. 31, p. 78.

41. Morga, Antonio de *History of the Philippine Islands from the discovery by Magellan in 1521 to the beginning of the XVII Century; with descriptions of Japan, China and adjacent countries* Volumes I and II translated and edited by Blair, E.H. and Robertson, J.A. (Cleveland, 1907, reprint New York, 1970). p.198.

42. San Antonio, Gabriel Quiroga de *A Brief and Truthful Relation of Events in the Kingdom of Cambodia* (originally published as *Breve y Verdadera Relacion de los Successos del Reyno de Camboxa* in 1604) (Bangkok, 1998), pp. 38-39.

Chapter 3

Defending the Faith: the Japanese 'mercenaries' of Fort Nagasaki

Reference was made in the previous chapter to the battle in 1565 between Japanese samurai and armed Portuguese merchants when the annual *naó* docked at Fukuda, a harbour controlled by the friendly local daimyo Ōmura Sumitada, whose support and influence would become crucial to the Portuguese effort in Japan. His port of Fukuda unfortunately had the disadvantage of being located on a small and vulnerable bay facing the open sea, so discreet enquiries by the Portuguese uncovered a further defensible alternative within Ōmura territory at a place called Nagasaki. The settlement possessed a deep natural harbour situated within a sea gulf protected by its *'naga saki'* (long cape). The land immediately around was almost completely undeveloped, but its defensive capacity was evident, and indeed a small fort had been erected at its highest point by Nagasaki Jinzaemon, a retainer of the Ōmura baptised as Bernardo, who guarded the place that bore his name.

After much land clearance and building Nagasaki became the preferred anchorage for the annual *naó* from 1571 onwards. It also became a safe refuge for any Christian families who had been uprooted from their homes for one reason or another, and Fróis notes people moving to Nagasaki from the Amakusa Islands and the Shimabara Peninsula.[1] It would play a vital part in the story of the Jesuit mission in Japan and would gain even more significance when the Portuguese were expelled from Japan in 1639 because, as the home of a handful of Dutch traders, Nagasaki became Japan's only window on the European world for over 200 years. The settlement's importance in the history of the Japanese mercenaries is twofold. First, because of the unique way in which Nagasaki was defended, it may provide the sole example of Japanese mercenaries serving a foreign power in their own country. Second, when that defence failed, the role that Nagasaki had played in Japanese politics meant that it was indelibly associated with the first Japanese Christian refugees who were exiled for their faith and joined the Wild Geese.

Ōmura Sumitada: daimyo of Ōmura

As a staunch supporter of the ongoing Jesuit mission, Ōmura Sumitada of Nagasaki had accepted baptism in 1563 under the Christian name of Dom Bartolomeu and had thereby become Japan's first *kirishitan daimyo*. Although lauded by the Jesuits for this act, Sumitada's opportunistic embrace of the faith and his limited sphere of influence brought the authenticity of the words 'Christian' and 'daimyo' into question. His Christianity may be a matter of subjective judgement, but in terms of his lordly pretensions it had to be recognised that Sumitada's domain was only one small territory among several within the general area of Hizen Province (modern Nagasaki Prefecture). This was a wild area where high cliffs, complex bays and hidden inlets provided the perfect stage from which petty rivalries could be defended and piracy pursued.

Unfortunately for Sumitada, his family ties were as complicated as the local terrain and even more threatening to his livelihood, so the area around Christian Nagasaki was rarely free from conflict. His domestic disputes arose ultimately from the fact that Sumitada had not been born into the Ōmura family but was in fact the second son of Arima Haruzumi 有馬晴純 (1483–1566), whose lands lay on the Shimabara Peninsula, the prominent lobe of Hizen Province that protrudes into the Ariake Sea to the east of Nagasaki. In a practice that was very common among Japan's daimyo, young Sumitada had been adopted into the Ōmura family in early adulthood to cement an alliance between the two families, at which his new father Ōmura Sumisaki promptly disinherited his own son and had him adopted in turn into the Gotō family as Gotō Takaakira 後藤貴明. This drastic decision led to a long period of antagonism between the two adoptees that was exacerbated by their subsequent marriage alliances with other families, and shortly after Sumitada received baptism Gotō Takaakira attacked him in his mansion at Yokoseura. That was the start of the incident noted earlier when Yokoseura and its church were burned to the ground.[2]

The Arima/Ōmura alliance held fast for most of Sumitada's lifetime, as did the bond between Ōmura Sumitada and the Portuguese. The latter friendship was strengthened by the dramatic demonstration of European military might at the battle of Fukuda Bay, and was further reinforced in 1566 when Gotō Takaakira attacked an Ōmura castle on the Sonogi peninsula. Sumitada was again forced to flee, but the sympathetic Captain-Major of the *naó* then lying at anchor in Fukuda heard of the plight of the Jesuits' great Christian supporter and supplied Sumitada with firearms so that the invaders might be driven back. In a quick attack even more dramatic than the battle of Fukuda Bay, western firepower triumphed once again.[3]

Gotō Takaakira was however not the only rival with whom Sumitada had to contend, because to add to the enmity engendered by his adoption Sumitada also faced antagonism from his wife's elder brothers: Saigō Sumitaka 西郷純堯, whose domain was nearby Isahaya, and Fukabori Sumimasa 深堀純賢, described by Luis Fróis as 'a great pirate', whose territory lay almost at the tip of Nagasaki's cape.[4] All three were intent on foiling Sumitada's accommodation with the foreigners and his embrace of their disruptive and destructive religion. To achieve this the brothers allied themselves with the most powerful daimyo in Hizen Province, whom they believed could help accomplish that goal: the firmly non-Christian Ryūzōji Takanobu 龍蔵寺高信 (1530–84). The Ryūzōji domain occupied much of the northern part of Hizen including what is nowadays Saga Prefecture, thus making Takanobu a near neighbour of Hizen's other anti-Christian daimyo: Matsuura Takanobu of Hirado Island.

In 1573 a dramatic reversal in Sumitada's fortunes gave his rivals the opportunity to strike, because instead of welcoming that year's *naó* into Nagasaki Bay, Sumitada had to contend with the dreadful news that the great ship had sunk with the loss of all hands along with its precious cargo. The disaster was a blow to Sumitada's fortune and prestige, and his brother-in-law Fukabori Sumimasa became the first rival to test the waters. Until the arrival of the Jesuits in Ōmura territory Fukabori's position at the entrance to Nagasaki Bay had allowed him to extract tolls from incoming shipping. Ōmura Sumitada's problems in 1573 presented the opportunity to re-establish local dominance without undue interference, and he chose his first target carefully. Francisco Cabral, the Jesuit leader in Japan, had to leave Nagasaki by ship, so Fukabori Sumimasa planned a *wakō* style attack on him. The Jesuits had, however, anticipated just such a move and assembled a fleet of seven ships equipped with firearms. Fukabori nevertheless attacked them with alacrity, killing five or six men using his own musketeers and capturing one of the ships. The other Portuguese vessels retreated hastily to Nagasaki, forcing Cabral to take a different route overland and giving the pirate leader a symbolic victory over the European incomers. It is however amusing to note that many centuries later the Christians of Nagasaki would exact a token revenge, because next to the small harbour now called Fukabori is its Catholic church, the car park of which is built on the site of Fukabori Sumimasa's headquarters![5]

The building of 'Fort Nagasaki'

The ambush by Fukabori Sumimasa confirmed the vulnerability of the seaborne approach to the Jesuits' precious settlement of Nagasaki as long as he was in control of it, and worse was to come later that same year. Following his brother's example of aggression, Saigō Sumitaka advanced overland against the Ōmura domain from Isahaya. Wild rumours soon reached Nagasaki that the Ōmura territory had fallen and that their great Christian protector Ōmura Sumitada was probably dead. The inhabitants fell into a panic and fled to the wooded hills around, taking with them their most precious sacred objects from the churches, which they believed would soon come under attack. Bernardo Nagasaki Jinzaemon, whose tiny castle alone protected the settlement, almost surrendered in face of the threat until a messenger arrived with the news that Ōmura Sumitada was still alive and was urging him and the Christian population of Nagasaki to stand firm and hold out until order could be restored. The Jesuits gathered their flock and the decision was made was to give Nagasaki its first proper fortifications by erecting a perimeter fence around the promontory and cutting a ditch through its land side. 'And so', writes Fróis in his *Historia*, 'it became a fortress: the place that is now Nagasaki'.[6]

Saigō Sumitaka moved quickly to stop the defence works being completed, bringing boats up close to the fence, discharging guns into the town and forcing the population to use the cover of darkness for their foraging and ditch-digging. His brother Fukabori Sumimasa – described now by Fróis as not only a pirate but the 'avowed enemy of God's laws' – joined in with what had developed into a siege of Nagasaki, which lasted throughout the winter of 1573–74. Frustrated by the continued resilience of the defenders, the brothers decided upon a major assault to wipe the Christian community from the face of Japan. Their attack was launched shortly after midnight during the week of Easter, and houses and other buildings outside the perimeter were burned in preparation for an assault through the fence. It was a demoralising experience for the defenders who were convinced that their end had come, but four Christian samurai originally from Shiki on the Amakusa Islands chose to disregard the advice of their priests to sit tight and instead sallied out from Nagasaki in a suicidal attack. They targeted the high-ranking officers in the Fukabori and Saigō armies, identifying them by their fine armour and weapons. So sudden and unexpected was the assault that nine of the enemy leaders were cut down before the brave Nagasaki men were themselves killed. Seeing what they had achieved by their example, their fellow defenders followed them in a furious advance and drove the besiegers back to their boats. The enemy commanders ordered a withdrawal and Nagasaki was saved.[7]

Following this remarkable demonstration of muscular Christianity Nagasaki received a new priest in the person of Father Gaspar Coelho (1529–90), a man who was destined to exert great influence on the Portuguese mission for many years to come. Coelho had the personality and the drive to push forward the Christian cause in newly liberated Nagasaki, and was determined to capitalise on Bartolomeu Ōmura Sumitada's genuine gratitude towards God, his Christian followers and Portuguese weaponry for this latest instance of a series of deliverances. Coelho therefore urged the complete extirpation within the Ōmura domain of any remaining vestiges of Buddhism and its replacement by Christian believers and Christian places of worship. His appeal did not fall on deaf ears, and large-scale services of baptism were soon being conducted to achieve the first conversion of an entire Japanese domain. This was followed by the destruction of shrines and temples by the fervent new converts.[8] By 1575 – a year when the *naó* docked at Nagasaki bringing further large supplies of guns and ammunition for Sumitada along with the usual silk – there were reckoned to be 20,000 Christians within his territory, all of whom were determined to defend Nagasaki to the death.[9]

This combination of mass conversions and European armaments seems to have ensured that Nagasaki remained unmolested for the next few years, which left the Jesuits free to concentrate on the conversion of the Amakusa and Arima domains. A similar process of mass baptism went smoothly on the Amakusa Islands, but the Arima territory threw up a few problems. It had been ruled from 1576 onwards by Ōmura Sumitada's nephew Arima Harunobu 有馬晴信 (1567–1612), who had first attracted the Jesuits' attention because of his persecution of Christians after inheriting the domain from his Christian father Yoshisada 義貞 (1521–76), Ōmura Sumitada's elder brother. Far from giving up on Harunobu as a hopeless case for conversion, Coelho decided to exploit his great fears of outside domination. A number of Harunobu's castles were currently being attacked by Ryūzōji Takanobu, so Coelho's superior Alessandro Valignano, the man who oversaw the entire Jesuit missionary effort in China and Japan from 1574 until 1606, ordered that, 'succour be given to the fortresses that were under fire, provisioning them with victuals, and some silver, as much as he could, and also provisioning them with lead and saltpetre, whereof he had laid in a good stock from the *naó* towards this effect'.[10] In 1579 the annual *naó*, once again laden with armaments, was ordered to dock at Harunobu's port of Kuchinotsu rather than at Nagasaki. The gesture was not lost on the aggressive Ryūzōji Takanobu, who ordered his forces to withdraw. Just as his uncle Ōmura Sumitada had done before, Arima Harunobu showed his gratitude to the Jesuits by accepting baptism and became the *kirishitan daimyo* Dom Protasio Arima.[11]

Ōmura Sumitada's nephew may have been saved from the Ryūzōji by this profound change of heart, but the setback gave Ryūzōji Takanobu the opportunity to concentrate his attentions on the uncle once again. The unholy alliance between the Ryūzōji and the Matsuura meant that Hizen's two most powerful anti-Christian daimyo could now exert joint pressure on the Ōmura domain. They conducted serious raids into the territory in 1577 and 1578, and by 1580 it was clear to Ōmura Sumitada that he would either be defeated in battle by Ryūzōji Takanobu or be forced to submit to him as a vassal to avoid certain destruction. Either way the Ōmura domain faced extinction, so Sumitada went even further in his accommodation with his Portuguese protectors, who fully appreciated that if the Ōmura domain succumbed to the pagan Ryūzōji then Nagasaki would be lost along with it. In June 1580, in a deal without precedent in Japanese history, Ōmura Sumitada handed Nagasaki over to the Jesuits for safe-keeping while retaining certain taxation rights. He then submitted meekly to the Ryūzōji as their vassal.

Nagasaki therefore became something unique on Japanese soil: a European colony in all but name, and within two weeks of the 'Donation of Bartolomeu' plans were being laid for Nagasaki and Mogi (the smaller harbour on the other side of the cape) to be fortified:

Both should accordingly be protected with forts and equipped with munitions, weapons and artillery for defence... In the first year [the Superior] should spend on the defence installations as much as necessary. Thereafter, 150 ducats out of the anchorage fees of the Portuguese should be applied to this purpose. Both fortresses are to be armed in a manner to withstand any attack. In order to secure Nagasaki even more, as many married Portuguese are to be settled there as will find accommodation in the town. In case of siege these will be taken into the fort and will reinforce it. The Superiors are to take care that the inhabitants increase, and that they are equipped with all necessary weaponry.[12]

By the end of 1581 the wooden perimeter fence and ditch that had served Nagasaki's inhabitants so well during the siege of 1573–4 had been replaced by something much more substantial, although both the walls and the motivation that led to their construction would be casually dismissed by Valignano in a document of 1598 as 'some very frail and tiny earthworks (quite ill-constructed)'.[13] By then Valignano was trying to downplay the extent of the control the Jesuits had over Sumitada by omitting any mention of the very impressive walls that had replaced the first ones within a few years. In 1598 Nagasaki was in fact a fortress town surrounded by water on almost all sides and strongly fortified where it joined the land, while the Jesuit headquarters were situated on Nagasaki's highest point like a separate citadel.[14] As for the mode of construction, it is inconceivable that the walls of Nagasaki (of which sadly no trace remains) would have been built to anything other than the highest standards then current in Japan, which consisted of the typically strong yet graceful sloping walls of interlocking stone blocks that had reached their peak of perfection in Azuchi Castle, the palace built for Oda Nobunaga in 1576. Azuchi was a place that Luis Fróis had seen with his own eyes, 'which as regards architecture, strength, wealth and grandeur may well be compared with the greatest buildings of Europe'.[15] We may therefore safely envisage that by the mid-1580s 'Fort Nagasaki' looked like a typical Japanese castle that doubled as a walled town for harbour defence, with impressive stone walls reaching down to the sea, topped by subsidiary corner towers that could provide storage and living accommodation, and overlooked by the Jesuit headquarters that doubled as the castle's 'keep'. The irony would no doubt have been lost on its Jesuit owners, but a fortified religious establishment such as this resembled nothing less in both structure and spirit than Osaka's Ishiyama Honganji, the fortress-cum-cathedral of the militant Buddhist True Pure Land sect, an institution for which the Jesuits had nothing but contempt.[16]

There is no indication in the 1580 document as to how Nagasaki was garrisoned other than the reference to its inhabitants being equipped with all necessary weaponry. In the document of 1598 it is claimed that these amounted to no more than 'two middling falconets... which the viceroys had sent to D. Bartolomeu, who kept them more for representation than for anything else'.[17] Most importantly, Valignano does not mention the presence of any foreign soldiery in Nagasaki and stresses that its defence was provided by local men who were presumably followers of Ōmura Sumitada, because 'never was any other fortress in the same town, nor a garrison of people other than from that same town'.[18] By this remark Valignano may have unintentionally revealed that Bartolomeu Ōmura's samurai were effectively acting as mercenaries for a foreign sovereign power on native Japanese soil.

Fears of invasion and Christian persecution

The defence of a Jesuit colony by local Japanese troops provides a further example of how Europeans could interfere in Japan's internal affairs, and side-by-side with their use of men who were virtually mercenaries in their own country went the possibility of an even greater intervention that within a few years would become an obsession with Japan's rulers: a Christian uprising in Japan supported by an invasion from abroad.

The earliest hint that such a course of action might even be possible is contained in a letter from Luis Fróis of 16 October 1578, where he reports widely believed rumours that were circulating in Bungo Province (modern Ōita Prefecture) to the effect that the Jesuits were waiting for the moment when they had sufficient converts to form an army. At that point a Portuguese armada would set sail and help them turn their spiritual conquest into a military one. Both Ōtomo Sōrin (1530–87), the daimyo of Bungo who was sympathetic to Christianity, and Oda Nobunaga (1535–82), the first of Japan's unifiers and a leader who favoured the missionaries, had laughed off that suggestion.[19] Nevertheless, in 1583 Valignano would revisit such fears in his arguments as to why only the Jesuits should be allowed to operate in Japan and why Spanish Franciscans should be excluded. After referring to the above rumours he notes that several non-Christian daimyo and Buddhist priests had surmised that they could not understand why the Spanish monarch would spend such vast sums on the mission if the end was not to conquer Japan.[20] That there were similar worries elsewhere in East Asia would be confirmed later by the Jesuit chronicler Fernão Guerriero, who wrote in 1602–03 in the context of India, 'Because as many heathen as are converted to Christ, just so many friends and vassals does His Majesty's service acquire, since they fight for the State and the Christians against the heathen'.[21]

These abstract fears – wild though they were – would be given some semblance of reality by Father Coelho because of his sincere, if somewhat clumsy, efforts to assist the Christian daimyo Dom Protasio Arima Harunobu in 1584. The fortifications of Nagasaki appear to have played the part envisaged for them in dissuading Ryūzōji Takanobu and his allies from attacking it, but with only that small scrap of former Ōmura territory still out of his hands Ryūzōji Takanobu could concentrate instead on Arima Harunobu, who had little to his name but a small strip of the Shimabara Peninsula. Showing considerable naivety about the nature of Japanese vassaldom, Coelho first tried to persuade Ōmura Sumitada to throw off his allegiance to the Ryūzōji and join his nephew in an alliance against them.[22] When Sumitada proved reluctant to betray his master, Father Coelho wrote to Manila on 3 March 1584 to ask for armed help from the Philippines, requesting four ships from the Spanish colonists laden with men, artillery and food 'to come to the aid of the Christians of Japan who are hard pressed by the heathen'.[23]

The request was turned down by Manila, but in the meantime Dom Protasio Arima Harunobu had made his own pact with the devil by seeking aid closer to home from the ancient and extremely belligerent Shimazu family of Satsuma Province (modern Kagoshima Prefecture). Together with the Ryūzōji and the Ōtomo the Shimazu made up Kyushu's influential 'big three' daimyo, and either fought each other or cemented temporary alliances over a period of several decades. The Shimazu ultimately proved to be the most successful of the trio, and by the early 1580s they had become masters of most of southern Kyushu. The Arima's problems with Ryūzōji Takanobu's aggression gave the Shimazu the opportunity to do to the Ryūzōji what they had already done to their other rivals the Ōtomo, over whom they had achieved a crushing victory at the battle of Mimigawa in 1578.

The Shimazu were however strongly biased against Christianity, a fact that seems to have been overlooked when the Jesuits celebrated the subsequent victory achieved by an Arima/Shimazu alliance over the Ryūzōji at the battle of Okita-Nawate on the Shimabara peninsula in April 1584. During the encounter one of Arima Harunobu's Christian followers, named by Fróis as Juan Zaemon, successfully conducted a bombardment of the Ryūzōji troops from the sea using two Portuguese cannon. The long and colourful account of the battle compiled by Fróis reveals the international make-up of the Portuguese contingent present on the ship, because 'in the absence of a gunner, a kaffir from Africa loaded the cannonballs and a Malabari lighted the touch hole'. Even more entertaining was the timing of the gun drill, which the untrained artillerymen had established by using their Christian piety, placing their hands together and reciting the Lord's Prayer, then (the barrels having presumably cooled down sufficiently) returning to their feet to reload, aim and fire, 'blasting the enemies's helmets into the air'.[24] When the battle was at its height a flying column of Shimazu samurai sought out Ryūzōji Takanobu and killed him as he sat in his palanquin.

The death of so great a pagan enemy must have seemed like divine intervention to the Jesuits because Ryūzōji Takanobu had made it known that his first act on gaining a victory would have been to sack Nagasaki and crucify Father Coelho.[25] In reality the removal of the Ryūzōji was due much less to the prayers of the Christians of Nagasaki than to the alliance that the desperate Arima Harunobu had made with the pagan Shimazu, who were now poised to fill the anti-Christian vacuum. Nevertheless, the victory at Okita-Nawate had saved the Christian Ōmura Sumitada from considerable embarrassment. As a reluctant Ryūzōji vassal he was on his way to aid his master while the battle was in progress, and must have been greatly relieved to encounter Ryūzōji troops fleeing in the opposite direction and confirming that his support was no longer needed.[26]

Once the new threat to Nagasaki from the Shimazu became apparent Coelho wrote again to the Philippines on 11 November 1584 and 24 January 1585 with requests for help against his new enemy the Shimazu rather than his old enemy the Ryūzōji.[27] No positive response was made to either request, so in 1586 Coelho wrote a third letter, which was taken to the Philippines by a group of Japanese Christians. The governor reported their arrival to the King of Spain, where their difference from the usual type of Japanese visitors — namely marauding *wakō* — was duly noted. 'Eleven Japanese Christians have arrived, vassals of King Bartholomew and inhabitants of Nagasaki; they brought me a letter from the Provincial and religious of the Society of Jesus there resident, requesting me to send help to the Christian kings. They are the first Japanese to have come here peacefully'.[28] Peaceful or not, once again no help was sent.

Hideyoshi and Kyushu

Within a few years' time the situation in Nagasaki would change dramatically, because the local wars between the daimyo of Kyushu were taking place to the backdrop of the seemingly unstoppable rise to national power of Toyotomi Hideyoshi. Coelho first met Hideyoshi in May 1586, having travelled to Osaka to seek his support against the

Shimazu. Hideyoshi was already planning a conquest of the Shimazu himself, so Coelho rashly promised to put all the Christian lords in Japan on his side. After Hideyoshi had sent him on his way with apparent encouragement for the gospel to be preached throughout Japan, a happy Coelho began a diplomatic offensive to create a Christian alliance in support of Hideyoshi, but returned to Nagasaki in December 1586, having failed utterly in his task. That a union of Christian daimyo was an impossibility even on Kyushu had been illustrated while Coelho was away because Ōmura Sumitada and Arima Harunobu, whose causes he had once so energetically embraced, had disgraced themselves by fighting a war over the control of the Sonogi peninsula.[29] Coelho was also unable to forgive Harunobu for choosing to ally himself with the Shimazu instead of joining the coalition of purely Christian daimyo against Ryūzōji that Coelho had proposed. In an apparent fit of pique Coelho ordered the Jesuits then in Arima to leave, and moved their seminary to Urakami, a village previously donated to the Order.

In 1587 Toyotomi Hideyoshi's armies swept down both coasts of Kyushu in an invasion so rapid that many daimyo were left stranded behind the advancing front line and came meekly to submit. Christian Nagasaki, geographically and politically isolated, remained grandly aloof, and in keeping with his dignity Father Gaspar Coelho travelled to meet Hideyoshi at Hakozaki (modern Fukuoka City) to congratulate him on his stunning victory. The meeting took place on Coelho's impressive private warship that was said to be the fastest vessel in Japanese waters. Coelho's other aim was to receive assurances from Hideyoshi that under his new regime the privileges the Jesuits had enjoyed in their defended colony would continue. The personal encounter was cordial, but it was to be followed quite unexpectedly a few days later by a decree from Hideyoshi condemning Christianity and ordering the fathers to leave the country. Japan, declared Hideyoshi, was the land of the gods, so Christian missionaries had no place within it with their forced conversions and destruction of temples. The supposedly *kirishitan daimyo* also bore an uncomfortable resemblance to the belligerent Buddhist sectarians of the True Pure Land who had defied Oda Nobunaga for ten years. Indeed, to Hideyoshi the Jesuits and their converts were even more dangerous than the True Pure Land disciples, because the Buddhist sectarians had seduced only the lower classes. The Jesuits had seduced upper-class influential daimyo, whose numerous followers had been sheepishly coerced into converting and then went around destroying Buddhist establishments.[30] It is highly likely that Coelho, who had sailed from his fortress town of Nagasaki like a prince on his own warship, had contributed not a little to Hideyoshi's suspicions.

Nagasaki was confiscated by Hideyoshi. The place was not given to a daimyo (the normal procedure elsewhere in Japan), but retained as crown property under Hideyoshi's *bugyō*, a word best translated as 'commissioner', who proceeded to rule Nagasaki with the support of *daikan* (magistrates).[31] The fortifications of Nagasaki were then demolished in front of Coelho's eyes.

Coelho was not a man to take humiliation lying down, so his earlier shuttle diplomacy among the Christian lords in support of Hideyoshi was revisited as he tried to persuade them to unite in armed resistance against Hideyoshi. Coelho stated that he would supply weapons and financial support, just as he had done for Ōmura and Arima against the Ryūzōji, but the situation in Japan had changed radically in seven years. It was no longer a case of supporting one petty Christian against an equally petty pagan; it was instead a pledge of European support for a *coup d'état* against the man who now ruled half of Japan and looked certain to conquer the other half too. To make matters worse, most of the Christian daimyo whom Coelho so naively approached had served Hideyoshi during the Kyushu campaign and had been richly rewarded for it. Even Arima Harunobu, whom Coelho believed to be in his debt, flatly rejected the alarming proposal.

Shunned by the Christian daimyo, the increasingly desperate Coelho looked again to the Philippines to help save the colony of Nagasaki. His subsequent letter to Manila echoed his earlier efforts of 1584 in its suggestion that 300 Spanish soldiers should invade Japan. The secular Spanish authorities sent his request on to Madrid (which was equivalent to ignoring it), while his Jesuit superior wrote back severely criticising him for his inflammatory suggestions. In 1589 the desperate Coelho turned instead to Macao, sending Father Belchior de Mora to ask for 200 Portuguese soldiers. The request produced no troops, although some weapons were sent to Japan. The appeal horrified Valignano, who accused Coelho of over-reaction because Hideyoshi's Christian expulsion edict had never actually been put into effect. Hoping against hope that the matter had not reached the ears of Hideyoshi, Valignano arranged for the personal armaments to be sold secretly to get rid of them and for the larger cannon to be sent back to Macao. Valignano then turned his attentions towards punishing Coelho, a course of action the rebellious priest avoided by dying in May 1590. The unlikely Spanish threat to Japan died with him.[32]

Even though Hideyoshi had not immediately enforced his new anti-Christian policy, the expulsion edict of 1587 was the beginning of a long process in which the considerable Christian advances made by the Jesuits in Japan were placed slowly but surely into reverse. Some churches were destroyed, but no missionaries were deported for the time being. The decree was nevertheless the first hint of the real persecution that was follow, so that Japanese travelling abroad for reasons of commerce, learning or pilgrimage would soon be joined by a slow trickle of voluntary and later compulsory exiles whose motivation was religious freedom. The *rōnin* among them would serve beside the adventurers in the military diaspora of the Japanese Wild Geese.

Notes

1. Fróis Part 1, Chapter 63 in Matsuda, Kiichi and Kawasaki, Momota (Trans.) *Kanyaku Furoisu Nihon shi Vol. 9:* (Tokyo: Chuokoron-Shinsha, 2000), pp. 328-329.
2. Fróis Part 1, Chapter 48 in Matsuda, Kiichi and Kawasaki, Momota (Trans.) *Kanyaku Furoisu Nihon shi Vol. 9:* (Tokyo: Chuokoron-Shinsha, 2000), pp. 94-96.
3. Fróis Part 1, Chapter 73 in Matsuda, Kiichi and Kawasaki, Momota (Trans.) *Kanyaku Furoisu Nihon shi Vol. 9:* (Tokyo: Chuokoron-Shinsha, 2000), pp. 255-257.
4. Fróis Part 1, Chapter 100 in Matsuda, Kiichi and Kawasaki, Momota (Trans.) *Kanyaku Furoisu Nihon shi Vol. 9:* (Tokyo: Chuokoron-Shinsha, 2000), p. 355; Fujita, Tatsuo 'Piracy Prohibition Edicts and the Establishment of Maritime Control System in Japan. c. 1585-1640' in Ota, Atsushi (Ed.) *In the Name of the Battle against Piracy: Ideas and Practices in State Monopoly of Maritime Violence in Europe and Asia in the Period of Transition* (Leiden: Brill, 2018), p. 181.
5. Fróis Part 1, Chapter 97 in Matsuda, Kiichi and Kawasaki, Momota (Trans.) *Kanyaku Furoisu Nihon shi Vol. 9:* (Tokyo: Chuokoron-Shinsha, 2000). pp. 326-327. For the remains of the Fukabori fortifications see Various Authors *Nihon Jōhaku Taikei Vol 17* (Tokyo: Shinjimbutsu, 1980), p. 160.
6. Fróis Part 1, Chapter 100 in Matsuda, Kiichi and Kawasaki, Momota (Trans.) *Kanyaku Furoisu Nihon shi Vol. 9:* (Tokyo: Chuokoron-Shinsha, 2000), p. 353.

7. Fróis Part 1, Chapter 100 in Matsuda, Kiichi and Kawasaki, Momota (Trans.) *Kanyaku Furoisu Nihon shi Vol. 9:* (Tokyo: Chuokoron-Shinsha, 2000), pp. 356-359.

8. Fróis Part 1, Chapter 104 in Matsuda, Kiichi and Kawasaki, Momota (Trans.) *Kanyaku Furoisu Nihon shi Vol. 10:* (Tokyo: Chuokoron-Shinsha, 2000), pp. 11-14.

9. Elison, George *Deus Destroyed: The Image of Christianity in Early Modern Japan* (Harvard, 1988), p. 92.

10. Elison, George *Deus Destroyed: The Image of Christianity in Early Modern Japan.* (Harvard, 1988), pp. 28 & 400.

11. Fróis Part 2, Chapter 19 in Matsuda, Kiichi and Kawasaki, Momota (Trans.) *Kanyaku Furoisu Nihon shi Vol. 10:* (Tokyo: Chuokoron-Shinsha, 2000), p. 144.

12. Alessandro Valignano *Regimen for the Japan Superior* (24 June 1580) in Elison, George *Deus Destroyed: The Image of Christianity in Early Modern Japan.* (Cambridge Mass., Harvard University Press, 1988), p. 98.

13. Alessandro Valignano *Apologia in which are answered divers calumnies written against the Padres of the Society of Jesus of Japan and of China* (1598) in Elison, George *Deus Destroyed: The Image of Christianity in Early Modern Japan.* (Cambridge Mass., Harvard University Press, 1988), p. 99.

14. Valignano, Alessandro; Alvarez-Taladriz, José Luis (Ed.) *Sumario de las comas de Japon (1583). Adiciones del sumario de Japon (1592)* Monumenta Nipponica Monographs 9. (Tokyo: Sophia University Press, 1954), pp. 79-80.

15. From Fróis *Historia* Part Two, as translated by Cooper, Michael *They Came to Japan: An Anthology of European Reports on Japan, 1543-1640* (London: Thames and Hudson, 1965), p. 134.

16. For an artist's impression of Ishiyama Honganji see Turnbull, Stephen *Japanese Fortified Temples and Monasteries Ad 710-1602* (Oxford, Osprey Publishing 2005), p. 38.

17. Alessandro Valignano *Apologia in which are answered divers calumnies written against the Padres of the Society of Jesus of Japan and of China* (1598) in Elison, George *Deus Destroyed: The Image of Christianity in Early Modern Japan.* (Cambridge Mass., Harvard University Press, 1988), p. 99.

18. Alessandro Valignano *Apologia in which are answered divers calumnies written against the Padres of the Society of Jesus of Japan and of China* (1598) in Elison, George *Deus Destroyed: The Image of Christianity in*

Early Modern Japan. (Cambridge Mass., Harvard University Press, 1988), p. 99.

19. Boxer, C.R. *The Christian Century in Japan: 1549-1650* (Berkeley, 1951), p. 151.

20. Boxer, C.R. *The Christian Century in Japan: 1549-1650* (Berkeley, 1951), p. 158.

21. Boxer, C.R. 'Portuguese and Spanish Projects for the Conquest of south-east Asia 1580-1600' *Journal of Asian History* III (1969) p. 136.

22. Elisonas, Jurgis 'Christianity and the daimyo' In Hall, John Whitney and McLain, James L. (eds.) *The Cambridge History of Japan. Vol. 4 Early modern Japan* (Cambridge University Press, 1991), p. 352; De Lucenza, Alfonso; Schütte, Joseph Franz (Trans. & Ed.) *Erinnerungen aus der Christenheit von Omura.* (Rome, 1972), pp. 112

23. Bernard, Henri and Tientsin, S.J. (1938) 'Les Débuts des Relations Diplomatiques Entre le Japon at les Espagnols des Iles Philippines' (1571-1594) *Monumenta Nipponica* 1,1, p. 113; Elison, George *Deus Destroyed: The Image of Christianity in Early Modern Japan.* (Harvard, 1988), p. 114.

24. Fróis Part 2, Chapter 51 in Matsuda, Kiichi and Kawasaki, Momota (Trans.) *Kanyaku Furoisu Nihon shi Vol. 10:* (Tokyo: Chuokoron-Shinsha, 2000), pp. 281 & 285.

25. Murdoch, James *A History of Japan Volume 2* (London, 1903), p. 220.

26. DeLucenza,Alfonso;Schütte,JosephFranz(Trans.&Ed.)*Erinnerungen aus der Christenheit von Omura.* (Rome, 1972), pp. 254-255.

27. Bernard, Henri and Tientsin, S.J. (1938), p. 113; Laures, Johannes, SJ 'An Ancient Document on the Early Intercourse between Japan and the Philippines' *Culture Social* XXXIX (1941), p. 7.

28. Santiago de Vera to the King of Spain (1586) in Bernard, Henri and Tientsin, S.J. (1938), p. 113.

29. Elisonas, Jurgis 'Christianity and the daimyo' In Hall, John Whitney and McLain, James L. (eds.) *The Cambridge History of Japan. Vol. 4 Early modern Japan* Cambridge University Press, 1991, pp. 352-353; De Lucenza, Alfonso de; Schütte, Joseph Franz (Trans. & Ed.) *Erinnerungen aus der Christenheit von Omura.* (Rome, 1972), pp. 110-124.

30. Boxer, C.R. (1951), p. 147.

31. Elisonas, Jurgis 'Christianity and the daimyo' In Hall, John Whitney and McLain, James L. (eds.) *The Cambridge History of Japan. Vol. 4 Early modern Japan* Cambridge University Press, 1991. pp. 363.

32. Boxer, C.R. (1951), p. 149; Moran, J.F. *The Japanese and the Jesuits: Alessandro Valignano in sixteenth-century Japan* (London, 1993), p. 73.

Chapter 4

Traders and Samurai: Japanese Mercenaries in Siam

Throughout the century of overseas mercenary activity by the Japanese no place would give them a warmer welcome than the kingdom of Siam, where their service was to be distinguished and long-lasting.[1] Relations between Japan and Siam dated back to 1385,[2] but Japanese mercenaries were not to become well-established there until the later 1580s.[3] There may have been some flight of Christians to Siam following Hideyoshi's threats of persecution, but otherwise the process of recruitment took place against a settled backdrop of extensive and peaceful commercial contacts between Japan and south-east Asia.

This would be greatly helped in 1604 by the establishment of the Japanese *shuinjō*, the maritime pass system, which meant that trade could be conducted within a stable framework. The *shuin* (red seal) licences, so called because they bore the vermilion seal of the shogun, authorised the recipient to make a particular voyage to a designated destination and promised him protection.[4] Information about the significance of the red seals was sent to the rulers of many East Asian countries urging that they should be honoured, and that any vessel not carrying one should be regarded a pirate vessel. In their first year of operation 356 passes were issued, and Iwao has identified 299 ships trading between Siam and Japan from 1604 until the imposition of restrictions in 1635. Deerskins for making decorative leather and ray skins for sword mounts were the products most valued in Japan and, just like the silk from Macao, they were paid for in Japanese silver.[5]

As noted earlier, the Japanese who served as mercenaries in the *nihonmachi* in Ayutthaya, Siam's capital, tended to switch between their two roles as merchants and fighters. The first Japanese to serve in this capacity acted as the king's *asa* (military auxiliaries) and would quickly have discovered that the employment of foreign mercenaries was already very well established.[6] They therefore joined many other nationalities in the Siamese armed forces, and from about the mid-1610s onwards an élite subsection of them would become hereditary bodyguards to the sovereigns of Siam. These highly regarded warriors were almost invariably compared very favourably to their counterparts, a fact picked up by Joost Schouten in 1636 in words not dissimilar to the comments about the 'Spaniards of Asia':

> The King's power by water and land consists most of his own Vassals and Natives, he hath indeed some few Strangers, as Moors, Malayers and some five hundred Japanners, the most esteemed for their courage and fidelity...[7]

Similar sentiments were echoed two years later in 1638 by Van Vliet in his *Description of the Kingdom of Siam*, concerning Japanese guardsmen who were 'gorgeously dressed and carry excellent arms'.[8] They were regarded as the best of all the king's mercenaries:

> The most numerous are the Pegus; further there are Moors, Portuguese mestizos, Malays and a few of other nationalities. But the Japanese (numbering 70 to 80) are the best soldiers and have always been highly esteemed by the various kings for their bravery. The greater number of the soldiers are cowardly Siamese.[9]

Admittedly, Van Vliet does refer to the Japanese mercenaries in another report as 'bald headed villains', although the context of that remark is the rivalry that developed between the Japanese and Dutch traders in Siam during the 1630s.[10] Otherwise the samurai were valued for their fighting skills, of which the Siamese had prior experience because of *wakō* attacks. The Chinese pirate Lin Daoqian had attacked Siamese ships in 1578 and is later noted as having Japanese followers.[11] The first Japanese auxiliaries must have been recruited about this time because the earliest surviving written record of Japanese mercenaries fighting anywhere in south-east Asia is to be found in Siam at the battle of Nong Sarai in 1593. It was a remarkable debut for them. One elephant unit at least was commanded by Japanese *asa*, because an account of the Japanese involvement at Nong Sarai appears in the *Royal Chronicles of Ayutthaya* as: 'Phra Sena Phimuk, mounted on the bull elephant Füang Trai and in command of the corps of five hundred Japanese volunteers'.[12]

Sadly, the above quotation is the only account to have survived of the Japanese auxiliaries' involvement in an epic struggle that is greatly celebrated to this day in Thailand. According to popular belief, the pivotal moment in the battle of Nong Sarai was a single combat on elephants between King Naresuan of Siam and the Crown Prince of Burma, an incident much cherished and depicted in Thai culture.[13] Accounts of the overall campaign and battle are very confusing, but the sequence of events seems to be that a Burmese army invaded Siam in February 1593. King Naresuan and his brother, the future king Ekathotsarot, planned to intercept the enemy before they had a chance to threaten the capital, and set in motion a rapid move that would hit the invaders before the Burmese could draw up fortified lines. It would appear that as the armies closed Naresuan had problems controlling his own elephant and may have advanced perilously close to the Burmese front line, where he was surrounded by enemy elephants. His brother came to his aid and engaged in combat with one of the Burmese leaders. At this point another Burmese general saw King Naresuan approaching the elephant of the Burmese Crown Prince. He uncovered his animal's eyes in preparation for a charge. The elephant was in the highly aroused state known as musth, but instead of furiously attacking the Siamese king it attacked his own prince's animal instead and wounded it. Naresuan took advantage of the situation and advanced on the Crown Prince. This is the point where the famous single combat is supposed to have occurred, but an alternative version has it that the Crown Prince was hit by a bullet and fatally wounded. Whatever the cause, the death of the heir to the Burmese throne forced the invaders to retreat and abandon the campaign.

King Naresuan died in 1605 and was succeeded by his brother Ekathotsarot (r.1605–1611), who also made considerable use of foreign mercenaries including some Japanese, and it is at the close of Ekathotsarot's reign that we first encounter the most famous Japanese ever to serve in Siam: Yamada Nagamasa (1578–1633). His romantic life has been much embellished by legend and propaganda,[14] so I will attempt to tease out the historical facts from the legend in the paragraphs which follow. To give an example of the use of his name for propaganda purposes, Nagamasa was 'discovered' during the early years of the Pacific War as an exemplar of a bold Japanese who travelled overseas and found adventure and service, spreading Japanese ideals in a way that was perfectly in accordance with Japan's current imperialistic expansion.

The historical Yamada Nagamasa was probably born in 1590 in Sumpu (modern Shizuoka City), where his memory is greatly honoured and includes a bust of him on the site of his supposed birthplace and an annual festival with a considerable Thai input. The principal Shinto shrine in Shizuoka is the Sengen Shrine, to which Nagamasa is believed to have donated an *ema* (votive painting) in 1626. Nowadays *ema* are small wooden boards inscribed by visitors with their petitions and prayers. They are often ritually burned, but the older style of *ema* were large paintings that were fixed permanently to the beams of a shrine. Nagamasa's *ema* was sadly destroyed by a fire in 1789, but a copy was made, which shows that the picture consisted of a large ship that was more warship than merchant vessel. It has two cannon in the bows and eight cannon along the side. The crew are all dressed as samurai warriors, but wearing armour of a design associated more with the twelfth century than Nagamasa's own time. If the original representation was identical, it must have been intended to show Nagamasa in a heroic light, sailing off on a great adventure. The inscription suggests that it was dedicated and commissioned while Nagamasa was in Siam, not before he departed, because it reads, 'As I leave Sumpu, I offer a prayer and make sacred vows at this shrine. By heaven's grace I have made many vows. Their fulfilment is my prayer. Born in Suruga Province, now in Asia. An auspicious day of the second month, Third Year of Genna Yamada Nizaemonno-jō Nagamasa'.[15]

Yamada Nagamasa is believed to have served as a palanquin bearer for the nearby daimyo of Numazu, Okubo Tadasuke, sometime around 1605. In early 1612 he went to Siam, where relations with Japan were somewhat strained because certain of his fellow countrymen had caused uproar the previous year. According to Peter Floris, a Dutch merchant employed by the English East India Company, a group of Japanese, whom he refers to as 'slaves', attacked the royal palace in Ayutthaya to take revenge on four Siamese noblemen who had killed their leader. The four suspects were killed on the spot. The Japanese then forced the young King Sisaowaphak (who would reign for only one year between 1610 and 1611) to sign a pledge of non-retaliation using his own blood, at which the Japanese departed. Another Dutch commentator rejoiced that the ultimate outcome of the riot would be that the Japanese would be sent away from Siam, which would have been good for their own business. The official Siamese account reads as follows:

At that time many Japanese boats had come to trade. The Japanese had been angry, claiming that ministers were unjust, and had conspired together to join with Phra Phimon to kill the Holy-Great-King. [Later] about five hundred Japanese managed to assemble together, march [on] the imperial plaza, and waited [to take prisoner] the Holy-Lord-Omnipotent [who] had come out to listen to the holy monks explicate books at the Còm Thòng Sam Lang Holy Throne. Just at that moment eight holy monks from the Monastery of the Pradu Tree and the Hall of the Law came in and escorted His Highness out right in front of the Japanese. After the holy monks had escorted the King away, the Japanese began shouting loudly: 'If you were going to seize His Highness, how come you just sat around doing nothing?' and the Japanese argued with each other in an uproar.

Meanwhile Phta Maha Ammat managed to assemble his troops and [attacked and killed] the Japanese in great numbers. The Japanese were routed from the holy royal palace, boarded their junks and fled.[16]

One interesting feature of all the accounts of the 1611 riot is the strong implication by omission that the Japanese bodyguard to the king of Siam had not yet come into existence. Had they been guarding the king's person it is difficult to see how he could have been intimidated by other Japanese rioters. The famous unit was therefore probably formed some time during the next few years under the reign of King Songtham (r.1611–1628), and it is tempting to see Yamada Nagamasa, who arrived in Siam in 1612, as having some involvement in its formation. Unfortunately, Yamada Nagamasa is not mentioned in any accounts of the Japanese community in Siam until about 1621, by which time he has risen to become one of the leaders of the *nihonmachi* in Ayutthaya, and has sufficient status to be able to send a letter to the shogun's council back in Japan:

I have been asked by the King of Siam to deliver a message to the great Shogun asking for his blessings and indulgences. As you are no doubt aware, the King of Siam has dispatched an envoy of two Siamese men and Ito Kyodayi, according to your august wishes. The King here also presented the envoys with letters of introduction, in which he asks that you grant them your favours. And one very small thing, please allow me to extend my personal courtesies, the envoys carry two sheets of decorative sharkskin and 200 *kin* (12kg) of gunpowder as a present for you.[17]

One remarkable thing about the letter is that its Japanese recipients had no idea who this Yamada Nagamasa was. They made enquiries of a monk who was employed to keep the shogun's diplomatic records, but all he was able to come up with was the reference noted above to a certain Yamada Nagamasa who had been a palanquin bearer. Nevertheless, the letter had the gravity that would be associated with an important official, so a suitable reply was framed to 'Yamada Jizaemonno-jō', thereby addressing him with a Japanese rank:

> I have received your letter… The two envoys have had an audience, and a letter in reply has been vouchsafed for them to carry back to their own country… The two shark skins and 200 catties of powder have arrived, and both of us are greatly obliged for your generosity. We send you a present of twenty pieces of bleached cotton cloth as a small compensation for the emptiness of this letter.
>
> A lucky hour [day?] in the 9th month of the 7th Year of Genna (October 1621)
>
> Honda Kōzuke no Suke Masazumi
>
> Doi Ōe no Suke Toshikatsu.[18]

An unusual incident in 1621 confirms the strong local influence that Yamada Nagamasa must have been exerting by then. John Dod, the second-in-command of the English factory in Ayutthaya, was on his way to visit Nagamasa when he was attacked by a mob. He was being escorted by two Japanese, who succeeded in getting a message through to Nagamasa. The latter despatched forty men armed with muskets who rescued Dod from his assailants.[19]

Three years later in 1624 we find a reliable record of the fully-fledged Japanese royal bodyguard taking action on a much larger scale on behalf of their sovereign King Songtham. The incident began when a Spanish ship arrived in Siam and attacked a Dutch ship on the spurious grounds that its crew had caused them some injury. King Songtham valued the presence of the Dutch merchants in his country, and ordered the Spanish to release their prisoners and the captured cargo:

> Don Fernando de Silva answered that he would not do so, and broke out in words that might well have been avoided toward the king. The latter quickly collected a numerous fleet of boats, and one day attacked our ships with Japanese (who form the guard of that kingdom) and many Siamese. Our men, fearing what would happen, were hurriedly embarking their merchandise, in order to come to Manila. Our men

began to serve the artillery, but there were so many hostile boats that they covered the water. The Spanish craft ran aground in the confusion and danger, whereupon the Siamese (and chiefly the Japanese) entered the ships. Don Fernando de Silva, with sword and buckler in hand, sold his life dearly, and others did the same. But the enemy killed them except those who fled at the first stroke of the victory, who remained alive. I think some thirty were captured.[20]

The Spanish prisoners were taken to Ayutthaya and paraded in disgrace. Insults were thrown at them when they appeared in public in manacles. It was a considerable triumph for the Japanese guards and, as subsequent events would show, Yamada Nagamasa was now as close to the king as they were. This was illustrated when King Songtham lay near to death and placed his succession in the hands of one of his ministers, Phya Sriworawong, a man who was possibly an illegitimate son of King Ekathotsarot and who had considerable personal ambitions towards the throne. In this he would be challenged by Yamada Nagamasa, who swore fidelity to King Songtham's wishes. When the king died Phya Sriworawong assumed the regency on behalf of the young king Chetthathirat who was then only fifteen years old. A bloodbath followed when the new regent tried to eliminate his rivals. It was a matter in which Yamada Nagamasa intervened, allegedly saving several lives by his personal action.[21] Shortly afterwards Phya Sriworawong achieved the rank of Kalahom, by which title he is usually known. His first move was to isolate Nagamasa, which he did by fomenting an alleged plot on behalf of Prince Sri Sin, a brother of the late King Songtham. The plot succeeded admirably, because Nagamasa took up arms against the rebel and obligingly dispatched him:

Upon learning of the Prince, his uncle, being alive and at liberty, of his proclamation and of the rising of several towns, the King at once caused all the roads to be closed off, thus preventing the further movement of people in the rebellious area. Soon he had gathered a considerable army, consisting of 15,000 to 20,000 soldiers and 700 to 800 Japanese... The Colonel of the Japanese contacted the Supreme Commander of the Prince's army and [deceitfully] told him that he and his Japanese soldiers wanted to come over to his side and join the troops of the Prince. They agreed that they should take to the field as of giving battle and charge each other 'without bullets' at which the Japanese would pretend to surrender. However when the day came the Japanese attacked ferociously.[22]

53

The other obstacle to the Kalahom taking the throne was the young King Chetthathirat, who was murdered in 1629, supposedly by his own Japanese guardsmen. This may sound surprising, but apparently the Kalahom had first ensured that Yamada Nagamasa was cognisant of the need to have a mature individual ruling Siam. Nagamasa apparently agreed to the Kalahom again becoming regent to another boy king and son of Songtham: Athityawong. He then got Nagamasa out of the way by sending him to quell a rebellion in Ligor (modern Nakhon Si Thammarat), and promising him the rule of Ligor once the rival was eliminated. Nagamasa agreed, and while he was away the Kalahom had the young king executed and became king himself as King Prasat Thong (r.1629–1656).[23]

Prasat Thong then ordered a massacre of the remaining Japanese in Ayutthaya, but the plot came to the ears of his intended victims, who took the initiative. Satow provides many lively details of the ensuing action in translations from the *Tsukō Ichiran* that rejoice in the martial qualities of the Japanese:

> They proposed therefore to proceed into the city with a small body of armed men, and as soon as the discharge of firearms was heard, everyone who felt like a man would hurry to the city, and die there fighting, to the exaltation of the military renown of Japan. This proposal was received with enthusiasm, and the others swore they would all die together.[24]

There was some bloodshed before the Japanese agreed to leave peacefully, but as the Japanese ships were departing they were attacked by Siamese ships. The Japanese drove them off and successfully made their escape. The Siamese then called upon a Portuguese vessel that lay at anchor nearby to intercept them. There was another skirmish, and the Japanese finally sailed away, counting forty-three dead among their number. Yet the Ayutthaya affair was by no means over. Eight samurai had been absent on a pilgrimage to a Buddhist temple, and when they returned to the capital they were arrested and put in jail. They did not stay there for long, because news arrived that Siam was in peril. Word had reached Siam's enemies that the Japanese had been expelled. It says something for the reputation the Japanese enjoyed overseas that some 'Java people', a vague expression that may have meant pirates, Dutch troops or even Portuguese, seized the opportunity to raid Siam. The king of Siam soon came to his senses, acknowledging that the Japanese 'belonged to a nation more feared by the Southerners than a fierce tiger'. He promised the captives their liberty if they would help rid his country of the invaders. The eight Japanese acted at speed and proposed that as many Siamese troops as possible should be equipped with Japanese armour and helmets, the sight of which would terrify the attackers. Seventy suits of Japanese armour were found, and this number of Siamese dressed up in them. Eight war elephants were also made available. The eight samurai took command of the disguised company together with an additional 500 Siamese soldiers, and placed a couple of small cannon on the back of each elephant. The army set out for the coast, and as soon as they came in sight of the Java ships, they began a furious cannonade, which would speedily have sunk the whole fleet, had they not prudently retreated.

The seemingly indispensable Yamada Nagamasa served King Prasat Thong with great loyalty until 1630. In that year he led an attempt to annex Patani to his own granted territory of Ligor, where 'Many were killed or cut down on both sides, but in the end the Japanese charged their enemy so desperately that the people of Ligoor took to flight, whereupon the Japanese burned and plundered the greater part of the town'.[25] Nagamasa is believed to have died from his wounds after the battle, but he may have been poisoned by a rival.[26] On his death the leadership of the Japanese in Ligor passed to Nagamasa's son Oin, but he was unable to control local rebels and the decision was made to evacuate to Cambodia where, as we noted above, there was already an established Japanese community:

> But having been warned of the evil resolve and desperate intent of the Japanese, the King decided to surprise them. On the night of October 26 1630, when the land around Iudia (i.e. Ayutthaya) was inundated by water from the river, he ordered the Japanese quarters to be set ablaze. In addition, heavy cannon fire was brought to bear upon the Japanese, so that they were forced to retreat in their junks. But since they were too few in numbers to adequately defend both junks, they embarked in just one of them and retreated down the river, fighting all the way. The King pursued them down the river, and with the loss of many Siamese lives, expelled them from the country.[27]

Cambodia also became the destination for other fugitive Japanese from Ayutthaya, who tried in vain to persuade the Cambodian king to launch a revenge attack.[28] King Prasat Thong nevertheless went on to make good use of the Japanese in Ayutthaya who had stayed behind as his loyal guardsmen. He must also have forgiven the community as a whole, because he later augmented the guard by recruiting Japanese auxiliaries who were used in an expedition against Chiang Mai, which King Prasat Thong attacked with an army of supposedly 90,000 men, foot and horse, accompanied by elephants, artillery and all necessities. He sent ahead 'a force of 9,000 soldiers to whom the captured Japanese were added'. His rival fled without waiting for the king of Ava, whose aid he had been expecting.[29] In 1634 another army of 30,000, including once again many Japanese, set out to subdue Patani. 'But due to poor leadership, inexperience in conducting military operations, and the staying away of Dutch assistance, they ran into difficulties and were forced to retreat with the loss of many of their soldiers'.[30] As Ibrahim Syukri writes about the incident, 'But the Malaya of Patani were quite accustomed to war, greatly treasured the sovereignty of the raja, and knew the advantage of a life of independence. The attack of the Japanese and Siam-Ligor did not succeed this time either. Finally, they were forced to return to Ligor, taking their defeat with them.[31] The Japanese auxiliaries and guardsmen continued to serve the king as mercenaries, but from about this time the Dutch East India Company was beginning to replace the Japanese from the valuable trading exchange between the two countries. To a large extent this was due to the eagerness of the Dutch to take advantage of the restriction the shogun had placed on his own citizens. The subsequent history of the Wild Geese in Siam under these very different circumstances will be described in a later chapter.

Notes

1. For a summary see Iwao, Seiichi *Nan'yō Nihonmachi no Kenkyū* (Tokyo, 1940), pp. 187-193.
2. Iwao, Seiichi *Nan'yō Nihonmachi no Kenkyū* (Tokyo, 1940), p. 118.
3. Baker, Chris et. al. *Van Vliet's Siam* (Chiang Mai, 2005), p. 4; Elisonas, Jurgis 'Christianity and the Daimyo' in Hall p. 360; Ribiero, Madalena. 'The Japanese Diaspora in the Seventeenth Century, according to Jesuit Sources' *Bulletion of Portuguese/Japanese Studies* 3 (2001) p. 55.
4. See Toby *State and diplomacy*, 61 n 30
5. Translated and tabulated in Reid, Anthony *south-east Asia in the Age of Commerce 1450-1680: Volume Two, Expansion and Crisis* (New Haven, 1993), p.18.

6. Charney, Michael *south-east Asian Warfare, 1300-1900* (Leiden, 2004), p.224.
7. Caron, François and Schouten, Joost *A True Description of the Mighty Kingdoms of Japan and Siam*. A Facsimile of the 1671 London edition in a contemporary translation from the Dutch by Roger Manley. Introduction and notes by John Villiers. (Bangkok, 1986), pp. 133-134.
8. Baker, Chris et. al. *Van Vliet's Siam* (Chiang Mai, 2005), p. 118.
9. Baker, Chris et. al. *Van Vliet's Siam* (Chiang Mai, 2005), p. 122.
10. Baker, Chris et. al. *Van Vliet's Siam* (Chiang Mai, 2005), p. 56.
11. Wolters, O.W. 'Ayudhyā and the Rearward Part of the World' *The Journal of the Royal Asiatic Society of Great Britain and Ireland* No. 3/4 (Oct., 1968), p. 171.
12. Cushman, Richard D (trans.) *The Royal Chronicles of Ayutthaya: A Synoptic Translation* (Bangkok, 2000) p. 128.
13. Damrong, Prince Rajanubhab *Our Wars With The Burmese: Thai-Burmese Conflict 1539-1767* (Bangkok, 2001) pp. 120-135; Terwiel, Barend Jan 'What Happened at Nong Sarai? Comparing Indigenous and European Sources for Late 16th Century Siam' *Journal of the Siam Society* 101 (2013), pp. 19-34.
14. Iwamoto, Yoshiteru 'Yamada Nagamasa and his relations with Siam' *Journal of the Siam Society* 95 (2007) pp. 73-84. A fine biography is Polenghi, Cesare *Samurai of Ayutthaya: Yamada Nagamasa, Japanese Warrior and Merchant in Early Seventeenth-Century Siam* (Bangkok, 2009).
15. Iwamoto, Yoshiteru 'Yamada Nagamasa and his relations with Siam' *Journal of the Siam Society* 95 (2007) pp. 77-78.
16. Cushman, Richard D (trans.) *The Royal Chronicles of Ayutthaya: A Synoptic Translation* (Bangkok, 2000) p. 208.
17. Baker, Chris et. al. *Van Vliet's Siam* (Chiang Mai, 2005), p. 329.
18. Satow, Ernest M. 'Notes on the Intercourse between Japan and Siam in the Seventeenth Century' *Transactions of the Asiatic Society of Japan* 13 (1885) p. 155.
19. Polenghi, Cesare *Samurai of Ayutthaya: Yamada Nagamasa, Japanese Warrior and Merchant in Early Seventeenth-Century Siam* (Bangkok, 2009), p. 44.
20. *Relation of 1626* (unsigned and undated) in Blair and Robertson 1903-09, vol. 24, pp. 137-139.
21. Wyatt, David K. *Thailand: A Short History* (Yale, 1982), p.106-107.
22. Baker, Chris et. al. *Van Vliet's Siam* (Chiang Mai, 2005), pp. 268-269.

23. Munro-Hay, Stuart *Nakhon Sri Thammarat: The Archeology, History and Legends of a Southern Thai* Town (Bangkok, 2001), pp. 130-136.
24. Satow, Ernest M. 'Notes on the Intercourse between Japan and Siam in the Seventeenth Century' *Transactions of the Asiatic Society of Japan* 13 (1885) pp. 193-194 & 196-197.
25. Baker, Chris et. al. *Van Vliet's Siam* (Chiang Mai, 2005), p. 305.
26. Nagazumi, Yoko 'Ayutthaya and Japan: Embassies and Trade in the Seventeenth Century' in Breazeale, Kennon (ed.) *From Japan to Arabia* (Bangkok, 1999) p. 93.
27. Baker, Chris et. al. *Van Vliet's Siam* (Chiang Mai, 2005), p. 306.
28. Baker, Chris et. al. *Van Vliet's Siam* (Chiang Mai, 2005), p. 314.
29. Baker, Chris et. al. *Van Vliet's Siam* (Chiang Mai, 2005), p. 308.
30. Baker, Chris et. al. *Van Vliet's Siam* (Chiang Mai, 2005), p. 313.
31. Syukri, Ibrahim *History of the Malay Kingdom of Patani: Serajah Kerajaan Malaya Patani* (Chiang Mai, 2005). P. 46.

Chapter 5

The King of Spain's Samurai

The positive impression made on the Spanish by Japanese warriors associated in one way or another with the Philippines ensured that it was not long before these fierce fighters were recruited as mercenaries, and it is interesting to note that the first time their service was considered was for the most grandiose project in the entire history of the Spanish colonial empire: the conquest of China. The invasion would be launched from the Philippines and, in the words of one enthusiast, would provide, 'the greatest occasion and the grandest beginning that ever in the world was offered to a monarch. Here lies before him all that the human mind can desire or comprehend of riches and eternal fame, and likewise all that a Christian heart, desirous of the honour of God and his faith, can wish for'.[1]

The audacious invasion schemes (three were discussed successively over a period of two decades) were based on the naive assumption that China would be as easy to conquer as Peru. The earliest written records of such optimistic deliberations are to be found in a letter of 8 July 1569, where the writer simply states that, 'the people of China are not at all warlike. They rely entirely on numbers and on the fortification of their walls. It would decapitate them, if any of their forts were taken. Consequently, I believe (God helping), that they can be subdued easily and with few forces'.[2] Further reports couched in a similarly positive vein followed over the next few years, in one of which – *News from the Western Islands* by Hernando Riquel and others, written on 11 January 1574 from distant Mexico – it was boldly claimed that even though, 'There are many very populous cities on the way... they could be subdued and conquered with less than sixty good Spanish soldiers'.[3] A less fantastic estimate of the number of troops that would be required comes from the incumbent Governor of the Philippines Francisco de Sande on 7 July 1576. He writes:

> The equipments necessary for this expedition are four or six thousand men, armed with lances and arquebuses, and the ships, artillery, and necessary munitions... With two or three thousand men one can take whatever province he pleases... This will be very easy. In conquering one province, the conquest of all is made.[4]

As to the question of how an invading army of 6,000 men might be raised, sufficient local recruitment of Europeans was impossible because a census of 1584 showed the existence of only 713 Spanish men throughout all the Philippine Islands.[5] Even if auxiliary troops could be transported from Spain, there was no guarantee that all would reach their destination, because in the parallel Portuguese experience it was not unknown for half the men shipped from Lisbon to Goa to die en route.[6] Mercenaries, particularly Japanese warriors hired in the Philippines from the expatriate community or from *wakō*, would provide the answer to the manpower problem. As the report notes optimistically, 'In all these islands a great many corsairs live, from whom also we could obtain help for this expedition, as also from the Japanese, who are the mortal enemies of the Chinese. All would gladly take part in it'.[7]

In spite of all this enthusiasm the 1576 scheme came to nothing, but ten years later the conquest of China was being seriously discussed again during a meeting held on 20 April 1586 in Manila, chaired by the new governor Santiago de Vera.[8] The fresh invasion scheme was the brainchild of the Spanish Jesuit Alonso Sánchez, concerning whose ideas Boxer comments that his report 'has to be read to be believed'.[9] Indeed, the first things that strike the reader of the long account are its supreme air of self-confidence and the immense detail that has already gone into planning the realisation of the vision.

Beginning with the troop requirements, by this time the numbers of the Spanish forces felt to be necessary to conquer the Ming had grown to a more realistic figure of between 20,000 and 25,000 men, involving several hundred soldiers drawn from the colonists themselves augmented by up to 12,000 men sent from Spain, local Indians and 'five or six thousand Japanese'.[10] Six thousand samurai could not be raised from the Philippine *nihonmachi* alone or from cooperative *wakō*, so the 1586 plan took the notion of mercenaries on to a different plane by envisaging for the first time that recruitment could be carried out within Japan itself. Governor Santiago de Vera was confident that this could be done. He knew that there were Jesuit missionaries in Japan who enjoyed a close relationship with the Christian lords, so by a supreme exercise of logic he envisaged them acting as recruiting sergeants.[11] De Vera was equally confident that the Spanish Crown would pay for the enterprise, so 'Have his Majesty send two hundred thousand pesos to cover and provide for these and many other things, and pay the Japanese, and other incidental expenses'.[12]

The above considerations reveal one of the most profound weaknesses in the scheme: the need for cooperation with the Portuguese in Japan. Not only was this officially forbidden by the strict rules that kept their spheres of influence apart, but Santiago de Vera also does not seem to have considered the embarrassment that the request might cause to the peaceful and somewhat precarious Jesuit mission in Japan, which was currently under threat from the Shimazu with Hideyoshi waiting in the wings. Yet the optimistic planners of the invasion had even worked out how the Portuguese contribution might best be gathered and deployed. The assembly point would be Cagayan because of its proximity both to China and Japan, but rather than attacking China as one force, the Spanish army would land in Fujian while the Portuguese entered Guangdong from Macao. The two armies, accompanied by Jesuits from Macao serving as interpreters and guides, would then make their way north and join forces for a triumphant assault on Beijing.[13] The authors also stated that if the Japanese mercenaries recruited by the Portuguese preferred to join the Spanish that would be acceptable, and if there was any reluctance on the part of the Jesuits in Japan to comply then the full authority of the King of Spain should be invoked.[14] The compilers of the report had also worked out that:

> The troops sent should be infantry with arquebuses, corselets, and pikes; and, besides, a few musketeers… there should be, for emergency, a number of coats of mail, and arquebuses; and, above all, five hundred muskets and three or four thousand pikes, a thousand corselets, and a thousand Burgundian morions from New Spain. Second: good flints and locks for the arquebuses can be had here cheaply; but the barrels must be brought from Spain, and should be all of one bore, so that the same bullets may be furnished for them. Third: from China we can procure very cheaply copper, saltpetre, and bullets; and in this island are ample mines of copper and sulphur.[15]

The prize was of course immense: nothing less than the conversion of the entire Chinese Empire to Christianity. Needless to say, the *Memorial to Council* dwells heavily on the benefits of so great a missionary enterprise, and goes into a surprising level of further detail over what local adjustments would be required once China was pacified. One pressing need would be to establish schools so that Spanish could replace three devices of the devil: the Chinese language, its writing system and its literature, 'which are extremely difficult, so much so that even they cannot understand them while still children... a diabolic invention to keep them busy all their lives with their whole minds'.[16]

As suggested above, the Portuguese element in the invasion plans eventually proved to be the main reason why the 'monstrous folly of so absurd an undertaking' was never implemented, although the fact that the proposal reached Madrid at about the same time as the news of the defeat of the Spanish Armada sent to England probably did not help.[17] Nevertheless, later correspondence reveals that overtures were indeed made to Japan and that they did not entirely fall on deaf ears. In a letter of 1587 to King Philip II, de Vera reports that he had entertained a visitor in the person of a 'captain of the king of Firando'. The so-called king would have been Matsuura Shigenobu (1549–1614), the incumbent daimyo of Hirado and the son of the late Takanobu whose men had once attacked the Portuguese in Fukuda Bay. The prime purpose of his captain's visit, as revealed in secret to the Governor, was to offer Philip II the military service of the Matsuura domain and that of 'another Christian king: his friend, by name Don Augustin'. This friendly daimyo was the Christian lord Konishi Yukinaga (?–1600), who:

> would send as many people and soldiers as should be requested. All these would come well-armed and at little expense, whether for Borneo, Siam, the Moluccas, or Great China (to which country they are hostile), without asking anything in return, for they only wish to serve your Majesty and to gain honour. This man has under him five hundred excellent soldiers, whose captain he is, who would come here willingly. These are his formal words. As a prudent man and experienced in war, he gave me certain advice, and a plan for bringing easily from those provinces six thousand men...[18]

Yet by the time of this remarkable meeting even the enthusiastic Governor Santiago de Vera seems to have had second thoughts about the proposal, so he simply notes in the letter that:

> I thanked him heartily in your Majesty's name for his offer, saying that your Majesty is not now thinking of the conquest of China or

other kingdoms; and that your Majesty's object has been, and is, to convert the natives, to preach the holy gospel to them, and to bring them to the knowledge of our Lord, so that all might be saved.[19]

With that letter the Spanish plans to conquer China were shelved indefinitely.

Japanese mercenaries in Spanish service

The invasion of China may have been abandoned, but the conquest of other lands was still on the Spanish agenda, and in 1596 the Spanish managed to use Japanese mercenaries for an invasion of Cambodia.[20] This temporarily successful operation was later claimed to be a victory whereby 'twenty-two Spaniards and as many Japanese were masters of the kingdom of Cambodia'.[21] It took place at a time described by David Chandler as Cambodia's 'Dark Ages', because the period of the great Khmer Empire had long passed into history. Cambodia was facing the high tide of Spanish imperialism by men who were 'masters of new military technology'.[22] Chandler is specifically referring here to firearms, but the fact that the Spanish were able to achieve victories using only a few hundred men also depended also on their use of Japanese mercenaries.

The operation had its origins in the invasion of Cambodia by Siam in 1593. The Siamese operation under King Naresuan had been an extensive one culminating in an attack on the then Cambodian capital Lovec, where 'the storming armies had elephants with iron face armours and iron clad feet, the men wore hats, coats and shoes made from thick hide. All the cannons were to fire at the battlements and gates'.[23] The gates were eventually forced open using the war elephants, and in January 1594 Lovec fell. The Cambodian King Sattha fled, while many member of the Cambodian royal family were taken prisoner to Ayutthaya.

Reports to the Philippines about the war lodged by the adventurers Blas Ruiz and the Portuguese Diego Belloso claimed that because of the Siamese incursions, the kingdom was weak and open to exploitation and that its king would welcome Spanish help to resist further attacks from Siam. The monarch was also willing to make an important concession reminiscent of Ōmura Sumitada's offer of Nagasaki to the Jesuits. 'He said that his final aim was to be a Christian, and that this I should tell the governor; and further that he wished to lend all his power to the Spaniards, so that they could conquer the surrounding kingdoms and possess them. As for him and his children, he wished no more than his own kingdom, converted to the faith'.[24] Much intrigue followed as the idea was formed of a Spanish expedition to assist Cambodia and advance thereby Spanish interests. One of the most enthusiastic supporters of the plan was the ruthless Dominican Diego Aduarte, noted earlier as a fighter against and later with *wakō*, and a man who later to be described by a modern Filipino scholar as being 'half warrior and half priest, brave and enduring, confessing, baptising and killing'.[25]

The expedition to conquer Cambodia set sail from Manila at the beginning of 1596 without approval from Madrid. Three ships conveyed 130 Spanish troops and about twice that number of Filipino natives and Japanese mercenaries.[26] Having established a foothold in Cambodia the Spanish prepared an embassy for the new king, but when they were forewarned that he planned to have them murdered, their plans changed dramatically to an attack on the palace:

> …having first done their duties as Christians, they decided to storm the king's residence. Blas Ruiz and Brother Diego Aduarte acting as captains and the others keeping their rank, with remarkable courage and valour, they crossed two rivers and having routed the guards who were on one of the river's bridges, arrived at the palace at two in the morning and attacked it as if they had been lions. They moved with lightning speed and brought down the walls, knocked down the partitions; assaulted the towers, broke the doors open and killed the men. The King fled with his wives, was hit by a bullet and died.[27]

When dawn broke the extent of the carnage was revealed, with 'the palace razed to the ground, the land strewn with corpses, the streets red with blood, the women clamouring, some for their husbands, some for their sons and some for the brothers…'[28]

Their next objective was to restore King Sattha, but when the Spanish discovered that he had died in exile in Laos they attempted to place another on his throne. In the resulting turmoil we are told that rival candidates for the sovereignty each received support (which may have had a military element) from different sections of Cambodia's expatriate Japanese community.[29] An uprising followed and the Cambodians fought back over the next three years, during which two further Spanish incursions were carried out. The first, in 1598, was a private enterprise expedition involving 200 Spanish soldiers, some Filipinos and some Japanese and was an unmitigated disaster.[30] A final attempt was made in 1599, again involving Japanese mercenaries, but this was to be thwarted not because of Cambodian resistance, but because of dissension between the Spanish and their Japanese mercenaries. Friction arose between them and their Spanish employers.[31] Trouble began when a Spaniard insulted a Japanese: this was the incident noted in an earlier chapter. The Cambodians, naturally enough, did all they could to make matters worse and a massacre of the colonists occurred.[32] Only one Franciscan, one Spanish soldier and five Filipinos survived.[33] The project was then abandoned leaving most of the original invaders dead.[34] The Spanish conquest of Cambodia was over.

The domestic use of Japanese mercenaries

In spite of the failure of the Cambodian expedition, the Spanish never lost sight of the qualities of the Japanese as fighting men, and in 1603 they also realised that such usefulness need not be confined to foreign conquest. The revelatory incident occurred in October of that year when Japanese mercenaries helped to put down with great brutality a local Chinese insurrection in Manila. Known as the Sangley Rebellion from the name given to pure-bred Chinese in the Philippines, it began with a curious incident whereby three mandarins arrived unexpectedly from China in search of a supposed 'mountain of gold' where trees with golden leaves grew. The ever-suspicious Spanish believed that the strange mission was a preliminary to an invasion of Manila, where the presence of ten Chinese to every one Spaniard implied the possible existence of a fifth column and likely annihilation.[35] The tragic events that followed were prompted by over-reaction on the part of Archbishop Benavides, whose suspicions that the Sangleys were about to rise up became a self-fulfilling prophecy:

> From that time, both in the city and its environs, where the Sangleys were living scattered, these people began to persecute the Sangleys by word and deed. The natives, Japanese and soldiers of the camp took from them their possessions and inflicted on them other ill-treatment, calling them dogs and traitors, and saying that they knew well that they meant to rebel…. This alone was sufficient to make it necessary for the Sangleys to do what they had no intention of doing.[36]

65

Forced to act to combat their oppression, the Sangleys did indeed revolt, capturing Spanish positions and creating havoc. On Monday 6 October 1603:

> Joan Xuarez Gallinato, accompanied by some soldiers and a Japanese troop, made a sally from the Dilao gate upon the Sangleys. They reached the church, when the Sangleys turned upon them and threw the Japanese into disorder. The latter were the cause of all retreating again to seek the protection of the walls, whither the Sangleys pursued them.[37]

Japanese mercenaries then took part in the counterattack:

> This man left with two hundred Spaniards – soldiers and volunteers – three hundred Japanese, and one thousand five hundred Pampagna and Tagál Indians, on the twentieth of October. He was so expeditious, that with little or no loss of men, he found the Sangleys fortified in San Pablo and Batangas, and after fighting with them, killed and destroyed them all. None escaped, except two hundred, who were taken alive to Manila for the galleys.[38]

The bloody conclusion of the Sangley Rebellion provided the first instance of what would become the Japanese mercenaries' most unsavoury role: that of acting as executioners. Their sharp swords and their skills in using them willingly, efficiently and rapidly made them ideal for such duties, and more than 23,000 Sangleys are believed to have been killed either in the fighting or during the executions afterwards. The accounts state simply that Don Pedro de Acuña ordered 'many Spaniards and natives' to 'hunt the disbanded Sangleys', while Hernando de Avalos seized more than 400 pacified Sangleys, 'and leading them to an estuary, manacled two and two, delivered them to certain Japanese, who killed them'.[39] The mercenary soldier's traditional desire for loot was also to be demonstrated when an attack was made on the Parián, the Chinese settlement.[40] 'The Japanese, seeing that the Pampanga Indians were destroying and sacking the Parián with great fury, gradually joined them. Together they killed all the Chinese whom they met, and went away, this man with a chest, this one with a pair of breeches, [and others with] bags filled with silks and rich articles'.[41]

The Japanese had served their masters well, but it was not long before suspicions would be entertained that these fierce warriors might one day rise up against the Spanish authorities. With this possibility in mind, in 1605 further restrictions were placed on the Japanese in Dilao because their numbers had reached 3,000.[42] Such an incident almost happened in 1606 while many Spaniards from the Manila garrison were taking part in an expedition to the Moluccas under the governor Don Pedro de Acuña, but the Japanese were eventually calmed by the local friars.[43] In de Morga's words:

> The Audiencia wished to drive a number of Japanese from the city, for they were a turbulent people and promised little security for the country. When this was attempted and force employed, the Japanese resisted, and the matter came to such a pass that they took arms to oppose it, and it was necessary for the Spaniards to take their arms also. The affair assumed definite proportions, and some on either side wished to give battle. However, it was postponed by various means until, through the efforts of certain religious, the Japanese were quieted; and afterward as many as possible were embarked on vessels, although they resented it greatly.[44]

De Morga adds with evident relief that because the Japanese are 'a spirited and very mettlesome race' it was fortunate that they had not come to blows, or the Spaniards would have come off worse.[45] Ironically, the Japanese mercenaries who had been included in Don Pedro de Acuña's expedition to the Moluccas were fighting bravely and well for their Spanish masters, leading to the recapture of a fortress on the island of Tidore,[46] so in spite of the unease caused by the presence of Japanese in Manila the use of them in a military capacity continued. Recruitment was still sought after another revolt in 1607, one of the number requested being a Japanese gunsmith.[47] Yet from this time onwards their main enemy would be the Dutch, a situation that threw up for the first time the possibility of Japanese mercenaries fighting on opposite sides at the same time, as a later chapter will describe.

Notes

1. Santiago de Vera and others, *Memorial to the Council*, 26 July 1586, in Blair and Robertson 1903-09, vol. 6, pp. 197-198.
2. Letter from Martin de Rada to the Marquis de Falçes, 8 July 1569, in Blair and Robertson 1903-09, vol. 34, p. 227.

3. Hernando Riquel and others, *News from the Western Islands*, 11 January 1574, in Blair and Robertson 1903-09, vol. 3, p. 247.
4. Francisco de Sande *Relation of the Filipinas Islands*, 7 June 1576 in Blair and Robertson 1903-09, vol. 4, pp. 58-59.
5. Boxer, C.R. 'Portuguese and Spanish Projects for the Conquest of south-east Asia 1580-1600' *Journal of Asian History* III (1969) p. 133.
6. Boxer, C.R. 'Portuguese and Spanish Projects for the Conquest of south-east Asia 1580-1600' *Journal of Asian History* III (1969) p. 135.
7. Francisco de Sande *Relation of the Filipinas Islands*, 7 June 1576 in Blair and Robertson 1903-09, vol. 4, pp. 58-59.
8. Santiago de Vera and others, *Memorial to the Council* 26 July 1586 in Blair and Robertson 1903-09, vol. 6, pp. 157-233.
9. Boxer, C.R. *The Christian Century in Japan: 1549-1650* (Berkeley, 1951), p. 257. Boxer is right in his suggestion to the reader, and the report may be found as Santiago de Vera and others, *Memorial to the Council* 26 July 1586 in Blair and Robertson 1903-09, vol. 6, pp. 157-233.
10. Santiago de Vera and others, *Memorial to the Council* 26 July 1586 in Blair and Robertson 1903-09, vol. 6, p. 200.
11. Santiago de Vera and others, *Memorial to the Council* 26 July 1586 in Blair and Robertson 1903-09, vol. 6, pp. 197-198.
12. Santiago de Vera and others, *Memorial to the Council* 26 July 1586 in Blair and Robertson 1903-09, vol. 6 p. 203.
13. Santiago de Vera and others, *Memorial to the Council* 26 July 1586 in Blair and Robertson 1903-09, vol. 6 p. 207.
14. Santiago de Vera and others, *Memorial to the Council* 26 July 1586 in Blair and Robertson 1903-09, vol. 6 pp. 208-209.
15. Santiago de Vera and others, *Memorial to the Council* 26 July 1586 in Blair and Robertson 1903-09, vol. 6 pp. 201-202.
16. Santiago de Vera and others, *Memorial to the Council* 26 July 1586 in Blair and Robertson 1903-09, vol. 6 p. 215.
17. Boxer, C.R. *The Christian Century in Japan: 1549-1650* (Berkeley, 1951). pp. 257-259.
18. Santiago de Vera, Letter to Felipe II, 26 June 1587, in Blair and Robertson 1903-09, vol. 6 p. 309.
19. Santiago de Vera, Letter to Felipe II, 26 June 1587, in Blair and Robertson 1903-09, vol. 6 p. 309.
20. Briggs, L.P. 'Spanish Intervention in Cambodia 1593-1603' *T'oung Pao* 39 (1950), pp. 132-160; Boxer, C.R. 'Portuguese and Spanish Projects for the Conquest of south-east Asia 1580-1600' *Journal of Asian History* III (1969) pp.130-131.

21. Boxer, C.R. *The Christian Century in Japan: 1549-1650* (Berkeley, 1951). pp 260-261.

22. Chandler, David *A History of Cambodia* (Boulder Colorado, 1983), p. 85.

23. Jumsai, M.L. Manich *History of Thailand and Cambodia (From the days of Angkor to the present)* (Bangkok, 1987), p. 41.

24. *Expedition to Camboja*. Gregorio da Cruz, and others; 1-3 August 1594 in Blair and Robertson 1903-09, vol. 9, p. 170.

25. Boxer, C.R. *The Christian Century in Japan: 1549-1650* (Berkeley, 1951). p 260.

26. Briggs, L.P. 'Spanish Intervention in Cambodia 1593-1603' *T'oung Pao* 39 (1950), p. 152.

27. De San Antonio, Gabriel Quiroga *A Brief and Truthful Relation of Events in the Kingdom of Cambodia* (originally published as Breve y Verdadera Relacion de los Successos del Reyno de Camboxa in 1604) (Bangkok, 1998), p.21.

28. De San Antonio, Gabriel Quiroga *A Brief and Truthful Relation of Events in the Kingdom of Cambodia* (originally published as Breve y Verdadera Relacion de los Successos del Reyno de Camboxa in 1604) (Bangkok, 1998), pp. 21-22.

29. Briggs, L.P. 'Spanish Intervention in Cambodia 1593-1603' *T'oung Pao* 39 (1950), p. 154.

30. Briggs, L.P. 'Spanish Intervention in Cambodia 1593-1603' *T'oung Pao* 39 (1950), pp. 155-156.

31. Briggs, L.P. 'Spanish Intervention in Cambodia 1593-1603' *T'oung Pao* 39 (1950), p. 157.

32. Tully, John *A Short history of Cambodia: From Empire to Survival* (London, 2005), p.61.

33. Briggs, L.P. 'Spanish Intervention in Cambodia 1593-1603' *T'oung Pao* 39 (1950), p. 157

34. Boxer, C.R. *The Christian Century in Japan: 1549-1650* (Berkeley, 1951). pp 260-261.

35. Borao, José Eugenio 'The massacre of 1603: Chinese perception of the Spaniards in the Philippines' *Itinerario*, vol. 23, No. 1, 1998, p. 22.

36. De Morga, Antonio *History of the Philippine Islands from the discovery by Magellan in 1521 to the beginning of the XVII Century; with descriptions of Japan, China and adjacent countries* Volumes I and II translated and edited by Blair, E.H. and Robertson, J.A. (Cleveland, 1907, reprint New York, 1970), Vol. II p. 32.

37. De Morga, Antonio *History of the Philippine Islands from the discovery by Magellan in 1521 to the beginning of the XVII Century; with*

descriptions of Japan, China and adjacent countries Volumes I and II translated and edited by Blair, E.H. and Robertson, J.A. (Cleveland, 1907, reprint New York, 1970). II p. 40.

38. De Morga, Antonio *History of the Philippine Islands from the discovery by Magellan in 1521 to the beginning of the XVII Century; with descriptions of Japan, China and adjacent countries* Volumes I and II translated and edited by Blair, E.H. and Robertson, J.A. (Cleveland, 1907, reprint New York, 1970). II p. 41-42.

39. De Morga, Antonio *History of the Philippine Islands from the discovery by Magellan in 1521 to the beginning of the XVII Century; with descriptions of Japan, China and adjacent countries* Volumes I and II translated and edited by Blair, E.H. and Robertson, J.A. (Cleveland, 1907, reprint New York, 1970). II p. 42 n.

40. Wickberg, Edgar *The Chinese in Philippine Life, 1850-1898* (Manila, 2000), p.11.

41. Miguel Rodriguez de Maldonaldo *The Sangley insurrection of 1603* (Sevilla 1606) in Blair, Emma Helen and Robertson, James Alexander (eds.) *The Philippine Islands, 1493-1803* (Cleveland, 1903-9), Part 14 p. 129.

42. Paske-Smith, T.R. 'Japanese Trade and Residence in the Philippines' *Transactions of the Asiatic Society of Japan* XLII (2) (1914, p. 699-670.

43. Boxer, C.R. *The Christian Century in Japan: 1549-1650* (Berkeley, 1951), p.261; Borao, José Eugenio 'The massacre of 1603: Chinese perception of the Spaniards in the Philippines' *Itinerario*, vol. 23, No. 1, 1998, pp. 22-39.

44. De Morga, Antonio *History of the Philippine Islands from the discovery by Magellan in 1521 to the beginning of the XVII Century; with descriptions of Japan, China and adjacent countries* Volumes I and II translated and edited by Blair, E.H. and Robertson, J.A. (Cleveland, 1907, reprint New York, 1970). II p. 61. ALSO BR 16 61

45. De Morga, Antonio *History of the Philippine Islands from the discovery by Magellan in 1521 to the beginning of the XVII Century; with descriptions of Japan, China and adjacent countries* Volumes I and II translated and edited by Blair, E.H. and Robertson, J.A. (Cleveland, 1907, reprint New York, 1970). II p. 61.

46. Boxer, C.R. *The affair of the Madre de Deus: a chapter in the history of the Portuguese in Japan* (London, 1929), p. 21n.

47. Paske-Smith, T.R. 'Japanese Trade and Residence in the Philippines' *Transactions of the Asiatic Society of Japan* XLII (2) (1914) p. 700; Boxer, C.R. 'Asian potentates and European artillery in the 16th-18th centuries: A footnote to Gibson-Hill' *Journal of the Malaysian Branch of the Royal Asiatic Society* XXXVIII (1966) p. 170.

Chapter 6

The Dutch East India Company and their *soldaten van Japon*

In spite of entertaining considerable misgivings about the Japanese that were broadly similar to the doubts expressed by the Spanish on the Philippines, out of all the colonial powers the Dutch would prove to be the most enthusiastic employers of Japanese mercenaries, wholeheartedly embracing their volatile ferocity and recruiting freely within Japan itself in a unique scheme that promised an extension of Dutch power and influence beyond anyone's wildest dreams. The Japanese mercenaries would become the first Asian soldiers to be recruited by the Dutch, and even though the programme only lasted for a few years and was far from being the golden age of Japanese mercenaries that the scheme originally promised, the service rendered to these particular European masters forms an important episode in the story of Japan's Wild Geese.

The actual agency that employed Japanese mercenaries in Dutch service was the remarkable entity known as the *Vereeinigde Oostindisches Compagnie* (VOC), the Dutch East India Company, which had been founded in Amsterdam in March 1602. It was formed (after long and tortuous negotiations) by merging a number of individual pioneering companies who since 1594 had been sending fleets to the East in defiance of the papal jurisdiction that had supposedly divided the world exclusively between Spain and Portugal. The earlier Dutch system had been inefficient; in 1598 fourteen different Dutch companies sent 65 ships.[1] The replacement of competition and duplication by unity and cooperation gave strength and enhanced ambition, both of which were backed to the hilt by the rulers of the States General of the Netherlands, who delegated power and responsibility to the 'Heeren 17', the seventeen-strong committee who ran the VOC. In the words of

Adam Clulow (from whose extensive works much of this chapter is drawn) their support meant that the VOC 'combined the attributes of both corporation and state'.[2] As a result, although it would become one of the greatest trading organisations in world history, commerce was never the VOC's only goal, because its mighty fleets sailed for the Indies under a charter that gave them full jurisdiction to exercise true rights of sovereignty.

The process whereby this blend of commerce and warfare might be achieved was set out clearly in Article 35 of the VOC's founding charter, which allowed the application of both diplomacy and warfare in the realisation of its chosen goals. The organisation was therefore permitted to 'enter into agreement with states and potentates' and could also 'build fortresses and strongholds, appoint governors, armed forces, officers of justice and officers of other necessary services'.[3] According to its early and very influential governor-general Jan Pieterszoon Coen, 'The Indies trade has to be pursued and maintained under the protection of one's own arms... the weapons must be financed through the profits so earned by trade. In short, trade without war and war without trade cannot be maintained'.[4] Japanese mercenaries would make up a small yet important part of those 'arms'.

Even though the aspirations of the VOC would prove crucial in determining the direction of Dutch-Japanese relations, the first contact between the two nations had already taken place a full two years before the organisation was founded. The innovative venture was the result of an ill-fated enterprise by one of the smaller pioneering companies that the VOC would replace, and was almost a complete disaster. In 1598 five ships set sail from Rotterdam. The fleet's route took it through the Straits of Magellan and across the Pacific, but after severe storms and fatal attacks from Portuguese and Spanish ships only the one vessel, the *de Liefde,* was left, and it was to run aground off the coast of Usuki on the Japanese island of Kyushu. The shipwreck happened in April 1600 and constituted the first arrival of any Dutch ship in Japan. The survivors included its captain Jacob Quaeckernaeck, senior officer Jan Joosten van Lodenstein and the ship's pilot William Adams, the first Englishman ever to reach Japan. The loss of the ship (which could not be salvaged) meant that their arrival was nothing like an ambassadorial approach from a new foreign contact. It also ensured that the survivors were effectively marooned in Japan, where they attempted to make the best of things. Lodenstein and Adams went on to play the roles of occasional advisors to Tokugawa Ieyasu, who was intrigued by the arrival of a type of European who was different from the Portuguese, although their influence was never as great as subsequent legends would claim.

Oblivious to the fate of the *de Liefde*, the VOC's efforts to extend its reach elsewhere in Asia were being pressed forward relentlessly, and in 1605 word reached the handful of pioneers stranded in Japan that a trading post had been established at Patani on the Malay Peninsula. After much negotiation and pleading the Bakufu (Shogunate) gave permission for the *de Liefde*'s former captain Quaeckernaeck to visit it. The party were conveyed to Patani on a ship provided by the Matsuura daimyo of Hirado, who was eager for them to make contact for his own purposes.

While waiting in Patani for the arrival of the next VOC fleet and a possible opportunity to make a proper show of opening up diplomatic relations with Japan, Jacob Quaeckernaeck received interesting if somewhat alarming news. His cousin, Admiral Cornelis Matalief de Jonge, was currently laying siege to the Portuguese colony of Malacca, a strategic base located on the opposite side of the Malay Peninsula. Quaeckernaeck resolved to join him, and when he arrived after a month's journey his cousin placed him in command of a Dutch ship. During the course of the fighting the unfortunate Quaeckernaeck received a Portuguese bullet in his head and died instantly. He would have perished in the certain knowledge that in the Portuguese army opposing him was a contingent of Japanese mercenaries. It was the first time that the Dutch had experienced at first hand the fighting qualities of the men with whom they were so keen to make official contact.

Their finest hour: Japanese mercenaries in the defence of Malacca

As the events concerning Nagasaki narrated above show, relations between the Portuguese and their Japanese converts in Japan itself were very cordial. In marked contrast, however, some of the Portuguese colonists elsewhere tended to be suspicious of Japanese people who were outside their own country. For example, in 1597 the Portuguese Viceroy in Goa expressly forbade any Japanese from landing there, even if they were Christians.[5] The mistrust may have sprung from Portuguese experiences of the *wakō*, but it is more likely to have had its roots in the diplomatic relations with China that were conducted through the valuable Portuguese colony of Macao, where the Japanese were treated with some suspicion even though Nagasaki lay at the other end of a major commercial enterprise.

The Chinese, who had strong views about *wakō*, regarded all Japanese as 'thieves, birds of prey and rebels against the sovereign emperor of China', and wished them to be excluded. Japanese were therefore officially forbidden to enter Macao, and tensions remained high. Sympathetic Portuguese however regularly defied the ban and took Japanese to Macao as servants, 'oblivious of the fact that they are rearing tigers'.[6] On occasions the enmity grew serious. In 1606 a rumour spread through Guangdong province that the Portuguese were planning an invasion of China from Macao in company with a force of Japanese Christian samurai, and as a result one Chinese Christian was tortured to death as a spy.[7]

The Portuguese in Malacca (modern Melaka) viewed the Japanese in a very different light because of what happened in 1606. On that occasion they were fighting for the Portuguese against the Dutch, and a glorious episode it was too. The area under contention was the strait of Malacca, which stretches for 800km and is the longest strait in the world. The settlement of the same name had controlled it for centuries under local jurisdiction, and in 1510 the Portuguese Tomé Pires noted that, 'Malacca is a city that has been built for trade; higher than any other in the whole world'.[8] For this reason it had long been harassed on all sides by hostile neighbours and coveted by the Portuguese.[9] Malacca was taken over in 1511 by the Portuguese as a means of guarding their access to the spice trade, and from that time onwards they faced almost continuous warfare with the surrounding Malay states, of which the most serious attack on the colony was the one in 1606. The state of Johor, from whom the Portuguese had originally taken Malacca, made common cause with Dutch adventurers in an attempt to win it back, although the Dutch were clearly resolved to make Malacca their own.[10]

The heavily fortified colony was under the command of André Furtado de Mendoça, a man who was already a hero of the Portuguese efforts in Asia. He had been governor of Malacca since 1603 and began to defend it against the Dutch from the middle of May 1606 onwards with a meagre garrison of only eighty Portuguese soldiers and a company of Japanese mercenaries, who may have been the 'black halberdiers' noted in the suite of the Captain of the Fortress, which consisted of forty Portuguese soldiers, twenty-four 'black halberdiers' with a drummer, a piper and an umbrella carrier.[11]

The Dutch under Cornelis Matelief de Jonge brought a fleet against Malacca and disembarked an army to carry out a siege, establishing a base in the nearby suburb of Camploclin and almost cutting Malacca off from the outside world. Some reinforcements managed to slip through the blockade to augment the garrison, but this raised the unwelcome prospect of having too many mouths to feed in a beleaguered city, so on 18 July André Furtado de Mendoça ordered sorties to be carried out in order to obtain more supplies. His Japanese mercenaries took part in this initial action and greatly distinguished themselves. Boxer quotes an unnamed writer noting them 'pouring out their blood, and it seemed from the way they precipitated themselves into danger that they sought only to lose their lives'.[12] The provisioning raid was otherwise unsuccessful because the raiding party returned from their expedition with nothing more than the quartered body of a drunken Dutch sentry which was then displayed upon pikes along the wall. The Dutch retaliated against the sight by hanging a Portuguese prisoner in full view of the Malacca garrison.

On 4 August a counterattack was made against the Dutch base in Campoclin by a force of 120 Japanese and Portuguese soldiers. Seven men were killed, among whom was the Japanese captain, while fourteen others were wounded.[13] By now only 6,000 out of the 12,000 inhabitants of Malacca were left alive after bombardment, starvation and disease had taken their toll. Relief eventually came on 14 August in the form of a Portuguese fleet that successfully engaged the Dutch at the Battle of Cape Rachado, and as the Dutch were re-embarking they were attacked for the last time in a fierce sortie that left six Portuguese and twenty-five Japanese dead, including their captain, the second time that the mercenaries had lost their leader in battle.[14] It was probably during this encounter that Jacob Quaeckernaeck lost his life, while a notable wounded hero on the Portuguese side was Andréa Pessoa, later to become notorious through the famous incident when the *Madre de Dios* was scuttled in Nagasaki harbour. At Malacca he fought alongside the Japanese mercenaries and may have had command of some of them. He is known to have been wounded in the right arm.[15] Japanese mercenaries may also have been used by the Portuguese during a retaliatory raid on the Dutch-held base of Pulau Pinang in 1608.[16]

The defence of Malacca was one of the proudest moments in the history of the Japanese Wild Geese and was much appreciated by the Portuguese colonists, but unfortunately for the future of both parties this positive attitude was to be short-lived following the death in 1609 of their great supporter André Furtado de Mendoça. His successor in the colony was Dom João de Silviera, who was to place Malacca's relationship with Japanese mercenaries in great peril. This was not because he despised them; far from it. He valued them so much that they effectively became de Silviera's own private army and were used for the furtherance of his own ends. For some reason de Silviera had a long-standing quarrel with the Bishop of Malacca, and in 1614 he pursued the argument using force. This involved breaking into the cathedral using Japanese mercenaries and ordering them to arrest the Bishop. The exact nature of the incident in 1614–15 is not known, but its seriousness may be guessed from the text of a letter sent to the Viceroy of India on 1 February 1618 by no less a person than the Iberian monarch concerning 'what passed in Malacca between the Captain João de Silviera and the Bishop'. It continues:

> and the fact that the said Dom João forced his way into the church with armed Japanese of his guard, – which it has been affirmed to me is composed of the said Japanese, – it is clear to me that grave disorder may arise therefrom; and seeing how perilous a thing it is to employ the said Japanese, since they are not a loyal race (as has been seen on many occasions in which they have proved so much), particularly in a stronghold as important as that, and one so menaced and on which the keeping of the South principally depends, I was greatly displeased that such wanton carelessness should have been permitted to allow armed Japanese, from whose infidelity such irreparable damage can arise, to enter a stronghold so surrounded by enemies...[17]

Having thus revealed an unfortunate lack of knowledge concerning the vital service rendered in 1606 to the Portuguese by these allegedly disloyal Japanese, His Majesty continues, 'I deem it good and hereby order that no Captain of Malacca shall ever have a guard of Japanese, Javanese, Malays or of any other nation of those regions, but only of Portuguese'.[18]

The Viceroy replied to the letter on 9 February 1619 to assure the King that the Japanese had already been dismissed from service and that the rule against employing any foreigners was being strictly applied. He did not however sound very optimistic about future compliance because he added the curious rider that, 'if the Captains should employ Japanese, Javanese or Malays in the said guard, the Factor is not to pay them nor are they to be included in the lists when they are made out'.[19] In the event the ban would be very firmly applied, so there were no Japanese around to defend Malacca when the Dutch again turned their attentions to it again in 1640.[20] During the rule of the Governor-General Anthonio van Diemen, 'of blessed, laudable memory', Malacca was besieged by sea and land, and after the death of the commander

Adriaen Anthonisz Coper, Malacca was taken by storm on the morning of 19 January 1641.[21]

Early in his account of the action (written in 1678) the Dutch governor of Malacca Balthasar Bort pays an honourable tribute to the 'great courage' shown by his Portuguese predecessor in fighting off the Dutch siege of 1606. 'Our forces hoped nonetheless to win the town, since it was already reduced to famine and much weakened by sickness and death, although the Captain General, Don Andrea Surtado de Mendonsa [Furtado de Mendosa] strove with great courage to hold the town'.[22] There is no mention of Japanese mercenaries fighting on either side in the 1641 action, so we may conclude that their contribution had indeed been discontinued, for which the Portuguese paid the ultimate price of the loss of their prized colony.

The founding of the Dutch factory in Japan

Throughout the time that Jacob Quaeckernaeck and his cousin had been fighting an army of Japanese warriors in Malacca, other influential figures within the VOC were trying to establish contact of a more peaceful sort with Japan. Victor Sprinkel, the chief executive officer of the Dutch factory in Patani – a position called the *opperhoofd* (literally 'supreme head') – put together his own version of a diplomatic address in the name of Maurits Prince of Orange, the Stadhouder of the United Provinces. This happened in 1605, but unknown to Sprinkel a fleet was already on its way to Japan from the Netherlands. The voyage was intended to be a diplomatic mission to the 'King of Japan', but while en route its commander Pieter Verhoeff was easily diverted from his primary task by the exciting news that the annual Portuguese *naó* was on its way from Macao. The prospect of capturing the ship was a huge lure to which opening up trade relations with Japan came a poor second so, pausing only at Patani to collect some token gifts for the shogun in case the piratical venture failed, the Dutch gave chase. The Portuguese out-sailed them, forcing the empty-handed Verhoeff to become an amateur ambassador once again. He made landfall in 1609 on Hirado, entering the same port from which Jacob Quaeckernaeck had sailed four years earlier, and with the warm support of the Matsuura set up the first Dutch factory in Japan.

Verhoeff's peaceful landfall in Hirado marked the beginning of an era, because from that moment on until their forced removal to Nagasaki Bay in 1641 the VOC's presence in Japan would be indelibly linked to that one small island off the north-western coast of Kyushu. By this time the daimyo Matsuura Takanobu had long passed on. In 1609 his son Shigenobu (1549–1614) still held some sway on Hirado even though power had officially passed to his grandson Matsuura Sōyō Takanobu II (r.1603–1637). Nowadays Hirado, with its fine harbour, restored castle and numerous monuments and memories of the European presence, is a charming place to visit, but earlier inhabitants were not so impressed. Richard Cocks, the director of the English factory which was established on Hirado in 1613 as a pale imitation of the Dutch effort, described it as a 'Fisher town and a very small & bad harbour, wherein not above 8 or 10 ships can ride at a time without great danger to spoil one another in stormy weather'. In Cocks's eyes Nagasaki was much to be preferred over Hirado, and as Nagasaki was under direct government control rather than being the possession of a local daimyo, it also did not suffer from a lord's pretensions and personal greed. Cocks notes the readiness of the Matsuura daimyo and his extended family to 'look for presents, or else it is no living among them'.[23]

The economics of Hirado also failed to live up to the promise of Matsuura Takanobu's warm welcome. The Dutch factory was not a commercial success during the first ten years of its existence, and this was partly due to the location.[24] Stuck on the western edge of Kyushu, Hirado was a bad choice for a purely trading post because it was so remote from the capital, so why had the Dutch not chosen somewhere in the vicinity of modern Tokyo Bay, which would have given them easy access to the shogun's headquarters in Edo Castle? The explanation was that trade had not been uppermost in Dutch minds when the location was selected, because Hirado was above all a good harbour from which raids could be launched against Portuguese ships away from any interference by the Japanese authorities in distant Edo.

Trade was nevertheless keenly pursued and kept the Dutch presence afloat when privateering was not being undertaken, and Hirado offered something more than trade in goods: it also promised a trade in soldiers, because Hirado would become the main source of supply of Japanese mercenaries fighting in Dutch service over the next couple of decades. This was of course not the first time that the Matsuura family had offered mercenaries for European service. As noted earlier, in 1587 the first Matsuura Takanobu had promised troops to the King of Spain for the invasion of China, and just as in the earlier example of the Spanish on the Philippines, the Dutch need for mercenaries arose from an identical manpower problem. Soldiers were wanted to defend the VOC's growing list of possessions and to extend its conquests, and an early estimate put the number required at between 3,000 and 5,000 men, of whom only 1,000 were actually available.[25]

As for supplying them from Europe, the voyage from Holland was long and hazardous with the prospect of many willing recruits dying on the way, so the hiring of local Asian troops was an obvious answer. Yet if native soldiers were to be used they had to be resourceful, reliable and willing to be posted away from home. Consequently, just as in the case of the Spanish on the Philippines, the recruitment of specifically Japanese fighters as mercenaries promised to provide the ideal solution to the company's desperate shortage of manpower. They fitted the bill perfectly, being brave, healthy and comparatively cheap to hire. Most importantly, there was a large local supply of them, because the founding of the Tokugawa shogunate and the apparent end of the bloody Sengoku Period had left hundreds of samurai without means of employment.

One of the earliest admirers of the Japanese was Admiral Cornelis Matelief de Jonge, who of course had experienced the mercenaries' fighting skills for himself when he and his men were driven back from Malacca by its Japanese defenders in 1606. A year later he became acquainted with Japanese military skills in a different context when he encountered a band of *wakō*. In June 1607 de Jonge had set sail for China, and after reconnoitring Macao from a safe distance, anchored off a nearby island where a local official, fearful of *wakō*, insisted on inspecting the Dutch vessels to ensure that no Japanese were on board. Not long afterwards some Portuguese vessels hove into view, so de Jonge made a prudent departure. He then dropped anchor off another island where he found three Japanese vessels stationed. They were commanded by *wakō* who asked to be treated as friends rather than enemies. De Jonge, with a firm eye on the development of links with Japan, responded in a positive manner. Their commander presented him with a sword and a suit of armour, and explained that they had recently been to Cambodia. When they parted company de Jonge asked the captain to put in a good word for him in Hirado, which was the *wakō*'s destination. De Jonge later wrote the following account of the incident, which echoes earlier Spanish impression of Japanese martial attitudes while adding a further observation of the Japanese readiness to perform *seppuku* (ritual suicide) to save their honour when all was lost:

> All these Japanese crews were robust men and had a marked appearance of being pirates, as in fact they were. They are of a firm and resolute nature, for when they see that the Chinese have the

upper hand of them, they slit their own bellies in order to avoid falling into the hand of these pitiless enemies, who would make them endure unspeakable torments, even going so far as to slice up their limbs one after another.[26]

De Jonge concludes with a note that the crew in question was acquainted with the fact that there were some Dutchmen already in Japan; they were of course the survivors of the *de Liefde*.

The VOC's new recruits

On its foundation the Dutch factory on Hirado came under the control of its own *opperhoofdt*, the first of whom was Jacques Specx (1585–1652) who was in office from September 1609 to August 1612. He was replaced temporarily for two years by Hendrick Brouwer (1581–1643) and then served again from 1614 to 1621. Both men became involved in the first recruitment of Japanese in 1613, although not all of those they enlisted were fighting men, as revealed by the first written document concerning them sent by Brouwer to Pieter Both, the Governor-General of the Indies, on 29 January. Their ranks included carpenters, blacksmiths, plasterers and grooms, although the rest were *barquiers ende soldate* (sailors and soldiers):

> We regard here the Japanese under good command to be bold men. Their monthly pay is also low and moreover they can be maintained with a small cost of rice and salted fish. With the oral instructions that you gave me last time, we wanted to send 300 men with these ships, but so as to bring more provisions, only 68 heads were shipped, including 9 carpenters, 3 smiths and 2 or 3 masons, the rest sailors and soldiers. If you value the service of these, there will always be enough people here [to recruit] as his majesty [the shogun] has given us his consent to take out as many as we desire.[27]

A further point in their favour that was soon to become apparent was that none seemed to suffer death from disease while being transported to their areas of operation. The Japanese appeared to be a perfect choice, and a great enthusiast for them would be found in the influential Jan Pieterszoon Coen, the man who was to set the direction for the development of Dutch power in the East. Born in Hoorn in 1586, Coen had witnessed at first hand the Dutch failure to capture the Moluccas in

1610. Skilled in languages and book-keeping, he returned to the Indies in 1613 and submitted in January 1614 a milestone report with a title that translates as *Discourse to the Honourable Directors touching the Netherlands Indies State*. The report envisaged taking the Moluccas, Manila and even Macao, and the participation of the impressive Japanese mercenaries was a vital element in the strategy:

> [By conquering Manila] the Spaniards shall be forced from the Moluccas, and indeed out of the East Indies [...] and along with this we shall get the riches of China. In executing such an important assault we can expect no small support from the islands of Manila as the poor subjects are weary of the Spanish yoke. For the execution [of the assault] we can get great help from Japan, because the Japanese soldiers are as good as ours and the Kaiser [shogun] has given us his promise that we can take out as many people as we can get hold of. We can get enough as they are ready and willing, as we have found from our experience. These same Japanese soldiers can be used to do great service in the expedition to Macao, and with whom this expedition can be effected. With these victories, we shall not only capture a great treasure but also the rich Chinese trade...[28]

Coen became Governor-General of the VOC in 1617, and under his guidance the numbers of Japanese mercenaries employed by the company grew from sixty-eight in 1615 to 100 in 1620, making 300 overall.[29] In his comments Coen echoed the positive impressions of the Japanese found in the Spanish reference to them as 'the Spaniards of Asia'. His support and approval also reflected the warmth expressed by Portuguese priests towards their Japanese Christian converts, yet just like the latter's dream of a Christian Japan, Coen's illusions would eventually be shattered when the conquests stopped happening. There were some personal misgivings too from other directions when disciplinary problems were discovered. 'We have the bellyful already; it is an excitable and difficult race', wrote Jacques Specx in 1620.[30] A further negative Dutch comment about the Japanese comes from Van Vliet, who describes them as 'bald-headed villains', although this was a specific reference to a boast by the Japanese leader in Siam that when the Dutch were eventually driven out of that country the Japanese would be back.[31]

The recruitment situation within Japan's home towns was of course totally different from the process that took place within Siam's *nihonmachi*. The VOC's *soldaten von Japan* would not be switching constantly between the roles of peaceful merchants and aggressive armies. They were sent overseas to do a specific job and, quite apart from their unique local origin, one major factor was that recruitment was done with the full permission of the shogun, who approved of his subjects being used in this way in apparently unlimited numbers. Perhaps not surprisingly, Tokugawa Hidetada was perfectly happy for hundreds of unemployed *rōnin* to be shipped overseas to fight and possibly die. It also soon became clear that once they were abroad the Bakufu took no further interest in them or their fortunes, just as it had no interest in nor responsibility for the activities of the merchants in the *nihonmachi*, whatever reasons may have lain behind their desire to emigrate. Letter after letter from the Bakufu attested that if anyone from the Japanese diaspora was unruly or violent, the local rulers should punish malefactors under their own jurisdiction and according to their local laws, even to the extent of executing wrongdoers who were still technically subjects of the Tokugawa shogun.

Before looking at the actions in which the mercenaries participated between 1613 and 1622, it is worth taking an overall view of the recruitment procedure and the conditions of service in the VOC. The best data available is for the year 1614, when Jacques Specx enlisted a second contingent of Japanese mercenaries on Hirado and arranged for them to be transported overseas in two ships. They were equipped with weapons listed as forty muskets, eleven bows and forty-five spears.[32] Their recruitment took almost a year, at the end of which the mercenaries were bound to a written contract designed to last for three years, but their service was not to be measured from the moment of enlistment. Instead they were 'Under engagement for three consecutive years after arrival at Bantam or elsewhere, to be employed as sailors, soldiers or otherwise insofar as capable of such'.[33]

To guard against any personal outrages the Japanese were held to strict rules that were written into their contracts. Example clauses include 'at no time or whatever place they will… instigate brawls or fighting… gambling or games… drink to drunkenness… hinder or assault married women or single girls… mutiny or difficulties'.[34] Should any mercenaries transgress then their own families would be punished.[35] A full list of names, duties and wages is also included with the document. Each man is noted as having a guarantor, who may have been a recruiting agent, because a certain 'Matsy Sejusteroo' is named as guarantor for eight individuals, and 'Amia' stands surety for five.[36]

The ease with which Specx obtained his men in spite of these punitive contracts with which they were forced to comply is a testimony to the men's thirst for employment, and the fact that some Christian names of Spanish or Portuguese origin appear in the list of recruits probably shows the influence of a factor of religious persecution. Most of the men were drawn from no further away than Nagasaki, whence they travelled to Hirado, which led to the Englishman John Saris describing a town filled with 'base people or Renegados … loytering vp and downe'.[37]

Sadly, their first behaviour was indeed to be like 'renegades', because long before any mercenary had drawn his sword in anger against the enemies of the VOC concerns were being expressed about some serious disciplinary issues. Their leader Kusunoki soon proved to be incapable of commanding a small group of men who were rapidly turning into a mutinous rabble, although the rebels' motivation was undoubtedly the appalling conditions of life on board ship. Under normal circumstances any European crewman who reacted similarly would have been subjected to the harshest discipline in order to bring him back into line, but the Japanese mercenaries lacked the command structure in which that could be applied successfully. Kusunoki then showed his own lack of self-discipline when a long-standing rival arrived on another ship. Kusunoki stabbed him to death.[38]

Although Coen remained very positive about Japanese mercenaries, as early as 1615 other Dutch commentators were starting to express fears about an inherent ferocity that was proving difficult to control. From Jacques Specx we have the devastating admission that, 'they are dangerous to govern outside their land … lambs [in their own country], but outside their land almost devils'.[39] Nevertheless, their overall contribution to the fighting strength of the VOC was regarded as very positive by all who came into contact with them, and Coen was so keen that recruitment should be continued at an accelerated pace beyond 1617 that he sent several urgently phrased letters to Hirado.[40] On 30 March 1618 he wrote to Hirado again and ordered Specx to recruit and send, '25 Japanese of the most suitable, brave young men that can be found'.[41] Such candidates were located, and in 1620 he wrote to the VOC directors that 'for the strengthening of all the garrisons we have sent for a good number of Japanese … a good number shall be sent to the Moluccas and up to 3 or 400 will be sent this year'.[42] Later that same year he demanded that Specx 'send here as many brave Japanese as time and circumstances permits. They will not be used for labour but for war'.[43] Specx sent at least two further contingents of recruits to Coen. In 1619 ninety set sail, and in 1620 another group of about 100 soldiers followed.[44] Yet still Coen insisted that more should come, and coupled these demands with further requests for troops from Europe.

In 1620 Coen called for the VOC directors to send 700 soldiers immediately. The troops sent in response were once again sourced from Hirado. Coen did not know it at the time, but they would be the last of the Japanese mercenaries, because the experiment had less than a year to run before being curtailed by the same shogun who had once given the scheme his official blessing. By then the Wild Geese had earned great glory for their Dutch employers, as the next chapter will explain.

Notes

1. Mulder, W.Z. *Hollanders in Hirado: 1597-1641* (Haarlem, Fibula-Van Dishoeck, 1985), p. 25.
2. This quotation is from Clulow, Adam. *Amboina, 1623: Fear and Conspiracy on the Edge of Empire* (New York: Columbia University Press, 2019), p. 15. His other works are Clulow, Adam 'Pirating in the Shogun's Waters: The Dutch East India Company and the San António Incident' *Bulletin of Portuguese/Japanese Studies* 13 (2006) pp. 65-80; Clulow, Adam 'Unjust, Cruel and Barbarous Proceedings: Japanese Mercenaries and the Amboyna Incident of 1623' *Itinerario* XXXI (2007) pp. 15-34.Clulow, Adam 'From Global Entrepôt to Early Modern Domain: Hirado, 1609–1641' *Monumenta Nipponica* 65 (2010) pp. 1-35; Clulow, Adam 'Like Lambs in Japan and Devils outside Their Land: Diplomacy, Violence and Japanese Merchants in south-east Asia' *Journal of World History* 24, 2 (2013), pp. 335-358; Clulow, Adam. "Commemorating Failure: The Four Hundredth Anniversary of England's Trading Outpost in Japan." *Monumenta Nipponica*, vol. 68, no. 2, 2013, pp. 207–231; Clulow, Adam. *The Company and the Shogun: the Dutch encounter with Tokugawa Japan* (New York: Columbia University Press, 2014); Clulow, Adam. '"Great help from Japan"' The Dutch East India Company's experiment with Japanese soldiers' in Clulow, Adam & Mostert, Tristan. *The Dutch and English East India Companies: Diplomacy, Trade and violence in Early Modern Asia* (Amsterdam: Amsterdam University Press, 2018), p. 179-210.
3. Clulow, Adam. *The Company and the Shogun: the Dutch encounter with Tokugawa Japan* (New York: Columbia University Press, 2014), p. 12.

4. Clulow, Adam. *The Company and the Shogun: the Dutch encounter with Tokugawa Japan* (New York: Columbia University Press, 2014), p. 14.
5. Boxer, C.R. *The Christian Century in Japan: 1549-1650* (Berkeley, 1951), p. 268.
6. Boxer, C.R. *The Christian Century in Japan: 1549-1650* (Berkeley, 1951), pp. 256-257.
7. Boxer, C.R. *The Christian Century in Japan: 1549-1650* (Berkeley, 1951), p. 269.
8. Pinto, Paulo Jorge de Souza 'Share and Strife: The Strait of Melaka and the Portuguese (16th and 17th centuries)' *Orientierungen Themenheft* (2013), p. 66
9. Marshall, P.J. 'Western Arms in Maritime Asia in the Early Phases of Expansion' *Modern Asian Studies* 14. 1 (1989), p. 19.
10. De Witt, Dennis *History of the Dutch in Malaysia* (Petaling Jaya, Selangor, 2008), pp. 46-50.
11. Winstedt, R.O *A History of Malaya* (London, 1935) p.86.
12. Boxer, C.R. *The affair of the Madre de Deus: a chapter in the history of the Portuguese in Japan* (London, 1929), p. 22.
13. Boxer, C.R. *The affair of the Madre de Deus: a chapter in the history of the Portuguese in Japan* (London, 1929), p. 22.
14. Boxer, C.R. *The affair of the Madre de Deus : a chapter in the history of the Portuguese in Japan* (London, 1929), p. 23.
15. Boxer, C.R. *The affair of the Madre de Deus : a chapter in the history of the Portuguese in Japan* (London, 1929), pp. 27, 39, 79.
16. De Witt, Dennis *History of the Dutch in Malaysia* (Petaling Jaya, Selangor, 2008), pp. 51.
17. Translated in Boxer, C.R. *The affair of the Madre de Deus : a chapter in the history of the Portuguese in Japan* (London, 1929), pp. 82-83.
18. Boxer, C.R. *The affair of the Madre de Deus : a chapter in the history of the Portuguese in Japan* (London, 1929), p. 83.
19. Boxer, C.R. *The affair of the Madre de Deus : a chapter in the history of the Portuguese in Japan* (London, 1929), p. 83; Teixiera, Manuel *The Portuguese Missions in Malacca and Singapore (1511-1958) Volume I – Malacca* (Macao, 1986) pp. 204-205.
20. For a full account see Leupe, P.A., and Mac Hacobian. 'The Siege and Capture of Malacca from the Portuguese in 1640-1641.' *Journal of the Malayan Branch of the Royal Asiatic Society*, vol. 14, no. 1 (124), 1936, pp. i-178.
21. Bremner, M.J. (trans.) 'Report of Governor Balthasar Bort on Malacca 1678, with an introduction and notes by C.O. Blagden' *Journal of the Malayan Branch of the Royal Asiatic Society* 5 (1927) p. 14.

22. Bremner, M.J. (trans.) 'Report of Governor Balthasar Bort on Malacca 1678, with an introduction and notes by C.O. Blagden' *Journal of the Malayan Branch of the Royal Asiatic Society* 5 (1927) p. 12.

23. Cocks, Richard. *Diary of Richard Cocks; Cape Merchant in the English Factory in Japan 1615-1622 with correspondence* Volume II (London, 1883), p. 314

24. Clulow, Adam 'Pirating in the Shogun's Waters: The Dutch East India Company and the San António Incident' *Bulletin of Portuguese/Japanese Studies* 13 (2006) p. 65; Clulow, Adam 'From Global Entrepōt to Early Modern Domain: Hirado, 1609–1641' *Monumenta Nipponica* 65 (2010) pp. 1-35.

25. Clulow, Adam. *Amboina, 1623: Fear and Conspiracy on the Edge of Empire* (New York: Columbia University Press, 2019), p. 74.

26. Boxer, C.R. *The affair of the Madre de Deus: a chapter in the history of the Portuguese in Japan* (London, 1929), p. 33.

27. Hendrick Brouwer to Pieter Both, 29 January 1613. Original text in *Dai Nihon Shiryō* XII Vol 10 p. 205. Translation in Clulow, Adam. *Amboina, 1623: Fear and Conspiracy on the Edge of Empire* (New York: Columbia University Press, 2019), p. 76.

28. As translated in Clulow, Adam. *Amboina, 1623: Fear and Conspiracy on the Edge of Empire* (New York: Columbia University Press, 2019), p. 80.

29. Clulow, Adam 'Unjust, Cruel and Barbarous Proceedings: Japanese Mercenaries and the Amboyna Incident of 1623' *Itinerario* XXXI (2007), p. 19.

30. Clulow, Adam. *Amboina, 1623: Fear and Conspiracy on the Edge of Empire* (New York: Columbia University Press, 2019), p. 75.

31. Baker, Chris et. al. *Van Vliet's Siam* (Chiang Mai, 2005), p. 56.

32. Clulow, Adam. *Amboina, 1623: Fear and Conspiracy on the Edge of Empire* (New York: Columbia University Press, 2019), pp. 85-86.

33. Mulder, W.Z. *Hollanders in Hirado: 1597-1641* (Haarlem, Fibula-Van Dishoeck, 1985), p. 243.

34. Mulder, W.Z. *Hollanders in Hirado: 1597-1641* (Haarlem, Fibula-Van Dishoeck, 1985), pp. 247-248.

35. Mulder, W.Z. *Hollanders in Hirado: 1597-1641* (Haarlem, Fibula-Van Dishoeck, 1985), p. 248.

36. Mulder, W.Z. *Hollanders in Hirado: 1597-1641* (Haarlem, Fibula-Van Dishoeck, 1985), pp. 243-247.

37. Satow, ed. *The Voyage of Captain John Saris to Japan* (London: Hakluyt Society, 1900), 172.

38. Clulow, Adam. *Amboina, 1623: Fear and Conspiracy on the Edge of Empire* (New York: Columbia University Press, 2019), pp. 88-89.

39. Boxer, C.R. *The Christian Century in Japan: 1549-1650* (Berkeley, 1951), p. 269; Clulow, Adam 'Unjust, Cruel and Barbarous Proceedings: Japanese Mercenaries and the Amboyna Incident of 1623' *Itinerario* XXXI (2007), p. 27.

40. Coen to Heeren 17, 26 October 1620, in Colenbrander, H.T. and Coolhaas, W.T. (Eds.) *Jan Pieterzoon Coen: Bescheiden Omtrent Zijn Bedriff in Indië*, (The Hague, Martinus Nijhoff, 1919-1954). Vol.1, p. 601.

41. Coen to Jacques Specx, 30 March 1618, in Colenbrander, H.T. and Coolhaas, W.T. (Eds.) *Jan Pieterzoon Coen: Bescheiden Omtrent Zijn Bedriff in Indië*, (The Hague, Martinus Nijhoff, 1919-1954). Vol. 2: 373.

42. Coen to *Heeren* 17, 22 January 1620, *in* in Colenbrander, H.T. and Coolhaas, W.T. (Eds.) *Jan Pieterzoon Coen: Bescheiden Omtrent Zijn Bedriff in Indië*, (The Hague, Martinus Nijhoff, 1919-1954). Vol. 1, p. 519.

43. Coen to Specx, 26 June 1620, in in Colenbrander, H.T. and Coolhaas, W.T. (Eds.) *Jan Pieterzoon Coen: Bescheiden Omtrent Zijn Bedriff in Indië*, (The Hague, Martinus Nijhoff, 1919-1954). Vol. 2, p. 748.

44. Pieter de Carpentier and Jacob Dedel to the directors, 8 March 1621 in Iwao, *Zoku Nanyō Nihonmachi no Kenkyū*, pp. 6-7.

Chapter 7

Heroism and Horror on the Spice Islands

The wealth of detail discussed above concerning the recruitment and conditions of service of Japanese mercenaries fighting for the Dutch is sadly not matched by any equivalent amount of data about how the *soldaten von Japan* were actually used during the few years of their existence, which begs the question of how effective they were or how far the harsh reality of their lives failed to live up to their employers' original expectations. They certainly did not get off to a good start. In Clulow's words, Coen envisaged the initial 1613 cohort serving 'in the vanguard of attacks against Spanish and Portuguese strongholds'. Instead they became engaged in 'minor marketplace skirmishes that erupted between the English and Dutch companies in Banten'.[1] Fortunately for all concerned, the mercenaries' later actions would be more in keeping with the roles originally assigned to them.

The first contingent of mercenaries shipped abroad from Hirado were taken to the above-mentioned Dutch base of Bantam on the island of Java. It provided a useful jumping-off point for other Dutch interests that needed defending, but Bantam was itself a place of violence because it had become the centre of the Anglo-Dutch contest for the pepper trade. The EIC, who employed Japanese only as labourers, had established their own base there in 1603. Fights were frequent, as recorded in the words of Richard Wickham, who begins his report with a note about the despatch of a Japanese-style gift:

> [I include] …a small remembrance of my love and duty, sent by Captain Harris, viz. a cuttane (*katana*) made up in a long square box… It was by a council thought necessary that myself, although

88

Above left: A Japanese expatriate and his wife living on the Philippines, from the manuscript of 1590 known as the Boxer Codex. The man is depicted wearing a *yukata* (robe) with a Japanese sword and has a classic samurai hairstyle. Men like this were being recruited as mercenaries by the Spanish colonists at around the time this picture was painted. (Picture supplied by courtesy of Indiana University).

Above right: A *wakō* raid on the Chinese coast is depicted in this life-sized diorama in a gallery within the Shaolin Temple (Henan Province, China). The *wakō* provided the first source of supply for any Japanese warriors who were used as mercenaries.

Below: The harbour of Hirado in Nagasaki Prefecture. This small island off the coast of Kyushu would play a vital role in relations between Japan and the European nations. Successive daimyo (lords) of Hirado offered samurai as mercenaries for the service of the Spanish and the Dutch.

Left: This statue of Naya Sukezaemon stands on the harbour of Sakai. He was a merchant who had close links with Cambodia, and is identified in some accounts with the *wakō* leader Taifusa, who attacked Manila in 1582.

Below: Matsuura Takanobu I (1522–99) was the daimyo of Hirado who in 1565 organised an attack on the Portuguese *naó* (annual trading vessel) as it lay at anchor in Fukuda Bay. The defeat of the Matsuura fleet was hailed as evidence of European military superiority.

Right: Bernardo Nagasaki, the Japanese Christian convert who shared his surname with the small fortified area that was to become the great city of Nagasaki.

Below: The large protected harbour of Nagasaki was to become the centre of both trade and missionary work for the Portuguese in Japan, and became Japan's window on the outside world when contacts were restricted in 1639.

The site of the headquarters of Fukabori Sumimasa, a great enemy of the Portuguese presence in Nagasaki and the arch rival of his brother-in-law the Christian daimyo Ōmura Sumitada.

Arima Harunobu (1567–1612) was the nephew of Ōmura Sumitada. Like his uncle, he converted to Christianity following support from the Portuguese in his battles with the Ryūzōji.

A map of 'Firando' (Hirado), the location of the first armed encounter between Japanese and European visitors. The so-called 'incident in front of the shrine' in 1561 arose over the price of a piece of cloth and ended with the death of fourteen Portuguese.

The Portuguese eventually shifted their attentions from Hirado to Nagasaki, but in 1609 Hirado would become the site of the first Dutch factory (trading post) in Japan. This headstone bearing the cipher of the VOC (the Dutch East India Company) was excavated from the site of the factory on Hirado.

King Naresuan the Great of Siam, depicted as young man in a heroic pose on his memorial in Ayutthaya. The incident depicted is his attack on a Burmese fortress in 1585, when he climbed a scaling ladder with his sword in his mouth. He was the first Siamese monarch to use Japanese auxiliaries.

A war elephant of King Naresuan appears on his memorial in Don Chedi. Some of his war elephants were commanded by Japanese mercenaries at the battle Nong Sarai against the Burmese in 1593. According to popular belief, the pivotal moment in the battle of Nong Sarai was a single combat on elephants between King Naresuan and the Crown Prince of Burma, an incident much cherished in Thai culture.

Above: The ruins of Ayutthaya, where Japanese served as loyal bodyguards to successive kings of Siam.

Below: The riverside site of the *Nihonmachi* ('Japan town') in Ayutthaya, where Japanese expatriates balanced the two roles of mercenary soldiers and enterprising merchants.

Above left: A bust of Yamada Nagamasa, the Japanese merchant adventurer who became an influential figure among the Japanese expatriate community in Ayutthaya and acted as a close confidant to successive rulers of Siam. This memorial to Nagamasa is on the site of his supposed birthplace in modern Shizuoka City.

Above right: King Ekathotsarot (r.1605–1611) succeeded his brother Naresuan on the throne of Siam. He made considerable use of foreign mercenaries including some Japanese, in whose ranks Yamada Nagamasa may well have served. This statue of him is in the grounds of Wat Phuttaisawan in Ayutthaya.

Below: A copy (on display within the museum of the *Nihonmachi* in Ayutthaya) of the *ema* (votive plaque) presented to the Sengen Shrine in Shizuoka by Yamada Nagamasa. The picture consists of a large ship that is more warship than merchant vessel. It has two cannon in the bows and eight cannon along the side, while the crew are all dressed as samurai.

Above: A display of trade items in the museum of the *Nihonmachi* in Ayutthaya. They include the highly prized deerskins that were exported to Japan in their thousands.

Below: An imaginative painting of the Portuguese settlement of Macao, one end of the thriving trade in silk and silver that was conducted by the Portuguese between China and Japan. This modern painting is in the museum at Azuchi (Shiga Prefecture).

Above: Matsuura Shigenobu (1549–1614), the son of Takanobu I, was the daimyo of Hirado who offered mercenaries to the Spanish on the Philippines to serve in their grandiose plan to conquer China.

Below left: On its foundation the Dutch factory on Hirado came under the control of its own *opperhoofdt,* (director) the first of whom was Jacques Specx (1585–1652). He was in office from September 1609 to August 1612 and then served again from 1614 to 1621. Specx was involved in the first recruitment of Japanese mercenaries in 1613. This statue of him is in Hirado.

Below right: In 1606 the Dutch Admiral Cornelis Matalief de Jonge (1569–1632) laid siege to the Portuguese colony of Malacca and was driven off by a determined resistance that included Japanese mercenaries fighting in on elf their most celebrated actions.

Above: The beautifully reconstructed Dutch factory on Hirado, viewed from Hirado Castle on the opposite side of the harbour.

Below left: Jan Pieterszoon Coen (1587–1629) set the direction for the development of Dutch power in the East. Born in Hoorn, Coen had witnessed at first hand the Dutch failure to capture the Moluccas in 1610 and became an enthusiast for the use of Japanese mercenaries in Dutch service. This display about him is in the restored Dutch factory on Hirado.

Below right: Japanese mercenaries were involved on both sides in the European contest to the Spice Islands. In 1570 the titular Portuguese governor of Ternate Island literally stabbed its sultan in the back, and according to some sources his mutilated body was then salted in a barrel. The sorry episode is now commemorated on a monument among the ruins of Fort Kastela, from where the new Sultan fought back to expel the Portuguese in 1575.

Left: Matsuura Takanobu II (r.1603–1637) was instrumental in making Japanese mercenaries available to the Dutch in a scheme unique to Hirado. This was done with the full approval of the shogun.

Below left: The involvement of Japanese mercenaries in executions on the Banda Islands is starkly commemorated in a painting on display in the museum on Banda Neira that shows them standing next to Dutch officials surrounded by dead bodies. It was commissioned by Des Alwi Abubakar (1927–2010), a man committed to developing the Banda Islands for modern tourism but who was also determined to educate visitors about Bandanese history.

Below right: The presence of peaceful Japanese visitors to Cambodia is shown by votive inscriptions in Chinese ink left on the pillars of one of the galleries of Angkor Wat by Japanese merchants from Sakai and Kyushu who were visiting that renowned Buddhist site in 1612. It was about this time that the Cambodian rulers employed Japanese mercenaries, and three decades later they would use them against the Dutch.

Above: The palace of the kings of Cambodia in Phnom Penh. In 1643 Japanese mercenaries in the service of the Cambodian king took part in a surprising victory over the Dutch including the capture of a Dutch ship.

Below: Fort Zeelandia was built at one end of a chain of islands that protected Tayouan Bay in Taiwan. It represented the Dutch presence on the island.

The army of Zheng Chenggong, popularly known as Koxinga (1624–1662), included a mysterious unit known as the Iron Men, who are believed to have been Japanese mercenaries.

Frederick Coyett (1615 or 1620–1687) was the last governor of Taiwan. He had only forty fighting men of any real experience to defend Fort Zeelandia against Koxinga, although there was enough food and gunpowder to last through a siege of six months.

Above: The surrender of Taiwan to Koxinga, as shown by a life-sized diorama in the museum at Anping, the site of Fort Zeelandia.

Below: The expatriate Japanese community had long played an important role in the ancient town of Hội An, and provided military service in 1631 when the son of the Nguyễn ruler of Champa fought off an attack from his brother and was supported by a group of Japanese. (Photograph by Ian Clark).

The 'Japanese bridge' in Hội An, built in the 1590s to connect the Japanese enclave with that of the Chinese (Photograph by Ian Clark).

King Taksin (r.1767–1782) of Siam is traditionally supposed to have made use of Chinese and Japanese mercenaries. Their payment in gold is supposed to have caused severe financial difficulties to the struggling Siamese kingdom after they had expelled the Burmese.

most unworthy, should undertake the command and conduct of a ship for Bantam, chiefly that there was an unruly company of English and Japons to govern'.[2]

More 'unruly Japons' arrived when the Dutch ship containing mercenaries docked at Bantam on 24 April 1616, where their leader soon had to deal with several disciplinary incidents. One Japanese with the name of Pedro was found asleep while on guard duty and was executed by firing squad. Another who committed a similar offence narrowly missed execution because of an absence of witnesses.[3] Over the ensuing months the mercenaries were moved in small groups to other Dutch outposts where they would be more useful. Some stayed in Bantam and took part in further squabbles with the English. Their attitude won them praise from the Dutch for their recklessness and courage, although disciplinary problems persisted. Among the conflicts was one of July 1617, when a fight started over the trivial matter of buying fish in the local market. One of the VOC mercenaries was so badly injured by a sword-cut through his shoulder blade that it left him permanently disfigured. In November of the same year some Portuguese and Spanish prisoners of the Dutch escaped and sought refuge in the English factory, and when the Dutch attacked it an English mob moved in turn against the VOC warehouses. The owners fled, leaving seven Japanese mercenaries to defend their property. This they did valiantly, cutting some of the English in half with their swords but losing three dead and one severely wounded in the process. Among five wounded Japanese one was reported as having died instantly, and four as being on the verge of death from severe wounds. Among these one died that night and another followed on the morrow, having had both arms severed and with injuries in ten places on his body.[4]

Apart from these petty skirmishes at Bantam, Japanese mercenary activity on behalf of the VOC between the years 1613 and 1621 was focussed almost exclusively on the complex and confusing series of battles that had already been taking place for over a decade for control of the spice-producing islands called the Moluccas. Now known as Maluku, this remote set of islands within the Indonesian archipelago stretches from east of Sulawesi to Papua in the east and Timor in the south. They still appear on glossy tourist brochures as the 'Spice Islands': the popular name they acquired because of the products derived from their unique and valuable flora. An insatiable and highly profitable demand for mace, nutmeg and cloves, for which all manner of beneficial properties were claimed, was the main reason why the pioneering fleets had set sail from Europe in the first place, a competition that developed into what one recent author has called a 'scramble for the spices'.[5] Of all the areas of south-east Asia that were contested by rival Asian and European powers, these little atolls changed hands more frequently than any other, and their political control shifted continuously between local chieftains, Muslim sultans, the VOC, the English East India Company, the Portuguese and the Spanish over a period of many decades.

Detailed European knowledge concerning the location of the Spice Islands was a comparatively recent phenomenon. Their valued commodities had been precious and expensive for centuries, yet until the sixteenth century very few people in Europe knew exactly from where they were ultimately derived, because spices were always traded as a monopoly by Venice, which controlled the trade routes to the east through a series of middlemen. It was the Portuguese who 'discovered' the actual source of supply, and their seizure of Malacca in 1511 was a decisive attempt to assert control over the international spice trade. Yet Malacca was only a waystation; it lay nowhere near the islands themselves, which fell into three broad geographical groupings. To the north lay Tidore and Ternate, where cloves grew. These two islands were ruled by rival sultans. Four hundred miles to the south was Amboina, famous also for its cloves, to the south-east of which lay the Banda Islands, the only places in the world where mace, the outer casing of the even more highly valued nutmeg, grew. Here the political system was very different because control was exercised at the level of villages or federations of villages.

By the mid-sixteenth century Portuguese forts had been constructed on each of these tiny places to protect trading posts and to make some small gesture of ownership when overall control was still impossible to guarantee. The Portuguese faced some rivalry from Spain, but the most important challenge to the Portuguese monopoly came in 1599 when a Dutch fleet sponsored by one of the predecessors of the VOC arrived on the scene. Its captains negotiated a spice cargo huge enough to generate a large profit and to open several eyes to future trading possibilities.[6] The establishment of the VOC shortly afterwards promised a coordinated approach that could further shift the balance of mercantile power in the spice trade in the Dutch direction.

From the time of the founding of the VOC the Dutch strategy with respect to the Spice Islands was to sign treaties with local elders or rulers, promising them protection against the imperial posturing and aggression of the Spanish and Portuguese. For the protective umbrella to be successful, of course, it meant the creation of Dutch forts on the sites previously or currently occupied by Iberian fortifications. In return for such cynical generosity the islanders would of course promise to sell their spices only to the Dutch. The Banda Islands provide a very good example of the process. Treaties were signed in 1602 and again in 1605 with local leaders called *orangkaya* (a word that literally means 'rich men'). The *orangkaya* had previously resisted all attempts by the Portuguese to gain control over the islands' affairs, an attitude that endeared them to the Dutch, although relations with the newcomers would not prove to be much more cordial.

The situation deteriorated very sharply in 1609 when the Bandanese ambushed and killed Pieter Verhoef along with forty of his men.[7] A further treaty followed which attempted to grant exclusivity of supply to the VOC. It was backed up by the threat of force, but the fact that the agreement was not honoured was due in part to the competition from the EIC, which was already trading freely with other Bandanese communities. Relations between the Dutch and the islanders eventually became so hostile that in 1612 Pieter Both, the first governor-general of the VOC, suggested deliberately burning down a large swathe of nutmeg trees as a sign of Dutch determination. This was followed by the even more drastic idea that the Bandanese should be 'totally conquered or with proper guarantee brought to reason or entirely exterminated'.[8]

The ensuing military invasions of the Banda Islands — an operation in which Japanese mercenaries would participate on the side of the Dutch — will be described below, because by this time Japanese mercenaries had already seen action on the other Spice Islands. In these first battles however, the mercenaries were fighting on behalf of the Portuguese against the Dutch, not vice-versa. The actions took place on the island of Ternate and its neighbour Tidore, which were highly prized for cloves and legendary for other riches:

> Tidore Island has its own king; very rich, he has a sapphire as big as an egg and a cornelian basin which belongs to the King of Cochinchina in which he washes his hands.[9]

Tidore was ruled by a sultan, and for most of its history the island had been involved in rivalry with the sultanate on nearby Ternate. The latter's first European visitor had been the Portuguese adventurer Francisco Serráo who was rescued from a shipwreck in 1512.[10] He was treated well, and in 1522 the sultan allowed the Portuguese to build a fort on Ternate and start the purchase of cloves. This peaceful coexistence did not last, and before long a confusing see-saw of military activity saw the islands change hands time and again between the Portuguese, the Spanish and the Dutch. In 1570 the titular Portuguese governor Mesquita literally stabbed the sultan in the back, and according to some sources his mutilated body was then salted in a barrel.[11] The sorry episode is now commemorated on a monument among the ruins of Portugal's Fort Kastela, from where the new sultan fought back to expel the Portuguese from Ternate in 1575 after a five-year siege.

At the same time neighbouring Tidore had been concocting an agreement with the Spanish as a way of asserting their own independence from Ternate, but any Spanish/Portuguese rivalry that might have been sparked by the issue was peacefully settled by a treaty of 1529, whereby the King of Spain nominally abandoned the right of Spanish presence on the island of Tidore in return for a payment. In 1585 the Spanish, now united with Portugal, tried to reconquer Ternate from its sultan, but it was not long before the Dutch threw their hats into the ring as well. In 1599 two VOC ships under Commander Wybrand van Warwijk arrived off Ternate. In 1601 Tidore fought off a Dutch attack, an action that forced Spain and Portugal into a fresh alliance, so the Portuguese André Furtado de Mendoça gladly received reinforcements from the Spanish.

In 1605 the Dutch returned and finally captured the fortress on Tidore. Its Portuguese survivors sought refuge in Manila and joined a Spanish expedition in February 1606 to win the island back. A fleet of thirty-two vessels and 3,000 men including Japanese mercenaries sailed from the Philippines under Don Pedro de Acuña. They crossed over to Ternate where a company under João Rodriguez Camello retook its own fort on 1 April. De Morga provides a vivid account of the fighting, but unfortunately he makes no specific reference to the Japanese who are definitely known to have been present within the Spanish contingent:

> The scouts in the trees gave information of what was being done, whereupon Captains Don Rodrigo de Mendosa, Alarcon, Cervantes, and Vergara reenforced him with their light-armed pikemen and halberdiers.They pursued the enemy with so great rapidity and resolution that they entered the walls behind them. However, some of the Spaniards were wounded, and Captain Cervantes was pushed down from the wall and his legs broken, which caused his death... The soldiers were stopped by a trench beyond the fort of Nuestra Senora, for the enemy had retreated to a shed, which was fortified with a considerable number of musketeers

and arquebusiers, and four light pieces. They discharged their arquebuses and muskets at the Spaniards, and threw cane spears hardened in fire, and *bacacaes* (darts?) after their fashion. The Spaniards assaulted the shed, whereupon a Dutch artilleryman trying to fire a large swivel-gun, with which he would have done great damage, being confused did not succeed, and threw down the linstock, turned, and fled. The enemy did the same after him, and abandoned the shed, fleeing in all directions.[12]

The year 1606 proved to be a busy one for the Japanese mercenaries in the service of Spain and Portugal, because a few months later they were assisting the Portuguese in the defence of Malacca. Meanwhile more violence was taking place back in Manila, where some of their fellow countrymen started rioting in the *nihonmachi*.[13]

VOC mercenaries in action

It would not be long before mercenaries appeared on the Dutch side in the long battle for the Spice Islands. The contest began in April 1610 when the Portuguese Viceroy sent a well-equipped fleet from Goa to join the Spanish in Manila in an attempt to expel the Dutch once and for all, but on arriving in Macao its cowardly commander refused to go any further. In 1613 the Dutch hit back, and for the first time used Japanese mercenaries of their own against Iberian possessions. The troops were fifty fighting men drawn from the sixty-eight recruits who had been hired in Japan by Brouwer and Specx and sent on from Bantam. They captured the fortress of Marieco on Tidore, where an observer wrote, 'the Japanese soldiers proved themselves to be as brave as our own [soldiers]. Their banner was first on the walls. Through their great boldness and fearlessness many were injured'.[14] In December 1615 the Portuguese and Spanish pooled their resources in order to make a final attempt to recapture the Moluccas from the Dutch, but the Portuguese contribution was completely destroyed off Malacca by Admiral Steven Van Der Haeghen (the conqueror of Amboina in 1605) long before their Spanish allies arrived. When Don Juan de Silva turned up with an army that included Japanese troops from Manila a few days later he was told of the defeat and withdrew to Malacca; he died there from dysentery a few days later.

The use of Japanese mercenaries by both sides during the same year throws up the intriguing possibility that had the earlier attack on the Spice Islands gone ahead, it could have provided the sole example in the history of Japan's Wild Geese of two units of them fighting each other. Instead the frustrated Spanish fleet returned to Manila, while a separate Portuguese fleet brought reinforcements to the Spanish in Ternate. Those troops allowed them to maintain a minor presence there and on Tidore until 1662, but from that time on Spanish/Portuguese cooperation faded from view, and trade with the Spice Islands would henceforth be a contest between the Dutch on one side and English rivals or native leaders on the other.[15]

Japanese mercenaries were also involved in the series of events that led to the founding of Batavia as the capital of the Dutch East Indies, but again specific details of their service are lacking. The move from Bantam to Jacatra, where Batavia would one day take shape, had its origins in 1618, when the fortunes of the VOC were at a low ebb. Coen had just been appointed as governor-general, and one of the first decisions he made was to threaten to move the factory from Bantam to Jacatra. He almost came to an agreement with the Chinese merchants located there and had forced the price of pepper down by fifty percent when English traders intervened by attacking Chinese ships. Fearing that Dutch vessels would be the next target Coen carried out his threat, but encountered armed resistance. His forces attacked and destroyed a gun battery and burned down the English trading post. It was the start of open warfare. When English ships intervened Coen prudently withdrew to seek reinforcements, leaving the garrison of the fort to defend it until his return. A quarrel between the English and local potentates then came most admirably to the aid of the Dutch defenders who, 'between hours of prayer and nights of orgies with wine and women they pledged themselves solemnly to defend the fortress as long as God will permit'. It was at this point that the garrison decided to name the place Batavia. On 28 May 1619 Coen returned in force and led his men, among whom were Japanese mercenaries, into the attack against the English and their local allies. Only one man was lost; the town was burned and became the site for a new fortress and a fine capital.[16]

The savage conquest of the Banda Islands

In 1621 Coen deployed Japanese mercenaries in a major operation to give the VOC complete control over the Banda Islands and the nutmeg trade. The action remains the best recorded operation by Japanese in the service of the Dutch, and it was also the most savage, both during the fighting and in its vicious aftermath. The Banda Islands consisted of a main island called Banda Neira and a number of smaller ones, the most

94

important of these being Run and Ai. In 1615 Japanese mercenaries in VOC service took part in an attack on the island of Ai, where the English East India Company had dared to set up a factory. They raised their company's flag and led the vanguard with the Dutch soldiers following along behind.[17] The attackers then found to their surprise that Ai was defended by walls that snaked up the hillsides from which muskets were fired with remarkable accuracy. Their successful defence was the result of being trained by the newly arrived English. Only their remorseless application of overwhelming force gave the Dutch confidence, and with only one small outpost left to fall, the invaders rested, but that night the Bandanese launched a counterattack and drove the Dutch into the sea.

The VOC returned in 1616, by which time the Bandanese had asked the EIC to strengthen their defences once again. Three ships set sail in January 1616, but a deal was struck with the Dutch, leaving the island vulnerable. When the Dutch and their Japanese troops attacked again they took better precautions than during the first invasion and secured Ai after much fierce fighting. To hold the island they erected a fort that would be given the appropriate name of Fort Revenge.

On 11 March 1621 Coen's new invasion force assaulted the strategic island of Great Banda. Its main strongpoint of Lontor was situated on the brow of a steep hill and covered by three lines of fortifications. They assaulted Lontor in a three-pronged attack. Two contingents of forty-five and forty-two Japanese mercenaries respectively were combined to mount an assault that was to be remarked upon for its fierce fighting. The unit stormed the well-defended heights and earned rewards listed as follows 'to the afore-mentioned leader of the Japanese, 60 *reals*… to fourteen Japanese 30 *reals* each'.[18] Coen also stationed a light ship armed by Japanese as a rapid-response force should trouble break out again.[19]

Helped by the great bravery of the Japanese and assisted not a little by some Bandanese treachery the Dutch had triumphed, so the *orangkaya* immediately sued for peace, but the Dutch did not trust them and hatched a plot to transport the entire population of Lontor to Batavia. A fresh rebellion began, and the Japanese mercenaries were also to become involved in the subsequent massacre of the defeated inhabitants, an incident that shocked the directors of the VOC so much that they reprimanded Coen for it. Two officers commented separately that, 'We must not forget the Bandanese fought for the freedom of their country, exactly in the same way as we have done in Holland for so many years', and the less ironic statement that 'Things are carried on in such a criminal and murderous way that the blood of poor people cried to heaven for revenge'.[20]

Two English merchants were caught up in the violence, as shown by the testimonies of Robert Randall and Abraham Woofe before the judge of the Admiralty Court the following year. They were 'pinioned and tied by the necks fast to a post, expecting to be presently executed, whilst the Dutch in inhuman manner, stood throwing the heads of the Chinese and Bandanese they had executed under their feet'. Abraham Woofe's deposition identifies the executioners as, '80 Japanese soldiers in the Dutch service'. He also believed that the Dutch made signs to the Japanese to kill the two Englishmen but that the gesture was misunderstood.[21] In all, forty-four *orangkaya* were executed because of alleged plots to revolt against the new treaty. The involvement of Japanese mercenaries in the executions echoes their earlier role in the Sangley massacre, and is starkly commemorated in a painting on display in the museum on Banda Neira that shows Japanese mercenaries standing next to Dutch officials surrounded by dead bodies. It was commissioned by Des Alwi Abubakar (1927–2010), a man committed to developing the Banda Islands for modern tourism, but who was also determined to educate visitors about Bandanese history.[22]

Macao, Amboina and the last *soldaten*

The securing of the Banda Islands was the greatest prize won by the Dutch using Japanese mercenaries. It was also the last, because in that same year of 1621 shogun Tokugawa Hidetada, who only eight years earlier had given the VOC a free rein to recruit mercenaries, completely reversed his position as one element of an attempt to control the VOC's activities on Hirado. No person could now be taken outside Japan on a foreign vessel, either as a slave or a hired man, without permission from the shogun, and it was made crystal clear that such permission would not be granted. The daimyo of Hirado was inevitably drawn in to police the edict and discharged his duties loyally, keeping a strict watch over Dutch ships leaving the ports of Hirado and Kōchiura. In October 1621 three Japanese who attempted to leave on the Dutch vessel *Zwaan* were discovered and crucified.[23] As Francois Caron, the current *opperhoofdt*, noted:

He would have no Arms transported out of his Empire, (which could not be hindered by no way but this) insomuch that two Chineses, Father and Son, were both crucified at Firando, for endeavouring to convey some away in private: and five Japanners, who had sold them the said Arms, without knowing their design, were beheaded.[24]

The 1621 ban was the first stage in the long succession of edicts that culminated in the expulsion of the Portuguese in 1639 and which are commonly referred to the Sakoku (the closed country) Edict. Although it is no longer claimed that Japan 'closed its doors' to the outside world these restrictions, which would eventually benefit the Dutch as the favoured nation of Europe through their outpost on Dejima in Nagasaki harbour, meant the end of direct recruitment for the VOC's most prized import: the Japanese mercenary. This was very bad news for Coen, who wanted Japanese troops for his next and most ambitious ventures: the capture of Macao from the Portuguese and Manila from the Spanish, so over the next few years he ordered his officers on Hirado to try and get the ban overturned.

The capture of the Portuguese colony had long been a prominent objective for the Dutch. They had first became aware of its importance in 1601 when, after taking part in an unsuccessful attack on Tidore, two Dutch vessels sailed close to Macao and were attacked and some of the crew imprisoned. On their return they informed the company of Macao's wealth and the fact that the profitable China-Japan trade depended on an annual voyage which left Macao once a year laden with silk and European goods and returned with gold and silver. In 1603 the annual ship was intercepted, seized, plundered and burned, and in 1607 the Dutch managed to enter the harbour of Macao and even began negotiations with the Chinese about trade until they were chased away by the Portuguese.

A twelve-year truce between the Netherlands and Portugal began in 1609, and during this time the Dutch established themselves in Hirado, but when the agreement expired in 1621 Coen decided to attempt an attack on Macao.[25] In this he would be helped by the sporadic enmity between Spain and Portugal, which even extended to the religious difference between them so that some of the exchanges between the Dominicans and Franciscans of Spanish Manila on one side, and the Jesuits of Macao on the other, are couched in language that would not be unexpected in matters relating to the difference between Catholic Iberia and Protestant Holland. In May 1619 the energetic and notorious Fray Diego de Aduarte even wrote a report to the king urging the destruction of Macao by Spanish troops and the forcible relocation of its inhabitants to Malacca. A similar report was lodged two years later. King Philip ignored both recommendations, reasoning sensibly that even though Macao was in the hands of his unwilling Portuguese subjects, that did at least prevent it from falling to the Dutch.

The Dutch confirmed the king's worst suspicions when they launched an attack on Macao in 1622 with some Japanese mercenaries in their retinue. These willing volunteers were, however, not mercenaries recruited within Japan. The ban was firmly in force, so this handful of mercenaries had joined the Dutch by a very circuitous route, because as the Dutch fleet bore down upon Macao they met a war junk of the King of Siam with twenty-eight Siamese and twenty Japanese on board. It turned out that the twenty Japanese were mercenaries recruited in the Philippines by Don Juan da Silva as reinforcements for Macao against the expected Dutch attack. The Spanish ship had been involved in a fight with the Siamese and their vessel was destroyed; the Japanese were saved. The twenty men offered their services to the Dutch, who willingly enlisted them.[26] Although the means of recruitment of these twenty Japanese is known, there may have been more. Boxer writes of possibly 200 being involved, while Murdoch puts the figures for the Dutch force as seventeen ships with 2,000 men: 900 Dutch and 1,100 Japanese and Malays; half of whom were killed.[27] We do not know precisely how the Japanese behaved during the unsuccessful attack, which was a Portuguese defensive triumph akin to their previous effort at Malacca in 1606. The near loss of Macao to their Protestant rivals concentrated a few Spanish minds, and reinforcements were sent under Don Fernando de Silva to help the Portuguese lest the Dutch return.

Recruitment in Japan was never revived. A few Japanese who were already overseas would continue to work for the VOC from within forts and garrisons; otherwise it was a failed experiment. Over a period of about two centuries the VOC would dispatch around 100,000 Asian troops overseas to defend its possessions, and the Japanese trial served to indicate the way recruitment had to develop. From this time on the only Japanese actions were by men who were already exiles, and in 1623 a handful of mercenaries stationed on the island of Amboina would become involved in a tragic event that sounded the final death knell for the notion of the loyal Japanese mercenary.

Jan Pieterszoon Coen, the great advocate of mercenary use, had left Batavia for the Netherlands; he was away for four years, and under his temporary successor Pieter de Carpentier a serious incident on the clove-producing island of Amboina encapsulated all the fears they had ever entertained about the loyalty and discipline of their Japanese mercenaries. Amboina was a place greatly coveted by the English, who also had merchants on the island. The Dutch employed Japanese mercenaries in its defence, numbering about a dozen in all, but they do not seem to have been wholly trusted by their employers, who kept them outside the castle and denied them the possession of firearms, their samurai swords being the only weapons they were allowed to bear.[28] In February 1623 this suspicion was heightened when one of the mercenaries was heard making intrusive enquiries into the defences of Amboina. He confessed under torture that he was involved in a plot to hand over Amboina to the English. More tortures followed which only added to the confessions, and arrests ensued. Eight English merchants and almost all the Japanese were summarily executed.[29]

The Amboina incident became a *cause célèbre* for the English as an example of Dutch perfidy, but the alleged treachery – revealed only after torture and unlikely to be true – changed the way mercenaries were regarded by the Dutch, and from that time onwards the VOC made no effort to revive the Japanese 'soldier trade'. Ironically, the tragedy was to add its own footnote to the image of the Japanese warrior. To Dutch people who were convinced of their guilt as conspirators, even a 'small number of Japonians were not to be slightly regarded on account of the valour & prowess of that nation'. To the English who believed that they had been framed the Japanese were no 'giants' and the stories about them were only 'apocryphal legends'.[30] The Japanese Wild Geese had passed from history, and no mercenaries are mentioned in official VOC correspondence after 1623. One final episode occurred when the Dutch had other Japanese mercenaries used against them in Cambodia, as will be described in a later chapter. Meanwhile the VOC representatives back in Japan had to contend with a comparatively menial role as the loyal 'servants of the shogun' and, as the next chapter will show, it must sometimes have felt as though the Japanese had hired them, rather than the reverse.

Notes

1. Clulow, Adam. *Amboina, 1623: Fear and Conspiracy on the Edge of Empire* (New York: Columbia University Press, 2019), p. 90.
2. Letter from Richard Wickham to Sir Thomas Smythe, Bantam, June (?) 1617 in Foster, William *Letters Received by the East India Company from its Servants in the East* (London, 1896-1902) Vol. 6, pp. 4-5.

3. Clulow, Adam. *Amboina, 1623: Fear and Conspiracy on the Edge of Empire* (New York: Columbia University Press, 2019), p. 90.

4. Iwao, Seiichi *Zoku Nan'yō Nihonmachi no Kenkyū: Nan'yō tōsho chiiki bunsan Nihonjin imin no seikatsu to katsudō* (Tokyo, 1987) p. 235; 'A French Account of Events at Bantam, July-Dec. 1617. Dieppe, 15/25 Aug. 1618' in Foster, William *Letters Received by the East India Company from its Servants in the East* (London, 1896-1902) Vol. 6, pp. 313-314; Clulow, Adam. '"Great help from Japan"' The Dutch East India Company's experiment with Japanese soldiers' in Clulow, Adam & Mostert, Tristan. *The Dutch and English East India Companies: Diplomacy, Trade and violence in Early Modern Asia* (Amsterdam: Amsterdam University Press, 2018), p. 203; Van Ittersum, Martine Julia. 'Debating Natural Law in the Banda Islands: A Case Study in Anglo-Dutch Imperial Competition in the East Indies, 1609-1621' *History of European Ideas* 42, 4 (2016), pp. 450-501.

5. Mostert, Tristan.. 'Scramble for the spices: Makassar's role in European and Asian Competition in the Eastern Archipelago up to 1616' in Clulow, Adam & Mostert, Tristan. *The Dutch and English East India Companies: Diplomacy, Trade and violence in Early Modern Asia* (Amsterdam: Amsterdam University Press, 2018), p. 25-54.

6. Clulow, Adam. *Amboina, 1623: Fear and Conspiracy on the Edge of Empire* (New York: Columbia University Press, 2019), p. 30.

7. Clulow, Adam. *Amboina, 1623: Fear and Conspiracy on the Edge of Empire* (New York: Columbia University Press, 2019), p. 35; Milton erroneously states that Verhoef was accompanied by Japanese mercenaries: Milton, Giles. *Nathaniel's Nutmeg: how one man's courage changed the course of history* (London, Hodder and Stoughton 1999), p. 135.

8. Clulow, Adam. *Amboina, 1623: Fear and Conspiracy on the Edge of Empire* (New York: Columbia University Press, 2019), p. 36.

9. De San Antonio, Gabriel Quiroga *A Brief and Truthful Relation of Events in the Kingdom of Cambodia* (originally published as *Breve y Verdadera Relacion de los Successos del Reyno de Camboxa* in 1604) (Bangkok, 1998), p.14.

10. Mostert, Tristan. 'Scramble for the spices: Makassar's role in European and Asian Competition in the Eastern Archipelago up to 1616' in Clulow, Adam & Mostert, Tristan. *The Dutch and English East India Companies: Diplomacy, Trade and violence in Early Modern Asia* (Amsterdam: Amsterdam University Press, 2018), p. 30.

11. Mostert, Tristan. 'Scramble for the spices: Makassar's role in European and Asian Competition in the Eastern Archipelago up to 1616' in Clulow, Adam & Mostert, Tristan. *The Dutch and English East India Companies: Diplomacy, Trade and violence in Early Modern Asia* (Amsterdam: Amsterdam University Press, 2018), p. 32.

12. Antonio de Morga *Sucesos de las Islas Filipinas*; Mexico 1609, in Blair and Robertson 1903-09, vol. 516, pp. 54-55.

13. Boxer, C.R. *The affair of the Madre de Deus: a chapter in the history of the Portuguese in Japan* (London, 1929), p. 21n; De Morga, Antonio *History of the Philippine Islands from the discovery by Magellan in 1521 to the beginning of the XVII Century; with descriptions of Japan, China and adjacent countries* Volumes I and II translated and edited by Blair, E.H. and Robertson, J.A. (Cleveland, 1907, reprint New York, 1970). II p. 61.

14. Clulow, Adam 'Unjust, Cruel and Barbarous Proceedings: Japanese Mercenaries and the Amboyna Incident of 1623' *Itinerario* XXXI (2007) p. 18.

15. Boxer, C.R. 'Portuguese and Spanish Rivalry in the Far East during the 17th Century' *Journal of the Royal Asiatic Society of Great Britain and Ireland* 2 (1946) pp. 153-155.

16. Vlekke, Bernard H.M. *Nusantara: A History of the East Indian Archipelago* (Cambridge Mass., 1945), pp. 122-123.

17. Iwao, Seiichi *Zoku Nan'yō Nihonmachi no Kenkyū: Nan'yō tōsho chiiki bunsan Nihonjin imin no seikatsu to katsudō* (Tokyo, 1987) p. 266.

18. Iwao, Seiichi *Zoku Nan'yō Nihonmachi no Kenkyū: Nan'yō tōsho chiiki bunsan Nihonjin imin no seikatsu to katsudō* (Tokyo, 1987) p. 268.

19. Clulow, Adam 'Unjust, Cruel and Barbarous Proceedings: Japanese Mercenaries and the Amboyna Incident of 1623' *Itinerario* XXXI (2007) p. 19.

20. Vlekke, Bernard H.M. *Nusantara: A History of the East Indian Archipelago* (Cambridge Mass., 1945), pp.125-126.

21. Sainsbury W. Noel (ed.) *Calendar of State Papers Colonial, East Indies, China and Japan*, Volume 4: 1622-1624, August 1622 in British History Online, http://www.british-history.ac.uk/report. aspx?compid=69749&strquery= (accessed 10 November 2011).

22. Tsuchiya, Kenji and Siegel, James 'Invincible Kitsch or as Tourists in the Age of Des Alwi' *Indonesia* 50, 25th Anniversary Edition (Oct., 1990), p. 64.

23. Murakami, N 'The Japanese at Batavia in the XVIIth Century' *Monumenta Nipponica* 2 (1939), p. 357.

24. Caron, François and Schouten, Joost *A True Description of the Mighty Kingdoms of Japan and Siam*. A Facsimile of the 1671 London edition in a contemporary translation from the Dutch by Roger Manley. Introduction and notes by John Villiers. (Bangkok, 1986), p. 83.

25. Boxer, C.R. 'The 24th June 1622 – A Portuguese feat of Arms' in *Estudos Para A História de Macau: Séculos XVI a XVIII (Obra Completa I)* Lisbon: Fundaçao Oriente, pp. 43-44.

26. Boxer, C.R. 'The 24th June 1622 – A Portuguese feat of Arms' in *Estudos Para A História de Macau: Séculos XVI a XVIII (Obra Completa I)* Lisbon: Fundaçao Oriente, p.49.

27. Murdoch Volume II p. 627; Boxer, C.R. 'The 24th June 1622 – A Portuguese feat of Arms' in *Estudos Para A História de Macau: Séculos XVI a XVIII (Obra Completa I)* Lisbon: Fundaçao Oriente, pp. 43-102.

28. Clulow, Adam 'Unjust, Cruel and Barbarous Proceedings: Japanese Mercenaries and the Amboyna Incident of 1623' *Itinerario* XXXI (2007), p. 27.

29. Clulow, Adam 'Unjust, Cruel and Barbarous Proceedings: Japanese Mercenaries and the Amboyna Incident of 1623' *Itinerario* XXXI (2007), p. 21; Iwao, Seiichi *Zoku Nan'yō Nihonmachi no Kenkyū: Nan'yō tōsho chiiki bunsan Nihonjin imin no seikatsu to katsudō* (Tokyo, 1987) pp. 252-258.

30. Clulow, Adam. '"Great help from Japan"' The Dutch East India Company's experiment with Japanese soldiers' in Clulow, Adam & Mostert, Tristan. *The Dutch and English East India Companies: Diplomacy, Trade and violence in Early Modern Asia* (Amsterdam: Amsterdam University Press, 2018), p. 180.

Chapter 8

Wars and Rumours of Wars: Japanese plans to invade the Philippines

The prevailing Dutch interpretation of the Amboina incident – that the English plot was genuine and that Japanese mercenaries were the key to its implementation – would appear finally to have confirmed the worst fears that the European colonists had entertained for half a century: one day these fierce troops might turn against their masters. This chapter will examine the specific history of that belief among the Spanish on the Philippines, where it remained a constant undercurrent almost from the time of their first encounter and would drag the VOC into one final major incident of Japanese foreign policy.

The Spanish fear of Japanese aggression may be traced back to the colonists' first experience of *wakō* on the Philippines, both in terms of the way it revealed the fighting potential of the Japanese warriors and their leaders' likely ambitions. The attack on Manila by the *wakō* Sioco in 1574 had been part of an overall plan to give his master Lin Feng control of the Philippines as a base for piratical activity. In the *Memorial to the Council* of 1586, cited earlier for the Spanish plans to invade China, we find renewed speculation that the Philippines were threatened by pirates, because *wakō* 'make a descent almost every year, and, it is said, with the intent of colonising Luzón'.[1]

These were no idle fears, because the following year something approaching that scenario actually occurred: a small-scale uprising known to history as the Conspiracy of the Maharlikas. On the face of it the 1587 incident was little more than another native rebellion, even though it was the brainchild of Agustín de Legazpi, the grandson of the original conqueror of the Philippines, who now wished to rule the islands himself in cooperation with certain native chieftains. In the 1598 report on the affair entitled *Conspiracy against the Spaniards* by Governor Santiago de Vera and others we read that de Legazpi had been in touch through an interpreter with a Japanese Christian called Juan Gayo, who is described as 'the captain of a Japanese trading boat', a term that probably indicates that he was a *wakō* leader. 'Don Agustin de Legazpi became very friendly to him, inviting him many times to eat and drink at his house', says the report. Meetings took place, and it was agreed that:

> the said captain should come to this city with soldiers from Japan, and enter it under pretext of peace and commerce, bringing in his ship flags for the use of the Spaniards, so that the latter should think his intentions peaceful. When they had conquered the Spaniards Agustín de Legazpi would be made 'king of the land', repaying the Japanese mercenaries with a share of the loot. They swore this after their fashion, by anointing their necks with a broken egg.[2]

The plot was however betrayed and the leaders hanged before any Japanese mercenaries arrived.[3]

The Conspiracy of the Maharlikas proved to be the last the Spanish were to hear of an invasion by *wakō*, but the authorities stayed on the alert for similar incursions while also preparing for something much bigger: a full-scale invasion of the Philippines that was officially sanctioned by the rulers of Japan. The idea may sound outlandish, but on four occasions between 1593 and 1637 serious consideration was given to precisely that scenario. None of the proposed invasions ever set sail, but an examination of the plans made and the reasons why they were not put into effect sheds considerable light on Filipino-Japanese relations during the late sixteenth and early seventeenth century. It also adds considerably to our knowledge of the Spanish attitude towards Japanese mercenaries, because even though their bravery was recognised and valued, there was a noticeable undercurrent of fear of a local uprising by a fifth column of expatriates in support of any invasion of the Philippines from Japan. Finally, as all four ventures foundered partly because of a lack of naval capacity, these little-known schemes also provide important information about Japan's military capabilities at that time in its history.

Hideyoshi and the Philippines, 1592–98

The first Japanese invasion scare began in 1591 when the Philippines entered the consciousness of Toyotomi Hideyoshi. Having reunified Japan after the chaos of a century of civil war, he now set his mind on overseas expeditions. The addition of the Philippines to Hideyoshi's megalomaniac aims, which happened shortly before he launched his better-known invasion of Korea, was credited to a certain 'Farandaquiemon — a Japanese of low extraction', who induced Hideyoshi 'to write in a barbarous and arrogant manner to the governor, demanding submission and tribute, and threatening to come with a fleet and troops to lay waste the country'.[4]

This 'Farandaquiemon' was a Japanese Christian merchant from Sakai called Harada Kiemon. He had visited Manila on several occasions, the first of which was as a member of Ōmura Sumitada's delegation of 1586.[5] His most recent misssion was in 1591 when, having studied Manila's defences, he returned to Japan convinced that the city could be taken quite easily.[6] Together with his colleague Hasegawa Sōnin, described as a 'court favourite', Kiemon persuaded Hideyoshi to write the above 'arrogant letter' to the governor of the Philippines.[7] Hideyoshi's military strength and his unification of Japan were already known about in Manila, so the bombastic letter began with a reference to those military triumphs and the miraculous birth that had augured Hideyoshi's destiny to rule other nations. The threats appeared later in the missive: 'If an ambassador is not sent, I shall unfurl my banner and send an army against that country to conquer it with a multitude of men; so that that country will repent at not having sent me an ambassador'.[8]

The Spanish sent back a reply dated 1 May 1592. It was delivered to Hideyoshi by the Dominican friar Juan Cobo. Cobo travelled to Japan with a Chinese Christian called Antonio López, who appears to have been sent as a spy. Cobo and López met Hideyoshi at Nagoya Castle, the military base in Kyushu built for the invasion of Korea, where 'Cobo showed the king of Japan the kingdoms of our king on a globe. He gave this to the king, with the names of the kingdoms written in Chinese characters, with the distances between them'.[9] Cobo was treated with great courtesy and even enjoyed the rare honour of joining Hideyoshi for the tea ceremony.[10] Harada Kiemon then took personal charge of a second Japanese embassy to Manila. The Japanese delegation and Cobo's embassy left for the Philippines in two separate ships, which was fortunate in view of the disaster that would overcome the embassy, because Cobo's ship was wrecked off Taiwan and he died at the hands of aboriginal headhunters. Antonio López arrived safely in Manila on board Harada's vessel.[11]

Harada Kiemon began his address to the council in Manila by stating that Hideyoshi had laid on the magnificent reception for Juan Cobo because he 'knew that the Spaniards are a warlike nation'.[12] Impressive though Kiemon was, the council gave much more attention to debriefing Antonio López, who certainly knew how to gather information. On 1 June 1593, López was questioned closely under oath about what he had seen and done in Japan, with most of the questions relating to his knowledge of the existence of any Japanese plans for an attack on the Philippines. López said first that he had heard that there were such and that Hideyoshi had entrusted the conquest to 'Kunquyn', which probably means Harada Kiemon.[13] There was also a possible motive, because '[i]n Japon there is universal talk of the abundance of gold in this land. On this account, the soldiers are anxious to come here; and are coming, as they do not care to go to Core [Korea], which is a poor country'.[14] López also stated that the Japanese had interrogated him in Nagoya about the military strength of the Philippines. He seems to have tried misinformation on that point, even though his initial reply had caused some arrogant amusement. 'The Japanese laughed when they heard Antonio say that these islands contained four or five thousand Spaniards. They said that the defense of these islands was merely a matter for jest, for one hundred of the Japanese were worth two or three hundred of us'.[15]

López also mentioned that three large ships were being built in Japan, although he did not know their purpose, and he warned his hosts that in his personal opinion the Chinese community in Manila could also not be trusted if an invasion took place.[16] López had even overheard the Japanese discussing the likelihood of the Philippines being reinforced when under attack. '[F]our months are needed to go from Mexico to Luçon,' said López, 'and on this account but few soldiers could come from Mexico. Japan is not more than twenty days' journey distant, and therefore it would be well for us to appreciate this fact'.[17] In terms of Harada Kiemon's personal ambitions, everyone López had met believed that when the Philippines were conquered he would become its governor.[18]

More interesting details then emerged about the size of the invading army, although the figures were very vague. López had heard 'in Hunquin's house' (Hunquin is probably Hasegawa Sōnin) that 100,000 would be sent, but when López (modifying his earlier figures) told them that the Philippines only contained 5-6,000 soldiers, of whom no more than 3–4,000 guarded Manila, the Japanese said that 10,000 would suffice. His host later told him that they had decided further that no more than 5–6,000 men would be needed, conveyed on ten large ships.[19]

The final point López covered was the invasion route. '[T]hey will come by way of Liuteui [the Ryūkyū Islands, modern Okinawa Prefecture]'.[20] An attack via the Ryūkyūs and then Taiwan was the sensible one; it avoided open seas for the maximum amount of time, and it is only 500 miles from Taiwan to Luzón. This was exactly the route the Japanese chose in the Second World War, when they attacked the Philippines from Taiwan, with additional forces landing farther south on Luzón from Amami-Ōshima.

The threat was sufficiently serious for the Spanish to take specific defensive precautions, and López's information, limited though it was, probably proved helpful in the planning. A document entitled *Luzón Menaced by Japanese* by Governor Gómez Pérez Dasmariñas ordered the citizens to stockpile food and arms, and all ships coming from Japan were to be searched. Twenty vessels would be stationed in the river below the artillery of the fort, with all other boats being moved upstream. The invaders could not then use the latter to build defences, and the seacoast would be kept clear for fighting. No ship was to leave harbour without permission lest its crew be caught and interrogated, nor should any gold or silver be moved out of Manila. It was also recommended that the Japanese residents of Manila should be moved to a settlement outside the city and all Japanese servants monitored closely.[21]

A review was then conducted of the available troops, including retired men who still held weapons. It was estimated that the defence of Manila alone required 1,000 men, or 600 at the very least. The latter figure was the one included in the document, which implies that 600men were all they had. Other strongpoints required fewer, and there would be twenty-five soldiers on board each of four vessels to guard the coasts. The total strength available to withstand a Japanese attack was put at a disappointing 1,517 men, only a quarter of the number that López had told the Japanese about in Nagoya. Spanish defenders were therefore outnumbered four to one, using his lowest estimate of the invading forces.[22]

The Philippines remained on high alert for four years after Harada's visit, and during that time the Spanish authorities closely monitored Hideyoshi's military expedition against Korea. It was launched during the summer of 1592 and rapidly changed from being a *blitzkrieg* success to a long and painful retreat. The Korean campaign revealed in particular a major Japanese weakness concerning naval warfare and support, and one of the main reasons for Japan's eventual defeat was that the Korean navy severed Japan's lines of communication between Busan and the Japanese island of Tsushima.[23] The encouraging lesson was not wasted on Manila. If Hideyoshi could not control the Tsushima Strait, how could he ever contemplate sending an invasion fleet as far as Luzón?

As his Korean incursion dragged on, Hideyoshi grew increasingly suspicious about the activities of Portuguese and Spanish missionaries in Japan. As we saw in an earlier chapter, an active persecution of Christianity followed, and Japan's first martyrs died in February 1597. One of them, Fray Martin of the Ascension, wrote a letter to the governor of the Philippines as he was on his way to his execution. It includes what he had heard about Hideyoshi's intentions toward the Philippines. 'It is said that next year he will go to Luzón, and that he does not go this year because of being busy with the Coreans'. Martin goes on to comment on the invasion route, whereby 'he intends to take the islands of Lequios and Hermosa [Ryūkyūs and Taiwan], throw forces from them into Cagayan, and thence to fall upon Manila, if God does not first put a stop to his advance'.[24] Manila gave some consideration to mounting a preemptive Spanish occupation of Taiwan but, as Fray Martin had hoped, God did indeed put a stop to Hideyoshi's plans. Hideyoshi died in 1598, the troops in Korea were recalled, and no fleet sailed for Manila. A Spanish reconnaissance of Taiwan may well have been carried out at this time, but no attempt was made to exert control over the island. That had to wait until 1626, when the Spanish established Fort San Domingo (modern Keelung).

Threats of invasion under the Tokugawa, 1614–16

Toyotomi Hideyoshi died in the way that all dictators dread, leaving a five-year-old son to inherit, and the questions over Hideyori's regency threatened to plunge Japan back into the military chaos from which Hideyoshi had rescued it. The end result was the displacement of Hideyori by Tokugawa Ieyasu (1542–1616), whose family were destined to rule Japan until 1868. The Japanese Christians held their breath when Ieyasu assumed the role of shogun in 1603, while concerns over Ieyasu's rise to power were also expressed in Manila. Ieyasu was believed to be suspicious of the motives of the priests who came from Manila, because 'what they call preaching the gospel is an artifice, and a means of conquering'.[25]

Ieyasu was far more concerned about the internal threat from Christianity within Japan than the existence of any external threat from the Philippines, and even though it was from the Philippines that most priests came, peaceful regulated trade was acceptable to both sides. Silver was an important commodity, and Japanese mines yielded perhaps a third of global silver production during the period covered by this chapter.[26] As Antonio de Morga wrote, '[I]t is well to keep the king of Japon friendly by this means. For if he were not so he would be the greatest enemy that could be feared, on account of the number and size of his realms, and the valour of the people therein, who are, beyond comparison, the bravest in all India'.[27] Elsewhere De Morga notes approvingly that when six shiploads of Japanese pirates had attacked Chinese ships bound for Manila, Ieyasu had them sought out and 400 were crucified.[28] Sensitive to Ieyasu's own concerns, Manila had responded by taking steps to control the flow of priests, stating quite clearly in 1606 that 'no religious shall pass to the provinces of Japan through these kingdoms'.[29] The prohibition was however piously ignored by the church, so the Philippines would remain the main conduit for missionaries entering Japan, to Ieyasu's growing annoyance.

Christianity held its own for the first few years of the Tokugawa regime in spite of sporadic instances of persecution, but the seamless robe of Catholic Christianity had been exposed as a sham by the arrival in Japan of Dutch and English Protestants in 1600. Richard Cocks, head of the East India Company's factory on Hirado, missed no opportunity to denounce his Catholic rivals in front of the Japanese and to play cynically upon the Tokugawa regime's deepest fears. In October 1615, for example, he wrote to his colleague Richard Wickham advising him to state before the Japanese authorities that King Philip had usurped Portugal and would do the same in Japan if he could, with the priests acting as his instruments of rebellion. On one occasion Cocks even suggested that two Spanish ships bound for the Philippines that had been unexpectedly driven to Japan by the wind had not arrived by accident:

> they were sent on purpose by the King of Spain having knowledge of the death of the old emperor, thinking some papistical *tono* (lord) might rise and rebel, and so draw all the papists to flock to them and take part, by which means they might on a sudden seize some strong place and keep it till more succours came, they not wanting money for men for the accomplishing of such a stratagem.[30]

Active persecution began in 1614 and many Christians sought refuge in Manila. It is possible that their arrival may have revived the old fears about a Japanese conquest, because in *Trade between Nueva España and the Far East,* which is unsigned and undated but of around this time, we read once again that the Japanese, 'have even thought of making war upon these islands in order to conquer them for themselves'.[31] There was no intelligence to suggest that an invasion was currently being planned by the refugees or anyone else, as indeed none was, although some unusual discussions are recorded in the diary of Richard Cocks.

In his entry for 18 September 1616 Cocks reports on a meeting between Captain William Adams and 'Mukai Shongo', who is described as a good friend of the English in Japan.[32] Adams was asked if he would act as a pilot for a Japanese invasion fleet, not of the Philippines but of the Ladrones Islands. The name means 'thieves' and referred to the behaviour of the inhabitants when Magellan discovered them in 1565. They are now known as the Marianas and were believed by the Japanese to be 'very rich in mines of gold and silver'.[33] Mukai also asked him if he was familiar with the island of Taiwan. Adams, perhaps playing for time, answered that the Marianas must be of little importance or the Spanish would already have taken them. The following day Cocks went to see Mukai, who repeated what he had said to Adams about the Marianas. Cocks answered in words similar to those of Adams, that if the Marianas had been any use to Spain they would already have seized them, but added rashly:

if the Emperor pretended to make a conquest of any, that the Philippines themselves were of more importance, and the Spaniards weak and ill-beloved of the country people, and that herein his Majesty needed not to doubt the assistance both of the English and Dutch, as the occasion should serve. At which speeches he seemed to make a pause, and in the end said that they wanted such ships as ours were.[34]

The matter was never discussed with the English again and no fleet sailed in 1616 to conquer either the Marianas or the Philippines. One possible reason is hinted at in Cocks's words relating to the Japanese naval capacity. As Hideyoshi's Korean disaster had shown, they simply did not have the number and quality of ships or the navigational expertise to contemplate such a move. It was one reason why the inhabitants of the Philippines now felt comparatively safe, a fact that is fully appreciated in *Reforms needed in Filipinas* by Hernando de los

Rios Coronel (1619–20), who wrote that the Japanese 'do not know how to navigate without a Spanish pilot and sailors'.[35] The contemporary Japanese military capacity on land was far more impressive: in 1609 the Shimazu daimyo of Satsuma had successfully annexed the Ryūkyūs and two unsuccessful attempts had been made against Taiwan in 1609 and 1616.[36] An attack on Manila was therefore feasible if the Japanese had the naval support that the Dutch or English could provide.

The Philippines and the Matsukura family, 1630–31

Japanese naval weakness would come up again as a crucial factor in 1630 when an invasion of the Philippines was considered for a third time.[37] The persecution of Christianity had intensified since 1616, and now the only contact Japanese Christians had with the outside world was through a handful of brave priests who entered Japan secretly. The Japanese authorities believed that they spread sedition and encouraged disobedience and most of them still came by way of Manila, so an invasion of the Philippines would be a heavy-handed way of closing the loophole once and for all.[38]

The 1630 invasion scheme would be associated almost completely with a single enthusiast: Matsukura Bungo-no-Kami Shigemasa (1574–1630), the notorious tyrant of Shimabara in Hizen Province, whose cruel treatment of his people and his persecution of Christians is very well recorded.[39] The Philippines had entered Shigemasa's consciousness in 1624 when two ships belonging to the Matsukura were blown off course and ended up on the islands. On returning to Japan, their captains spoke enthusiastically about the considerable mercantile activity that existed between Japan and the Philippines and how Shigemasa might be able to gain control of it by means of a military expedition.[40] Shigemasa took no immediate action because it would have been without precedent for any daimyo to act in such a manner purely on his own initiative, rather than by direction of the shogun, but then an incident occurred that provided him with the ideal opportunity for an authorised expedition to the Philippines. It would be carried out to avenge an insult to Japan.

The affront had its roots in the 1622 attack on Macao described above, where the Portuguese had heroically beaten off the Dutch attack and a handful of Japanese mercenaries had served on the Dutch side.[41] The Dutch attempt caused such alarm in Manila that the Spanish sent further reinforcements to Macao after the campaign in case of a renewed incursion. These Spanish troops were ordered to stand down in 1624 when the situation quietened, but instead of sailing straight home to the Philippines their leaders chose to engage in a leisurely piratical expedition.[42] Among their targets was Siam, where they preyed on the local freight vessels 'carrying as merchandise, rice, a considerable amount of pepper, and some cloth. The last named was much needed by the infantry, who already had no shirts on account of the long voyage'.[43] One of the ships they attacked and burned belonged to the king of Siam, but the Spanish pirates really exceeded their brief when they attacked a Japanese 'red seal' ship. It had been sent to Siam by the *machidoshiyori* (town elder) of Nagasaki, Takaki Sakuzaemon.[44]

The Spanish account of the affair is very shamefaced. It admits that '[o]ne [ship] was Japanese, and carried drugs and merchandise. It was captured in good faith, but the justification of this act is being discussed. It is thought that the Japanese will be remunerated for the injury received, as they ought not to have been harmed'.[45] The most serious aspect of the incident was the appropriation of the red seal; an act that amounted to an attack on the shogun's personal authority.[46] A profound apology was subsequently conveyed to Nagasaki.

No acknowledgement came from the Japanese side, and at its meeting in Manila on 16 January 1629 the Council of the Philippines decided to take the matter no further, while minuting four reasons why relations between Spain and Japan were at such a low level. The first was that Spanish trade had been embargoed, not for commercial reasons but because of its links to Christianity. The second point was that the Japanese had refused to receive any Spanish ambassadors. The third referred to the 'old time robberies' of the Hideyoshi era and his threats of invasion, a theme echoed in the Spaniards' understanding of the current situation in their fourth point:

> [T]he Japanese had news of the riches of these islands, they have always tried to conquer them, by endeavouring to get a foothold on the island of Hermosa, in order to make it a waystation for the conquest of Luzón. That has caused the governors of Philipinas to make great expenditures and vast preparations during the past few years; and but recently it is learned that discussions of this kind are rife in Japon and that their reason for not doing it is not lack of malice but of power.[47]

Matsukura Shigemasa possessed both malice and power. He realised the opportunity that had fallen into his lap, and addressed the *rōjū* (the shogun's senior advisory council) in Edo as follows:

Luzón is governed by the Western country [Spain], and that country in conjunction with Namban [Portugal] is ever looking for an opportunity to invade this empire. For that reason there is a fear that our country will be disturbed. All who come from Spain to Japan touch at Luzón. Therefore if I shall conquer that country with my own troops, place my own agents there, and thus destroy the base of the Westerners, this country will be secure for years to come. If I be permitted I will cross over to Luzón and conquer it. I pray that the red seal of the Great Lord, giving me an estate of 100,000 *koku* there, may be granted me.[48]

To his own desire for territorial expansion and personal wealth Shigemasa therefore had added the frustration of any invasion of Japan by Spain. While holding back from a binding commitment to send Japanese troops to Manila, the shogun gave Shigemasa permission to investigate it as a potential target and to make military preparations. On 14 December 1630, with the cooperation of the Nagasaki *bugyō* Takenaka Umene,[49] Shigemasa sent two retainers called Yoshioka Kurōemon and Kimura Gonnojō to Manila to spy out the Spanish defences.[50] They were disguised as merchants and their cover story was that they wished to discuss the development of trade. Each had ten *ashigaru* (foot soldiers) under his command, but during a stormy return crossing all ten of Kimura's men perished.

While they were away, Shigemasa continued with his military preparations. The paucity of sources for what appears to have been the most serious plan to invade the Philippines is regrettable, although the omissions may indicate simply that certain crucial aspects were never considered. All that is known for certain is that Shigemasa amassed 3,000 bows and muskets for his army.[51] As these are foot-soldier weapons, one might envisage an additional 1,500 foot-soldier spearmen and half that number of samurai with noncombatant support troops, making the total numbers in Shigemasa's army about the same as the 5–6,000 suggested by Antonio López in 1593. There is no mention of naval support within the very meagre historical sources, nor is any indication given that Shigemasa might be aware that the important waystation of Taiwan had acquired a Spanish fort since the time of Hideyoshi. Finally, no consideration was given to the need for artillery against the walls of Manila, but that omission could possibly be explained by the fact that Shigemasa was awaiting the arrival of his spies with the relevant information.

The men returned to Japan in July 1631. No records of the intelligence they brought back with them have survived, but their information is unlikely to have been either profound or accurate, because they were a far cry from the *ninja* of Japanese martial fantasy. The authorities on the Philippines knew exactly who they were and the real purpose of their visit, as is confirmed by the unsigned *Events in Filipinas* of 2 July 1632:

> In Japon they are still pricked with the thorn of the ship which some years ago our galleons captured and burned on the bar of Sian. To avenge this, notable councils have been held in Japon, in order to come and wage war against this land; in order beforehand to have it well explored, they sent last year in January two merchant ships, under cloak of trade and traffic. Although in Manilla warning of this double object had been received, this was not made known; and they were received and regaled as ambassadors from the Tono of Arima and Bungo. A ceremonious reception and very handsome presents were given to them; but the city was put in readiness for whatever might happen.[52]

A separate Jesuit source suggests that a deliberate attempt was made to impress on the spies the futility of attempting to take Manila by force. It comes in a report sent to Spain on 29 July 1631 by Hernando Perez. In it he stated unambiguously that Yoshioka and Kimura were 'sham envoys sent to investigate our situation in order to have an easy conquest of our country'. Perez confirmed that presents were given and banquets were held. 'However, although on the surface there was a warm reception, in reality there was a display of military strength in accordance with a situation of war. As the envoys passed through the town the army units were lined up from the seashore to the governor's residence'. Perez concluded that the envoys were 'amazed' by what they saw.[53] Their undercover mission therefore came to nothing, but was nullified anyway by the unexpected death of the invasion commander Matsukura Shigemasa.[54] He had died suddenly in a bathhouse in Obama while his spies were still in Manila. Murder was suspected.[55]

The Dutch and the final invasion plans, 1637

No further considerations were given to an expedition against the Philippines for another five years, but while Christian refugees from Japanese persecution continued to arrive in Manila, so also persisted the much smaller reverse flow of secret priests to Japan. The last of the line, Father Sidotti, would arrive in Japan in 1708. That incursion may have been only a trickle, but it was enough evidence of a continuing

Christian problem to ensure that the idea of an invasion of the Philippines rumbled on after Shigemasa's death.

Shigemasa was succeeded by his son Matsukura Nagato-no-Kami Katsuie, who proved to be as much of a tyrant and enemy of Christianity as his father, and it is during Katsuie's reign as daimyo of Shimabara that we encounter the hatching of the last ever scheme to invade the Philippines. Once again there was concern about the lack of Japanese naval capacity, a deficiency that possibly could be made up by the men who were now Japan's most loyal trading partners: the Dutch East India Company. In two decades their position had slipped from arrogant recruiters of *rōnin* for their own imperial pretensions to a status as subservient – albeit highly trusted – servants of the empire of Japan as it was manifested in the shogun.

The instigator of the 1637 invasion plans was neither Matsukura Katsuie nor his master the shogun Tokugawa Iemitsu, even though the Dutch were convinced that the shogun was to blame.[56] Instead it appears to have been the brainchild of the two current *bugyō* of Nagasaki: Sakakibara Hida-no-Kami Toshishige and Baba Saburōzaemon Motonao, who hoped thereby to curry favour with their superiors. The matter of Dutch cooperation was first raised at a meeting held towards the end of September 1637 with François Caron, the *opperhoofdt* of the VOC.[57] Caron had long been insisting that all Japanese trade should be shifted from the Portuguese to the Dutch, and one plank in his argument had been to contrast the Portuguese willingness to flout Japanese laws with the Dutch attitude of docile obedience to the shogun as his loyal vassals.[58]

The *bugyō* listened respectfully to Caron, then changed the subject to a request for help from the loyal Dutch to destroy the Iberian bases of Manila, Macao, and Keelung.[59] Of these three potential targets, the *bugyō* believed Manila was the top priority because its status as the source of supply for Catholic priests would be the best bargaining counter to use with their superiors in Edo when the time came to gain official permission to invade. That was of course essential, but so was an army, and the *bugyō* were civilian officials, not commanders of samurai. The invading army would have to be supplied either by the shogun or a daimyo, such as Matsukura Katsuie, acting on the shogun's behalf. As for numbers, apparently an expeditionary force of 10,000 men was envisaged, although this is only a supposition based on comments made after the expedition had been cancelled.[60] That figure would have been twice the estimated number that Matsukura Shigemasa had planned for 1630, so other daimyo would have had to be involved as well. The *bugyō* were, however, astute enough to realise that once again naval power would be a serious weakness, so a guarantee of Dutch naval support would ensure that the army could be transported. It also would reduce the costs of the operation, which was another positive point to place before the shogun.

The *bugyō* did not approach the matter as supplicants. Instead they broached the subject in an assertive manner by challenging the Dutch to explain why, if they had the command of the sea, as they so often claimed, Manila had not become theirs already? Was it not also true that they had made an attack on Macao in 1622 and had been repulsed? Caron replied with a long and not entirely accurate account of the 1622 expedition that sidestepped the reasons for the defeat. The inclusion of Japanese mercenaries in the Dutch attacking force was not mentioned. The *bugyō* were unlikely to have heard of it, and the Dutch would not have wanted to admit that Japanese had been involved on the losing side.[61]

As for the means of attacking Manila, by 1637 it had become one of the most heavily fortified places in East Asia. Caron had no desire either to assault it or even to transport samurai to do so, and he finished his presentation by suggesting meekly that the Dutch were now more merchants than soldiers. Besides that, he said, their fleet was already fully committed because of their existing responsibilities. One of the *bugyō* seemed to accept Caron's excuses, while the other kept shaking his head, but neither was inclined to give up. The next day Heizō Ietsugu, the *daikan* of Nagasaki, presented a document for the Dutch to sign that would commit them in no uncertain terms to supporting an invasion:

> Recently we have understood that the people of Manila are breaking the emperor's prohibitions and are sending priests, who are forbidden in Japan. As a result, they are viewed as criminals by Your Honours. If the High Authorities decide to destroy this place, the Hollanders, who bring a good number of ships to Japan every year, are always ready, in time or opportunity, to present our ships and cannon for your service. We ask that Your Honours trust and believe that we are, in all matters without exception, ready to serve Japan.[62]

The text of the document contained such a firm commitment to act that Caron could not have signed it there and then; it would have to be passed up the company's chain of command. The *bugyō* were not surprised by that response, but before taking their leave they took pains to remind the Dutch that their reputation for loyalty was regarded as akin to the fidelity pledged to the shogun by his own daimyo. That point was not lost when the document came to be discussed by the Dutch at a higher level, where the choice was clear. They had to decide between abandoning their reputation as servants of the shogun, with all the implications for trade such a move would have, and the huge dangers of committing men and resources to an overseas military expedition that could result in the destruction of the company's entire fleet. They chose danger, and agreed to convey the Japanese army of invasion to the Philippines on six Dutch vessels.

Dutch support having been pledged, the matter was placed before the shogun, who agreed that the invasion should go ahead. His decision may have been influenced by the recent arrival of another group of missionaries from Manila under Father Marcello Mastrilli.[63] No mention was made of who would supply the invading army. Matsukura Katsuie was the obvious candidate, but he soon became involved in a serious development that would sound the death knell for the entire operation. An uprising on the nearby Amakusa Islands quickly spread to the Matsukura territory of Shimabara. The predominantly Christian rebels barricaded themselves inside Hara Castle, the dilapidated fortress that Matsukura Katsuie's father had replaced by nearby Shimabara Castle. The quelling of what became known as the Shimabara Rebellion soon proved to be beyond the capabilities of Matsukura Katsuie. It sucked in all the military resources of the Tokugawa shogunate for well over a year, and the Dutch naval support promised so loyally for the Philippines expedition was used instead for a reluctant and largely ineffective bombardment of the rebel castle.[64] There was no spare military capacity for an invasion of the Philippines, and even less of a stomach for one.

The final reckoning

When the shogun's advisers reviewed the Shimabara Rebellion a few months later, the inevitable comparison was drawn between the efforts needed to take flimsy Hara Castle and the plans to transport a similar-sized army with similar naval support many hundreds of miles through occupied territory to take on the European fortifications of Manila. The comment was made that the 10,000 men they had earmarked for the Philippine invasion should have been 100,000: exactly the number of troops that had to be deployed against Hara to overcome one-third that many rebels.[65] Yet such a calculation was now only an academic point, for no further attempt would be made against the Philippines for over 300 years.

The shock caused by the Shimabara Rebellion then brought about the worst fears for the remaining Portuguese in Japan. The shogun decided they should follow the Jesuits in being deported. With the Sakoku Edict of 1639, all contact was cut with Catholic Europe, and even the loyal Dutch were confined to the artificial island of Dejima in Nagasaki Bay, from where they would exercise their role as servants of the shogun in a very different manner.

Of the three schemes for invading the Philippines between 1593 and 1637, the vast armies at Hideyoshi's disposal in his 1593 plan could well have succeeded against the meagre garrison of Manila had he not been humiliated already in Korea by a woeful lack of naval support. The two seaborne attempts against Taiwan in 1609 and 1616 were also failures, and the annexation of the Ryūkyūs in 1609 was to be contemporary Japan's only overseas gain. The 1630 effort against the Philippines was to be led by someone who was committed to the scheme, but there was apparently no improvement in the seaborne capacity. The chances of success were reduced also because the defences of Manila were by then stronger than in 1593 and Taiwan had a Spanish fort on it instead of a Japanese one. These points alone may well have led to the cancellation of the project if the Matsukura spies had ever had the chance to report back to Shigemasa.

The popular view of the final attempt in 1637 gives the impression that a fleet was ready to set sail and was stopped only by the Shimabara Rebellion, but this does not appear to have been the case. The Dutch had made a genuine commitment to provide naval support and the shogun had approved the scheme, but there is no evidence that Matsukura Katsuie was waiting for the go-ahead. It is more than likely that the invasion plans had advanced no further than the two Nagasaki officials with their ill-informed 'back-of-an-envelope' calculations. The subsequent experience at Hara Castle then betrayed a huge Japanese deficiency in siege artillery.[66] The walls of Manila would have been safe even if the Japanese had succeeded in getting beyond fortified Taiwan.

The issue of Japanese naval capacity would not be resolved until the twentieth century, so when the Shimabara Rebellion forced the cancelation of the 1637 Philippines expedition it marked the point in time when Japan turned its back on the notion of an overseas empire for 300 years. As for the problem of Christianity, an invasion of the Philippines would have cut off the supply of subversive secret priests, but the flow was always only an ideological annoyance, never an armed flood. Instead Japan responded to this minor threat by the dramatic and fateful decision to isolate itself from European nations.

Throughout the decades under discussion, the Spanish took the Japanese threats seriously and always responded on the basis of good intelligence. Their exposure of Matsukura's spies showed that the considered response to a notional Japanese threat was as carefully managed in 1630 as it had been in 1593. Spanish preparations always involved the monitoring of a potential fifth column of Japanese residents in Manila, but even when brief uprisings occurred, other Japanese could be found fighting as loyal mercenaries for their Spanish masters elsewhere, so the Spanish never feared any great threat from that quarter. Their defensive actions were prompted only by rumours of war, not war itself.

Notes

1. *Memorial to the Council*, 1586, in Blair and Robertson 1903-09, vol. 6, p. 183.
2. Santiago de Vera and others *Conspiracy against the Spaniards*, in Blair and Robertson 1903-09, vol. 7, p. 99.
3. Agoncillo, Teodoro A. *History of the Filipino People* (Quezon City, 1960), pp. 103-104; Corpuz, O.D. *The Roots of the Filipino Nation* Volume I (Quezon City, 1989), p. 134.
4. Antonio de Morga, *Sucesos de las Islas Filipinas* 1609, in Blair and Robertson 1903-09, vol. 15, p. 67.
5. Laures, Johannes, SJ 'An Ancient Document on the Early Intercourse between Japan and the Philippines' *Culture Social* XXXIX (1941), p.7.
6. Governor Gómez Pérez Dasmariñas to the Ruler of Japan, 11 June 1592, in Blair and Robertson 1903-09, vol. 8, p. 264, note 45.
7. Henri Bernard and S. J. Tientsin, "Les Débuts des Relations Diplomatiques Entre le Japon et les Espagnols des Iles Philippines (1571–1594)," *Monumenta Nipponica* 1, no. 1 (1938), p. 120; Kiichi Matsuda, *Hideyoshi no Nanban gaikō: San Feripe Gō Jiken* (Tokyo: Shin Jinbutsu Ōraisha, 1972), p. 132.
8. Toyotomi Hideyoshi, *Letter from the King of Japan*, in Blair and Robertson 1903-09, vol. 8, p. 261. A slightly different translation of the letter and the reply can be found in Yoshi S. Kuno, *Japanese*

Expansion on the Asiatic Continent (Berkeley: Univ. of California Press, 1940), vol. 1, pp. 308–309.

9. *The second embassy to Japan* by Gómez Pérez Dasmariñas and others to the King of Spain; April-May 1593, in Blair and Robertson 1903-09, vol. 9, p. 45.

10. *The second embassy to Japan* by Gómez Pérez Dasmariñas and others to the King of Spain; April-May 1593, in Blair and Robertson 1903-09, vol. 9, p. 36.

11. M. T. Paske-Smith, "Japanese Trade and Residence in the Philippines," *Transactions of the Asiatic Society of Japan* 42, no. 2 (1914), pp. 696–97.

12. *The second embassy to Japan* by Gómez Pérez Dasmariñas and others to the King of Spain; April-May 1593, in Blair and Robertson 1903-09, vol. 9, p. 27.

13. Francisco de Lorduy, statement incorporated in report by Governor Gómez Pérez Dasmariñas to the King of Spain on the second embassy to Japan, April–May 1593, in Blair and Robertson 1903-09, vol. 9, p. 39. The reference may be to Kiemon's close associate Hasegawa Sōnin instead.

14. Francisco de Lorduy, statement incorporated in report by Governor Gómez Pérez Dasmariñas to the King of Spain on the second embassy to Japan, April–May 1593, in Blair and Robertson 1903-09, vol. 9, p. 41.

15. Francisco de Lorduy, statement incorporated in report by Governor Gómez Pérez Dasmariñas to the King of Spain on the second embassy to Japan, April–May 1593, in Blair and Robertson 1903-09, vol. 9, p. 39.

16. Francisco de Lorduy, statement incorporated in report by Governor Gómez Pérez Dasmariñas to the King of Spain on the second embassy to Japan, April–May 1593, in Blair and Robertson 1903-09, vol. 9, pp. 39–41.

17. Francisco de Lorduy, statement incorporated in report by Governor Gómez Pérez Dasmariñas to the King of Spain on the second embassy to Japan, April–May 1593. in Blair and Robertson 1903-09, vol. 9, pp. 47–48.

18. Francisco de Lorduy, statement incorporated in report by Governor Gómez Pérez Dasmariñas to the King of Spain on the second embassy to Japan, April–May 1593. in Blair and Robertson 1903-09, vol. 9, p. 48.

19. Francisco de Lorduy, statement incorporated in report by Governor Gómez Pérez Dasmariñas to the King of Spain on the second

embassy to Japan, April–May 1593. in Blair and Robertson 1903-09, vol. 9, pp. 51–53.

20. Francisco de Lorduy, statement incorporated in report by Governor Gómez Pérez Dasmariñas to the King of Spain on the second embassy to Japan, April–May 1593. in Blair and Robertson 1903-09, vol. 9, p. 54.

21. Governor Gómez Pérez Dasmariñas, *Luzón Menaced by Japanese— Precautions Submitted to the War-Officials and Certain of the Cabildo of the City,* 1591, in Blair and Robertson 1903-09, vol. 8, pp. 284–85.

22. *Memorandum of troops required in the Philippines* 1593?, in Blair and Robertson 1903-09, vol. 9, pp. 74–75.

23. Park, Yune-Hee. *Admiral Yi Sun-shin and his Turtleboat Armada* (Seoul: The Hanjin Publishing Company, 1978).

24. Martin de la Ascencion to Doctor Morga, 28 January 1597, in Blair and Robertson 1903-09, vol. 15, p. 125.

25. *Passage of missionaries via the Philippines to Japan.* Conde de Lemos, and others; Madrid, 1606-07 in Blair and Robertson 1903-09, vol. 14, p. 219.

26. Dennis O. Flynn, "Comparing the Tokugawa Shogunate with Hapsburg Spain: Two Silver-based Empires in a Global Setting," in *The Political Economy of Merchant Empires: State Power and World Trade, 1350–1750,* ed. Cambridge: Cambridge Univ. Press 1991), pp. 332–59.

27. Antonio de Morga, *Report from the Council of the Indias* 31 March 1607, in Blair and Robertson 1903-09, vol. 14, p. 229.

28. De Morga, Antonio *History of the Philippine Islands from the discovery by Magellan in 1521 to the beginning of the XVII Century; with descriptions of Japan, China and adjacent countries* Volumes I and II translated and edited by Blair, E.H. and Robertson, J.A. (Cleveland, 1907, reprint New York, 1970), I p. 203.

29. *Passage of missionaries via the Philippines to Japan.* Conde de Lemos, and others; Madrid, 1606-07 in Blair and Robertson 1903-09, vol. 14, p. 218.

30. Boxer, C.R. *The Christian Century in Japan* (1951), pp. 310-311.

31. *Trade between Nueva España and the Far East.* [Unsigned and undated; ca. 1617] in Blair and Robertson 1903-09, vol. 18, p. 62.

32. He was the son of Mukai Shogen Tadakatsu (1582-1641) the Admiral of the Tokugawa.

33. Cocks, Richard. *Diary of Richard Cocks; Cape Merchant in the English Factory in Japan 1615-1622 with correspondence* (London, 1883), Volume I p. 177.

34. Cocks, Richard. (1883), Volume I p. 178.
35. *Reforms needed in Filipinas* by Hernando de los Rios Coronel; [Madrid?], 1619-20 in Blair and Robertson 1903-09, vol. 18 p. 295.
36. For a full account of the Taiwan expeditions see below and also my article 'Onward, Christian Samurai! The Japanese Expeditions to Taiwan in 1609 and 1616' *Japanese Studies* Vol. 30 No. 1 (2010) pp. 3-21. For the Ryūkyūs see my *The Samurai Capture a King, Okinawa 1609* (Oxford, 2009) for a good introduction.
37. The most detailed account of the 1630 venture is Iwao, Seiichi "Matsukura Shigemasa no Ruzonto ensei keikaku," *Shigaku Zasshi* 45, no. 9 (1934), pp. 81–109.
38. Iwao, Seiichi "Matsukura Shigemasa no Ruzonto ensei keikaku," *Shigaku Zasshi* 45, no. 9 (1934), p. 83.
39. *Nagasaki-ken shi* [History of Nagasaki prefecture] (Tokyo: Yoshikawa Kōbunkan, Shōwa 48, 1973), pp. 242–43.
40. Hayashi, Senkichi (ed.), *Shimabara Hantō-shi* (Shimabara: Minamitakaki-gun Shi Kyōikukai, Shōwa 29, 1954), vol. 2, p. 980.
41. C. R. Boxer, "The 24th June 1622—A Portuguese Feat of Arms," in *Estudos para A História de Macau: Séculos XVI a XVIII (Obra Completa I)* (Lisbon: Fundacao Oriente, 1991), p. 49.
42. C. R. Boxer, "Portuguese and Spanish Rivalry in the Far East during the 17th Century," *Journal of the Royal Asiatic Society of Great Britain and Ireland* 2 (1946), pp. 158–59; Iwao, "Matsukura Shigemasa," pp. 87–89.
43. *Relation of 1627-28*, [Unsigned]; Manila 1628, in Blair and Robertson 1903-09, vol. 22, p. 193.
44. The *machidoshiyori* had responsibility for affairs in the inner wards of Nagasaki and was equivalent to the *daikan* (magistrate) who covered the outer wards.
45. *Relation of 1627-28*, [Unsigned]; Manila 1628, in Blair and Robertson 1903-09, vol. 22, p. 193.
46. Michael S. Laver, *Japan's Economy by Proxy in the Seventeenth Century: China, the Netherlands and the Bakufu* (London: Cambria Press, 2008), p. 72.
47. Juan Niño de Tavora to Philip IV, 1 August 1629, in Blair and Robertson 1903-09, vol. 23, p. 65.
48. James Murdoch, *A History of Japan* (London: Kegan Paul, Trubner, 1903), vol. 2, p. 631.
49. The Nagasaki *bugyō* were the chief representatives of the Tokugawa regime in the city. For most of the period under discussion there were two *bugyō* in office at the same time. As part of their duties

involved the supervision of international trade, it was only appropriate that Terazawa was involved in the espionage.

50. Iwao, "Matsukura Shigemasa," p. 98.
51. Hayashi, ed., *Shimabara Hantō-shi*, p. 980; *Nagasaki-ken shi* [History of Nagasaki prefecture], p. 246.
52. Antonio Yxida (?), *Events in Filipinas, 1630–32* 30 March 1632, in Blair and Robertson 1903-09, vol. 24, pp. 229–30.
53. Schwade, Arcadio "Matsukura Shigemasa no Ruzonto ensei keikaku," *Kirishitan Kenkyū* 7 (1964), p. 345.
54. Iwao, "Matsukura Shigemasa," p. 101.
55. Hayashi, ed., *Shimabara Hantō-shi*, p. 980; the theory about his assassination is discussed in detail in Schwade, "Matsukura Shigemasa," pp. 346–48.
56. Hirofumi Yamamoto, *Kanei Jidai* (Nihon Rekishi Sōsho vol. 39) (Tokyo: Yoshikawa Kobunkan 1989), pp. 54–55.
57. François Caron and Joost Schouten, *A True Description of the Mighty Kingdoms of Japan and Siam. Reprinted from the English Edition of 1663 with Introduction, Notes and Appendices by C. R. Boxer* (London: Argonaut Press, 1935), pp. xlii–lv.
58. The status of the Dutch as the Shogun's "loyal vassals" is brilliantly analysed in Adam Clulow, *The Company and the Shogun: the Dutch Encounter with Tokugawa Japan* (New York: Columbia Univ. Press, 2014).
59. Caron and Schouten, *A True Description*, p. xliv.
60. Ibid. p. xlv.
61. C. R. Boxer, "The 24th June 1622," p. 49.
62. Clulow, *The Company and the Shogun*, pp. 123–24.
63. C.R. Boxer, *The Christian Century in Japan 1549-1650*. (Berkeley: University of California Press 1951), p. 373.
64. C. R. Boxer, *Jan Compagnie in Japan, 1600–1850: An Essay on the Cultural, Artistic and Scientific Influence Exercised by the Hollanders in Japan from the Seventeenth to the Nineteenth Centuries* (The Hague: Martinus Nijhoff, 1950), p. 29.
65. Caron and Schouten, *A True Description*, p. xlv.
66. Within a year of the Shimabara Rebellion the Dutch were demonstrating mortars to the Japanese. Mortars, with their higher trajectory, could have been useful at Hara and against Manila. For a full description of the trials see Boxer, *Jan Compagnie in Japan, 1600–1850*, pp. 32–37.

Chapter 9

The Wild Geese and the Defence of Cambodia

By 1643 the activities of the VOC in Japan had been firmly confined to the tiny artificial island of Dejima in Nagasaki Bay, from where the once haughty *opperhoofdt* made an annual visit to the shogun to pay tribute in gratitude for the blessings the VOC had received. Elsewhere in Asia, however, the advancement of Dutch interests was being pressed forward with confidence and pride, and one of those places was Cambodia. As noted earlier, the Spanish had used Japanese mercenaries in their attacks on Cambodia in the 1590s, but sometime after that we have records of other Japanese Wild Geese serving the king of Cambodia as his guards, and that was the capacity in which they would deal the Dutch their last great military surprise.

The Japanese in Cambodian service who would fight the Dutch in 1643 had not of course been recruited in Japan. Those days had long gone, and by the 1640s any Japanese mercenaries serving any masters could only come from the particular country's expatriate community. Cambodia was but one among a number of countries including Siam and Cochinchina that now housed Japanese emigrants whom their native country had forgotten about. It was noted earlier that the shogun would have nothing to do with these exiles, and one of the best examples of the official Japanese attitude comes from 1623 in the form of a remarkable exchange of correspondence between the shogun and the king of Siam concerning the behaviour of Japanese in Ayutthaya. Specifically discussed is the possibility that the king of Cambodia might use his own Japanese mercenaries against Siam. Cambodia had first renounced its dependence on Siam in around 1618, and war was threatened. In 1623 King Songtham wrote to Tokugawa Hidetada:

My government intends therefore to take a convenient opportunity of training forces by sea and land, in order to overrun and subdue his territories. If the merchants of your honoured country who trade thither should be so misguided as to render him assistance when the war breaks out, they will run the risk of being hurt in the melee, which would I fear not be in accordance with the friendly feelings I entertain towards you.[1]

Keeping to the convenient euphemism of 'merchants', the shogun replied:

If merchants of my country resident there should aid them to repel the attack of your honoured country, you wish to exterminate them, although it is not in accordance with the friendly relations existing between Japan and Siam. This will, however, be perfectly just, and you should not hesitate for a moment.[2]

International exchanges like this took place against a background of a number of disturbances associated with the Japanese within these countries. This bad behaviour, however, was less to do with the settled expatriate communities than with Japanese traders visiting on a short-term basis. Such trade was conducted under the red-seal system of approved ships, which had supposedly meant that trade would be carried on within a stable framework. It failed, however, to ensure the good behaviour of the crews, whose 'riotous behaviour' was to be noted in several diplomatic exchanges. In this the Japanese differed markedly from other Asian settlers. Instead they were demonstrating arrogant behaviour that had more in common with arrogant Western colonists.

Clulow suggests two reasons why the Japanese acquired a unique reputation for violence. First, memories of *wakō* raids confirmed that Japanese mariners had a long history of mixing trade and warfare in an unstable but effective mix. Many came from ports that once were pirate bases. Second, force was a tool, a way to succeed when other avenues were closed.[3] So bad did the situation become that in 1604 shogun Tokugawa Ieyasu had been forced to send a diplomatic letter to Nguyễn Hoàng (1523–1613), the ruler of Cochinchina. The missive began with pleasantries, but the main thrust of the letter was to respond to serious complaints about the violent behaviour of certain Japanese inhabitants. In a second letter of 1605, the shogun explained how merchants were driven by greed to take great risks, and then behaved badly, 'breaking laws and disrupting trade', while a letter of 1606 spelled out the direction that punishment for such misdemeanours should take. 'If the merchants from Japan who go to your country do not obey [the rules of] your government, please inspect the severity of their crimes, and punish them heavily or slightly in accordance with their guilt'.[4] Nguyễn Hoàng was sent a notice board in Japanese that conveyed these sentiments, and it was ordered to be displayed in public places. In 1606 he wrote back to the shogun, updating him on the situation. Sadly, three Japanese ships had arrived the previous year, but instead of engaging in peaceful trade the Japanese merchants had behaved like raiding pirates. They ran 'rampant in my lands stealing goods and money belonging to Fujianese merchants and abusing neighboring residents and women'. Their hosts had to use force to control them.[5]

Cochinchina also proved to be the site of some international rivalry which was to have indirect repercussions in Japan. In June 1643 a VOC fleet under Pieter Baeck intent upon attacking Cochinchina was intercepted by fifty ships of the Nguyễn, who fought back valiantly and well. 'The battle was a total disaster', reported the Dutch. 'The de Wijdenes [the Dutch flag ship] was destroyed. Baeck was killed and another two ships took great pains to escape'. Apparently the flagship caught fire and was blown up by its own stock of gunpowder. The news of the disaster travelled as far as Japan, where 'the Japanese started to think that we are nothing to be afraid of and so started looking down in us, and our company's credit has been lost a great deal'.[6]

Even the minor state of Patani suffered enough from Japanese visitors for a letter to be sent about them. In reply Ieyasu noted that, 'Japanese merchant ships go to your country and engage in violent plunder and harmful disruptions. These are serious offences'.[7] As a consequence, he asked the queen of Patani to punish the 'villains aboard Japanese ships' appropriately for their crimes, which included 'murder, arson, and disturbing the peace'.[8] Similar problems in Cambodia in 1610 are tackled in another letter sent by Ieyasu to a fellow sovereign:

In the first place, merchants from my country [Japan] go to several places in your country [Cambodia] as well as Cochin-China and Champa. There they become villains. I have received information that that these men cause terrible damage and there are no peaceful days in these areas. Already because of this we have explained in past years to the merchants of our country who remain in Japan, that we will execute all those [who committed such crimes]. Those villains now abroad must be punished when they return to Japan.

Probably because they are afraid of this, they have not returned. Furthermore, we have heard that they hide [in south-east Asia]... and when the right circumstances present themselves they commit crimes and cause suffering to people in those areas. Their offences are extremely serious. Please punish them immediately according to the laws of your country. It is not necessary to have any reserve in this regard.

On a more positive note, the violent reputation of the Japanese encouraged local rulers to enlist them as mercenaries, just as had happened half a century before in other lands, and the area that is now modern Vietnam provides a further example of the situation whereby Japanese could be recruited from among the diaspora on an *ad hoc* basis. The expatriate Japanese community had long played an important role in the ancient town of Hội An,[9] and provided military service in 1631 when the son of the Nguyễn ruler fought off an attack from his brother and was supported by a group of Japanese.[10] The rulers of Cochinchina do not appear to have had a Japanese palace guard but were certainly aware of the quality of Japanese swords, as revealed by the traveller Christopher Borri in 1633, where the king's 'continual commerce with Japan hath brought into his Countrey great store of Swords and Cemiters of that Countrey which are of an excellent temper'.[11] Japanese traders supplied arms to both sides during a dispute between the rulers of Cochinchina and Tonkin in 1628, prompting a letter from the former to the shogun urging exclusive support for his cause.[12]

The Japanese defence of Cambodia

The incident that occurred in 1643 in Cambodia provides the outstanding example of the loyalty rendered to the king of Cambodia by his own Japanese bodyguard. We noted earlier the use of Japanese mercenaries by the Spanish in their expeditions against Cambodia, and the presence of peaceful Japanese visitors to Cambodia is shown by votive inscriptions in Chinese ink left on the pillars of one of the galleries of Angkor Wat by Japanese merchants from Sakai and Kyushu who were visiting that renowned Buddhist site in 1612.[13] It must have been about this time that the Cambodian rulers acquired Japanese mercenaries of their own, and three decades later they would use them against the Dutch.

The VOC had turned their attentions to Cambodia only recently, and it had happened almost on a whim. Anthony van Diemen was

Governor General of the Indies when news reached Batavia of the 1636 edict restricting Japanese travel abroad. He immediately realised that the Dutch were not to be expelled from Japan like the Spanish and Portuguese but were merely to be restricted in their movements. The 1636 edict was therefore an excellent business opportunity for the Dutch, so within days of van Diemen's deliberations a Dutch trading post was established in Cambodia as one element in a rapid development of trade at the expense of their Catholic rivals.

All went well until the Cambodian king died in 1640 and a succession dispute broke out, led by Prince Sattha, who was supported by the local Japanese community among others. His rival was however stabbed to death by the court chamberlain using a Japanese dagger. Prince Sattha then carried out a bloody purge of his enemies, and soon had himself crowned as King Ramadhipati.[14] The new Cambodian king then decided to rid his kingdom of the Dutch with the help of his Japanese followers. It was to be the first time the Dutch had Japanese fighters used against them since Malacca in 1606, and the effect was devastating.

The head of the Dutch trading post was summoned to a friendly meeting with the king in November 1643, but the gesture proved to be a trap. The king had placed 200 of his finest troops, who included both Portuguese and Japanese in their ranks, in hidden positions around the market square, while others blocked all roads and waterways out of the capital. Early in the morning of 27 November 1643 the Dutch assembled and proceeded towards the royal palace. Surrounded by hidden enemies, the entire Dutch party was slaughtered, and because there were no survivors no warning could be sent to the Dutch factory. This was the next place to be attacked, and its inhabitants were killed to a man along with the crew of the *Rijswick*, a Dutch ship lying at anchor nearby.

A more astonishing action followed shortly afterwards when a group of eleven samurai led by a certain 'Captain Soyewon', who clearly spoke Dutch, drew up alongside the Dutch vessel *Orangienboom*. Oblivious of the massacre that had taken place on land, the unsuspecting ship's captain invited them on board and accepted the generous gifts of Chinese beer and *arak* that the visitors brought with them. The samurai were fortunate that most of the crew were ashore. As soon as the remaining Dutchmen were sufficiently intoxicated the Japanese drew their swords, killed most of the crew and captured the ship. Some of the Dutch sailors who were caught below decks extricated themselves through portholes and swam to the shore.[15]

Dutch retribution followed a year later in the form of a military expedition from Batavia. Among the orders given to its commander was the firm demand that the Japanese who had dared to capture a Dutch ship should be arrested and sent back to Batavia to await punishment. The expedition resulted in a prolonged battle at Ponumpingh (modern Phnom Penh), which the Cambodians had protected by building two pontoon bridges across the river approach. They were built from thick bamboo rafts that were tied together and tightly secured to the river bank by stout ropes. Each of the bridges was protected by cannon batteries, some of which were manned by Japanese, erected on either side of the river's banks. When darkness fell hundreds of torches were lighted on the bridges to show the approaching Dutch ships that they should proceed no further, and salvoes of cannon fire followed as a further warning to the invaders. Captain Harouse, the commander of the Dutch fleet, decided that an attempt had to be made to destroy the bridges. Four ships should attack the first pontoon. As they approached the vessels came under intense fire, causing much damage to the ships and many casualties among the crews, although a handful of determined men managed to mount the bridge and began hacking away at its bamboo core. A sufficiently large breach was made and just allowed the fleet through to confront the second bridge, which had as its own core a stout iron chain. It was desperately defended, and one of the Cambodian cannon balls from the shore decapitated Captain Harouse during the assault. An incredibly brave attack by a landing party then disabled one of the artillery batteries. A fierce battle followed that forced the Dutch into a fighting retreat, their honour being saved only by the welcome recapture of the *Orangienboom* from the samurai and the liberation of ten Dutch captives who were still being held on board.[16]

For several years afterwards the Cambodians expected further Dutch retaliation, which was indeed considered in alliance with King Prasat Thong of Siam, but in the event the battle of Ponumpingh proved to be the last conflict between the Dutch and Japanese mercenaries in that area of south-east Asia. Much further afield in distant Taiwan, however, the Dutch would soon lose one of their prized colonial possessions in a unique campaign that may mark the last hurrah of Japan's Wild Geese.

Notes

1. Satow, Ernest M. 'Notes on the Intercourse between Japan and Siam in the Seventeenth Century' *Transactions of the Asiatic Society of Japan* 13 (1885) p. 157.
2. Satow, Ernest M. 'Notes on the Intercourse between Japan and Siam in the Seventeenth Century' *Transactions of the Asiatic Society of Japan* 13 (1885) p. 178.
3. Clulow, Adam 'Like Lambs in Japan and Devils outside Their Land: Diplomacy, Violence and Japanese Merchants in south-east Asia' *Journal of World History* 24, 2 (2013), pp. 347-348.
4. Clulow, Adam 'Like Lambs in Japan and Devils outside Their Land: Diplomacy, Violence and Japanese Merchants in south-east Asia' *Journal of World History* 24, 2 (2013), p. 344.
5. Clulow, Adam 'Like Lambs in Japan and Devils outside Their Land: Diplomacy, Violence and Japanese Merchants in south-east Asia' *Journal of World History* 24, 2 (2013), p. 346.
6. Li, Tana *Nguyễn Cochinchina: Southern Vietnam in the Seventeenth and Eighteenth Centuries* (New York, Cornell University, 1998), pp. 178-179.
7. Kondō, *Gaiban tsūsho*, p.198.
8. Kondō, *Gaiban tsūsho*, p.198.
9. Chen, Chingho A *Historical Notes on Hội An (Faifo)* (Carbondale, Illinois, 1974), pp. 12-23; Vu Minh Gang 'The Japanese presence in Hoi An' in *Ancient town of Hoi An : International Symposium held in Danang on 22-23 March 1990* (Danang, 1990) pp. 135-141.
10. Tarling, Nicholas (ed.) *The Cambridge History of south-east Asia Vol 1 from Early Times to 1800* (Cambridge, 1992), p. 433-444.
11. Borri, Christoforo *Cochin-China* (originally published in 1631 as *Relatione della nuova missione delli pp. della Compagnia di Giesu al regno della Cocincina)* (Rome, 1970), p. 53.
12. Péri, Nöel, 'Essai sur les relations du Japon et de l'Indochine aux XVIe et XVIIe siècles' *Bulletin de l'Ecole française d'Extrême-Orient* 23 (1923), p. 70.
13. Shimizu, Junzo 'The Inscriptions by some Japanese Found at Angkor Wat' in Matsumoto, Noburo (ed.) *Indo-Chinese Studies. Synthesis Research of the Culture of Rice-Cultivation Races in south-east Asia* (Tokyo, 1965), p. 265.

14. Van der Kraan, Alfons *Murder and Mayhem in Seventeenth-Century Cambodia: Anthony van Diemen vs. King Ramadhipati I* (Chiang Mai, 2009), pp. 9-10.
15. Van der Kraan, Alfons *Murder and Mayhem in Seventeenth-Century Cambodia: Anthony van Diemen vs. King Ramadhipati I* (Chiang Mai, 2009), pp. 29-31.
16. Van der Kraan, Alfons *Murder and Mayhem in Seventeenth-Century Cambodia: Anthony van Diemen vs. King Ramadhipati I* (Chiang Mai, 2009), p. 61.

Chapter 10

Japan, Taiwan and the 'Iron Men'

Until the seventeenth century, in the words of two recent historians of the island, 'Taiwan remained an unclaimed land',[1] that lay 'on the outer edge of Chinese consciousness and activity',[2] whose head-hunting aboriginal inhabitants were ignored and overlooked at an official level by both China and Japan. Yet, although unclaimed, Taiwan was far from being a land unknown either to its neighbours or to European voyagers. For example, by 1615 the East India Company was referring to it both by its Japanese name (variously written as Takasago or Tarosakun) and its more familiar Portuguese name of Formosa, hence William Adam's phrase 'by takkasan or the Ill. of formosa',[3] which is one of several reference he makes to Taiwan, while in the logbook of John Saris of the EIC for 13 July 1617 we read of a typhoon blowing, 'with mighty great gushes and storms with the wind at north East beating it to and again between the Coast of China and bewe[4] within the straits of tackasanga'.[5]

The East India Company, however, made no moves to extend its trading interests in the direction of Taiwan, while any relations that existed between Taiwan, China and Japan were conducted unofficially by fishermen, pirates and traders. Such entrepreneurs interacted with the Taiwanese aborigines on a wholly unregulated basis until the latter half of the sixteenth century. When the restrictions on Chinese maritime trade were partly relaxed in 1567 a few official licences were granted for trade with Taiwan, where Chinese traders would meet their Japanese counterparts.[6] During the 1560s Taiwan also provided a refuge for certain Chinese pirates fleeing justice in Fujian. The inhabitants fled inland at this particular incursion, but not long afterwards there are records of other pirates trading peacefully with the Taiwanese, mainly for deerskins.[7] These were the exports most prized in Japan, where the demand for leather for use in military equipment was enhanced by the current experience of civil war, and records exist of the export of 18,000 deerskins on one single Japanese ship in 1624.[8]

Long before this date, however, three attempts had been made by Japan's rulers to establish some form of official relationship. The first, in 1593, consisted of no more than a letter that proved impossible to deliver, while the 1609 and 1616 efforts took the form of quite substantial overseas expeditions, although they paled by comparison with the explicit and successful invasion of Ryūkyū in 1609. That action resulted in a king being brought as a prisoner before the shogun. Taiwan lay a scarce 110km beyond Yonaguni, the most remote island of the Ryūkyūan archipelago, yet somehow Japanese expansion was to stop at that very point.

Hideyoshi and Taiwan

There appears to be no official record of contact between Japan and Taiwan at any time prior to 1593, an impression strengthened by the involvement of comparatively lowly Japanese traders in the mission of that year. The attempt, along with the two that followed, lay within the context of contemporary East Asian trade, which was based around the tributary system: that strange historic conceit whereby China, the dominant power in the region, regarded itself as a universal and benevolent empire whose sovereignty had to be acknowledged by its less fortunate barbarian neighbours before the benefits of commerce could be bestowed. These supplicant barbarians first paid homage to the Chinese Emperor, who then graciously bestowed upon them titles and privileges such as being acknowledged as rulers of their own countries. In deep gratitude they would then bring tribute to his feet, and gifts would be showered upon them in return. This exchange of tribute for gifts contained the essence of trade, and further commercial transactions flowed from it.

By the sixteenth century the actual practice of paying homage and receiving investiture had largely been replaced by the issuing of permits for foreigners to trade in the form of tallies, but in 1549 even this came to an end as far as Japan was concerned when the Ming closed the door to trade because of the activities of the *wakō*. Japanese demand for Chinese goods continued in spite of the prohibition and was met either indirectly through intermediaries, of which the Portuguese in Macao provided a profitable example, or directly by illegal trade that was often overseen by erstwhile pirates. Even the rulers of Japan took part in this huge 'black market', and any desire for trade to be made official once again was always tempered by the fear of domestic reaction should a ruler pay homage, even nominally, to the Chinese Emperor; a fear which Toby calls 'the Japanese ambivalence towards recognition of China's ecumenical legitimacy'.[9] It was, however, possible simply to ask for tallies to be restarted. This involved less humiliation than seeking investiture, but did involve assuring the Chinese of the ruler's own legitimacy. A third alternative was to try an indirect approach, and the three instances in this chapter represent attempts to use Taiwan for this purpose.

In spite of the frustrations caused by the tributary system, it was so engrained in the Japanese mentality that when Japan had dealings with other rulers whom it wished to dominate the initial approaches were invariably couched in the accepted language of homage. This comes over very clearly in the wording of the first attempt by a Japanese ruler to establish formal contact with Taiwan. It was made by Toyotomi Hideyoshi at a time when his invasion of Korea, launched in 1592, appeared to him, at least, to have been a success. As the conquest of China, rather than merely Korea, had always been Hideyoshi's main objective, he was the last person to have considered paying homage to the Chinese Emperor.[10] Instead rulers of other countries such as Taiwan and the Philippines should pay homage to him, so the letter that Hideyoshi composed to a supposed ruler of Taiwan was an extraordinarily bombastic document:

The Philippines and Liu Chiu (Ryūkyū) have sent tribute-bearing envoys to our country, thus showing due reverence. These nations have learned to establish relations with us by utilising both water and land facilities. Your country, however, has not yet sent any envoy to our military headquarters. This lack of loyalty will certainly bring the curse of Heaven upon you. Because of geographical disadvantage, however, your country has not been kept informed of conditions in the outside world, and has therefore unintentionally disregarded our authority. We hereby send Harada to you as our envoy, bearing this letter. He will soon sail to your country. If you should fail to pay due reverence to us after having received our instructions, we shall immediately instruct our military leaders to invade your country and inflict severe punishment. We wish to remind you that it is the sun which makes all things in the universe to grow, and it is the sun that makes all things to dry up and perish. We leave the entire matter to your conscientious consideration.[11]

Harada Magoshichirō, named in the above account as Hideyoshi's envoy, was a merchant from Sakai who was already an experienced diplomat. Together with his cousin Harada Kiemon he had been involved in 1591 in the mission to the Spanish Governor of Manila on behalf of Hideyoshi. That initiative had prompted a response in the person of the Dominican friar Juan Cobo, who was then shipwrecked on his return voyage and lost his life to the head-hunters of Taiwan.[12] Undaunted by this example, Harada Magoshichirō carried out his own mission to Taiwan, but finding neither a central government nor any ruling authority, was unable to deliver the letter. Being a merchant rather than a military man Harada may not have wished to risk his life by being too insistent, and he returned safely. The threats of military intervention included in the letter were never followed through, even though the use of terms such as 'the curse of heaven' suggests that Hideyoshi was fully prepared to invade Taiwan as he had invaded Korea. In fact, a 'southern invasion route' of China conducted via the Ryūkyū Islands had indeed been a consideration entertained during the initial planning of the Korean expedition. Hideyoshi had also been concerned that Ryūkyū, which conducted active trade with Ming China, might alert the Chinese to his plans, so King Shō Nei was ordered to break off all trade relations forthwith. The king refused to do this, and instead reported the matter to a group of Chinese envoys, urging them to inform their emperor of a possible attack on China through Ryūkyū as well as through Korea.[13] Such a move would probably have involved using Taiwan in some way, but King Shō Nei's intransigence put paid to any 'second front' through Ryūkyū and Taiwan until 1593 when Hideyoshi composed his letter to the supposed ruler of the latter island. By the time that his envoy had returned empty-handed Hideyoshi's mind had moved on to other matters and Taiwan was forgotten.

The 1609 expedition

When Tokugawa Ieyasu became shogun in 1603 he made no attempt to follow Hideyoshi's example of trying to invade China and Korea. Instead the first priority of the Tokugawa *bakufu* in that area was the normalisation of relations between the three countries. The restoration of relations with Korea was to be rightly celebrated as an outstanding diplomatic achievement,[14] yet when it came to China Ieyasu shared with

Hideyoshi a similar concern over the tributary system and its threat to his position. Nevertheless Ieyasu was keen to restore the tally trade, and as no direct diplomatic link to the Ming existed he tried to use the three intermediaries of Korea, Ryūkyū and Taiwan.

Ryūkyū passed under Japanese control after a well-planned and efficiently executed invasion in 1609 under Kabayama Hisataka, the general appointed by Shimazu Iehisa, daimyo of Satsuma, to command the expedition.[15] Taiwan came back into the picture that same year when Arima Harunobu was commissioned to send an expedition.[16] Dom Protasio Harunobu was of course the nephew of the man who had donated Nagasaki to the Jesuits, and became the first of two Christian leaders to undertake an official voyage to the island.[17] The command to Harunobu to sail for Taiwan came from Tokugawa Ieyasu via Honda Masazumi. The original orders have not survived, but a copy, addressed to Tanigawa Sumitsugu Kakube'e was preserved within the Arima household. It reproduces the wording of the commission that Harunobu had received and includes the regulations set out by Harunobu to ensure a successful voyage.[18] The commission reads as follows:

1. Siam, Cambodia and many other distant nations have paid homage to us by sending annual trade ships, but Taiwan, which is located so close to our country, has not established any relations with us. This is an international outrage which we cannot overlook. You are hereby authorised to send a military expedition to that island and take all necessary steps.
2. If matters relating to Taiwan are settled without appeal to arms, you are to return to Japan accompanied by envoys from Taiwan.
3. If a peaceful settlement is reached, you shall arrange things so that ships from the Great Ming and Japan may meet in Taiwan and engage in trade.
4. Your officials must prepare a sketch map of Taiwan from west to east and from north to south, which is to be brought to us.
5. Any items or goods that the Taiwanese people desire shall be generously supplied to them.
6. Should you fail to come to a peaceful settlement after having made every possible effort, and if the Taiwanese people defy you, you should resort to arms and bring back to Japan a large number of Taiwanese prisoners.[19]

The soldiers placed under the command of Chijiwa Umene, Harunobu's chosen leader, were subject to strict military discipline, as shown first by the rider attached to the above commission requiring any disobedience to be punished by compelling the malefactor to commit *seppuku*,[20] and second by the regulations drawn up for conduct on board ship, which are reminiscent of the rules governing the Japanese mercenaries in Dutch service:

Item: All those presently making the crossing to Taiwan must display no violent behaviour or licentiousness either at sea or on land; such things are strictly banned.

Item: All those making the crossing, regardless of rank, must obey Chijiwa's commands.

Item: All those making the crossing must do nothing without [Chijiwa] Umene's permission. This will not be allowed even for one moment.

Item: Heavy drinking on board ship is forbidden to all, regardless of rank.

Item: Both at night and at early dawn great care must be taken concerning fire

Item: No one must belittle another or play the fool.

Item: Any punishment due will be inflicted upon the wrongdoer's family an addition to the perpetrator.

Item: If any unexpected difficulty arises, consult [your superior] and take appropriate action.

Item: Exceptional acts of loyalty will earn exceptional rewards. These regulations and their requirements must be kept. There must be no slacking, regardless of rank down to the common sailors.

If these regulations are transgressed then previous acts of loyalty will not count in that person's favour.[21]

The above documents imply two things. First, that the aim of the 1609 expedition was to secure Taiwan as an intermediate trading base, thus circumventing the Ming ban on the tally trade. Secondly, that the expedition was officially commissioned, well planned and run on strict military lines. Just as in Hideyoshi's letter, the language is derived from the tributary system but is backed up by the threat of force, yet in Arima's expedition we see the actual deployment of that military threat. No records of troop numbers have survived, but in the light of subsequent events the force was not large, nor did the commission contain any orders to permanently occupy Taiwanese territory.[22]

In spite of all the preparations the disappointing outcome of the expedition is summarised in the Jesuits' Annual Letter for that year. Just like Hideyoshi's envoy, Arima's men found no central authority with whom to make contact. Instead they were attacked by aboriginal tribesmen and responded in kind. Following Ieyasu's orders they took some aborigines prisoner and transported them back to Japan. These unfortunates were presented to Ieyasu, who soon realised that he was not dealing with ambassadors, so the Taiwanese were given presents and allowed to return home.[23]

Ieyasu's desire to reopen trade with China was undiminished by this failure to exploit the Taiwan route, and in 1610 an unusual opportunity to deal directly with the Ming presented itself when Zhou Xingru, a merchant of Fujian, arrived on the Gotō Islands. He was received by Ieyasu and on his return in 1611 was requested to deliver a letter drafted by Hayashi Razan, the great Confucian scholar, asking the Ming to start issuing tallies for Japanese trade once again.[24] The carefully worded missive, the first to be sent from Tokugawa Japan to Ming China, has been analysed by Toby, who identifies an attempt to steer a difficult course between the assertion of Ieyasu's legitimacy in Ming eyes and compromising that legitimacy in Japanese society, although the attempt to proclaim Japanese legitimacy by stating that 'Ryūkyū calls herself Japan's vassal' could have been interpreted as an attempt to usurp China's place in the world order.[25] No reply was ever received, nor was any official letter sent from the Ming to Japan until 1621, a unique event that had its origins in the next expedition to set sail for Taiwan.

The 1616 expedition

In 1616 a second Taiwan expedition was launched under very different circumstances from the first. This was no military expedition led by an experienced soldier following a commission from the *bakufu*. The 1616 venture was instead a desperate attempt to regain official favour by a very wealthy Christian merchant of Nagasaki called Murayama Tōan, who held the office of *daikan* of Nagasaki, second in command only to the Nagasaki *bugyō*. The position of *daikan* had been created by Hideyoshi and was chiefly concerned with commercial matters. All the new commander had in common with Arima Harunobu was his Christian faith; although a few years earlier their names had been linked at an official level through their joint involvement in the notorious affair of the *Nossa Senhora da Graça*, the ship scuttled in Nagasaki Bay by its captain to frustrate Japanese attempts to impound it.[26] According to the Jesuits, Tōan and his superior Hasegawa Sahyōe, *bugyō* of Nagasaki were jointly responsible for persuading Arima Harunobu to seize the vessel in the first place.[27]

Murayama Tōan is one of the most interesting and complex characters in early Tokugawa Japan. His initial rise to prominence had much to do with an interview he had, probably in 1594, with Hideyoshi, who was unable to pronounce Murayama's baptismal name of Antonio and instead referred to him as Tōan, an appellation that stuck.[28] His commercial skills were considerable; he was a gourmet and a good cook, and took a keen interest in European food.[29] His elevation to the position of *daikan* of Nagasaki in 1605, this time through the patronage of Tokugawa Ieyasu,[30] ensured that his name also became well known to any European having dealings with that area of Japan. Thus Richard Cocks of the EIC's factory on Hirado Island, whose diary provides important primary source material for Tōan's Taiwanese adventure, entertained one of Tōan's sons when he visited the English house in secret in 1617:

> April 20 Easterday. ...but I was informed per one of our servants who he was, and so gave him the best entertainment I could. This Towan (*sic*) is held to be the richest man in Japon, and come up from base parentage by his subtle and crafty wit.[31]

The exercise of Tōan's 'subtle and crafty wit' as he rose in society made him many enemies, including the Jesuits, who were sceptical about his allegiance to Christianity. That he favoured the Dominicans was the least of his crimes in their eyes, while more serious allegations included abduction and apostasy.[32] Even the neutral observer the Spanish merchant Bernadino de Avila Girón felt able to comment on Tōan's alleged sexual excesses, but it was this same Avila Girón who was to bear witness to Tōan's staunch defence of the Christian faith, even when that faith was threatened by his own superior Hasegawa Sahyōe. In 1614 Tōan was the recipient of a letter from Hasegawa requiring the Christians of Nagasaki to abandon their faith. Instead of carrying out the order Tōan joined his fellow Christians in an extraordinary outburst of religious fervour as a series of religious processions became transformed into political theatre with Murayama Tōan, the leading Christian layman in Nagasaki, topping the bill. On 9 May 1614 Nagasaki witnessed a procession of 3,000 flagellants soaked in blood. Another procession three days later included participants tied inside sacks, bound by chains or staggering under the weight of huge stones, each object being indicative of a form of execution or torture used on their fellow believers. On 14 May Avila Girón witnessed Tōan's wife Justa wearing a crown of real thorns and with her arms tied back as if being crucified, and then on 20 May the participation of the Murayama family reached its climax. While Tōan's son, the priest Father Francisco Murayama, followed him holding a silver reliquary, a man believed to be Murayama Tōan himself staggered forward in the role of Christ of Nazareth, carrying his cross and with blood streaming from his aching back. [33]

Having set himself so publicly against the religious policies of the retired shogun who had put him in so exalted an official position, Tōan then exacerbated the situation by favouring the cause of Toyotomi Hideyori, son of the late Hideyoshi, whose inheritance had been lost to the Tokugawa. In 1614 Hideyori crammed into his father's great fortress of Osaka the troops of other daimyo who had suffered from the Tokugawa ascendancy together with tens of thousands of *rōnin* (masterless samurai). Tōan provided men and supplies for the defenders. [34] Also present in Osaka was Father Francisco Murayama, son of Tōan, eager to minister to his fellow Christians within Osaka Castle, but during the attack Father Francisco received a blow from a samurai sword that split his head open. Two other priests present with him in Osaka, one Spanish and one Italian, survived the siege. [35]

The death of his son while apparently fighting alongside the greatest enemy of the Tokugawa boded further ill for Tōan, who endeavoured to extricate himself from growing disfavour by offering to organise and finance an expedition to Taiwan. [36] As a merchant with no military experience Murayama Tōan would have been an unlikely choice for an official commission to lead an armed embassy, but his offer was nonetheless accepted. The commission to sail was delivered in the form of a red seal letter dated the ninth day of the ninth lunar month of the First Year of Genna (31 October 1615) from his superior the *bugyō* of Nagasaki, Hasegawa Sahyōe. Tōan's commission is briefly worded, simply authorising him to take ship from Japan to Taiwan. [37] If any additional orders or detailed regulations similar to Arima's were issued then none has survived.

Murayama Tōan immediately began to collect warships, men and provisions to make up a fleet that was to sail under the command of his second son Juan (sometimes written as Chūan or Shuan) Murayama. [38] Further information is provided by Richard Cocks, who had heard rumours about a possible expedition to Taiwan. Cocks's first reference appears in his diary for 12 October 1615, where he briefly mentions seeking confirmation as to 'whether Twan is appointed to make wars against China.'[39] In a letter to the East India Company of 23 February 1616 Cocks also writes:

> Also it is said that the Emperor hath appointed one Tuan Dono, a rich man of Langasaq', that at his own charge [he shall go to the wars] and take in an island called Fermosa [off the coast of] China, for wh'ch occasion he is now making [ready junks?] and other provision.[40]

The Dominican Father Diego Aduarte noted the departure of Juan Murayama's fleet from Nagasaki on 4 May 1616, observing that three of the ships, including Juan Murayama's flagship, were much larger than the others.[41] Cocks refers to the commencement of the voyage in his diary entry dated the following day, the impossibly fast transmission of information being simply explained by the fact that Cocks used the Julian calendar, so the date of the diary entry according to the Gregorian calendar as used by Aduarte would be 15 May, eleven days later:

> May 5 The son of Tuan Dono of Langasaque departed to sea with 13 barkes laden with soldiers to take the island Taccasange, called per them so, but by us Isla Fermosa. And it is reported he is at Goto, staying for more succours which are to come from Miaco...[42]

The rendezvous with reinforcements on the Gotō Islands suggests that Juan Murayama had chosen to sail directly for Taiwan to avoid the political sensitivity of making his way by means of the Ryūkyūs, which had so recently passed under the control of Satsuma.

Both of Cocks's comments cited above contain a similar and remarkable rider. That within the letter to the EIC reads, 'But some are of the opinion it [is to seek for] Fidaia Samme the fugitive prince, either in the Lequeas or elsewhere he may be found'.[43] This rumour, that Juan Murayama was not actually heading for Taiwan but instead for Lequea (Ryūkyū) to look for Toyotomi Hideyori who was presumed to have escaped death at Osaka, is not as fanciful as it might first appear. Cocks was aware of the rumour of Hideyori's survival as early as 27 July 1615,[44] and Ryūkyū did indeed provide a refuge for at least one fugitive from the great siege. This was an anonymous samurai who came to the attention of William Adams while the latter's ship lay at anchor in Naha harbour. Adams records in his logbook:

> The 21 being Saturday here Cam a noble man to Ceeoree (Shuri) which fled from the wars in Osaka his name was [here there is

a gap in the manuscript] which day I heard that the Emperor (i.e Tokugawa Ieyasu) had got the victory of which news I was glad to hear...[45]

In some quarters the rumours of Hideyori's survival were even more alarming. Cocks, for example, also heard that the 'King of Xaxma (Satsuma) meaneth to make wars against the new Emperor in right of Fidaia Samme whom they report to be alive, and that he meaneth to begin with Langasque'.[46] Seen in this light, for Juan Murayama to be seeking out Hideyori could be regarded as a brave endeavour to save Nagasaki from attack, and was certainly one that would encourage people to forget that Juan's brother Father Francisco had perished at Hideyori's side.

Regardless of any motivation behind sending the Murayama fleet to Taiwan, the fact that there were only thirteen ships in the fleet indicates that the use of the term 'invasion' to describe the expedition would be inappropriate. The Satsuma invasion of Ryūkyū, by comparison, involved 3,000 soldiers conveyed on between seventy and 100 ships.[47] The only source to mention the number of men taken to Taiwan by Murayama is Dutch and consists of a letter written from Batavia to Amsterdam almost certainly by Jacques Specx, the former head of the VOC factory in Japan, in 1629. It deals very briefly with Murayama's expedition, neatly summarising the motivation behind it in the words 'it was taken in hand by a particular gentleman to curry His Majesty's favour'. Specx concludes that between 1615 and 1616 Teijouhan (Taiwan) was 'conquered' by a 'swiftly sent armada' from Japan manned by 3–4,000 men, but that 'because of faults of the subsidiaries, left again'. The figure of 3–4,000 men is clearly exaggerated, and one tenth of the number would give the same average men per ship as for the Ryūkyū expedition, a reasonable figure.[48]

No Japanese records of the voyage have survived, a loss explained by the expedition's ultimate failure to redeem Tōan in the eyes of the shogun. Instead, he and most of his family were to perish in the Christian persecutions that followed shortly afterwards. If any plans or regulations for his men were drawn up they no longer exist, so it is impossible to draw any direct comparison with Arima Harunobu's expedition in terms of planning and preparation. However, it is possible to piece together a reasonable narrative of Murayama's expedition using Chinese and European sources, an exercise which results in a much better understanding of Murayama's voyage than of Arima's.

Father Diego Aduarte records that after leaving the Gotō Islands Juan Murayama's fleet met with an early disaster in the shape of a fierce storm that drove the ships on to 'Ryūkyū, a territory controlled by the Lord of Satsuma'. Some stayed there to pass the winter, while the remainder sailed back to Nagasaki and did not restart the expedition until the following November. Here Aduarte's account is at variance with Cocks's contemporary dated reports, which suggest instead that there was no return to Nagasaki but that the fleet continued the voyage. It is likely that Aduarte is confusing reports he had heard of the Taiwan expedition and Murayama Tōan's embassy to Ming China the following year; two voyages that were closely related, as will be described below. There then appears to have been a further storm which scattered the fleet.[49]

Whether or not there was one storm or two, the dispersal of the ships is a confirmed fact and was instrumental in shaping the subsequent course of events, which may be summarised briefly as follows. Out of the thirteen ships that set sail only one reached Taiwan. Three reached China and carried out a pirate raid. Two also sailed to China and brought back a hostage. The three largest ships in the fleet, the group that included the flagship of Juan Murayama, ended up in Cochinchina and only returned to Japan over a year later. Four ships remained unaccounted for, although their fate may have been recorded in Japanese documents since destroyed, and as Cocks mentions only one ship being lost (ironically the only one that made it to Taiwan) we may presume that they returned safely to Japan at some stage.

Cocks tells us first about the group of three ships that went raiding in China. He makes no direct reference to a storm, although this is of course implied, but the implication is that the deviation towards the Chinese coast, however it was caused, resulted in a conscious decision to engage in a spell of piratical activity. In a letter to Richard Wickham 'at Osaka, Kyoto or elsewhere' for 12 July 1616 he writes that the three ships 'went upon the cost of China, where they have killed above 1,200 Chinas & taken all the barkes or junkes they met withall, throwing the people overboard',[50] while in his diary entry dated a few days earlier he records:

> July 7 ... 3 of Twans barkes are returned, which should have gone for Tacce Sange, or the Island Formosa, but went no thither, but rather a boot-haling on the cost of China, where they have taken 11 boats or junks, and put all the people to death because they stood out and fought with them...[51]

For a voyage that had begun with peaceful intentions to have degenerated into a *wakō* raid would be to Murayama Tōan a lasting disgrace, as was the fate of the sole vessel to reach Taiwan, where the crew suffered disastrous consequences:

> Yt is said that one boat of Twans men put into a creek at Island Formosa, thinking to have discovered further into the country; but, before they were aware, were set on by the country people, and seeing they could not escape, cut their own bellies because they would not fall into the enemies hands.[52]

A similar account appears in his letter to Richard Wickham of 12 July 1616:

> And the barks which Towan sent to conquer the islands Fermosa missing of their purpose (their pretence being discovered before they came), lost only one bark & all them w'ch were in her, who cut their own bellies, being compassed by the islanders & seeing no means to escape.[53]

The same letter continues with the gloomy thought that as a result of the appalling behaviour in China no Chinese junks would visit Japan that year, and that as a result 'Twan will loose his life & all which he hath'. On 8 August John Osterwick at Hirado was indeed able to confirm in a letter to Richard Wickham that 'The China junks likewise have failed in coming this year by reason of Twann his fleet of barkes, who hath done much spoil upon the coast of China...'[54]

The three ships that went raiding must have returned safely to Japan some time during 1616, but the flagship group containing the commanding officer Juan Murayama was away for almost a year. In a final reference to the Taiwan expedition, in his diary entry for 12 July 1617 Cocks notes receiving a letter reporting the sighting of these three ships as, '3 barkes of Twans are returned, which were sent out to have taken Taccasango (or Isla Fermosa), but could effect nothing, yet were put into Cochinchina, where they saw Capt. Adam's junk...'[55] Aduarte also includes the Cochinchina episode, and adds that Juan Murayama was on board.[56]

The fate of the other two ships that were driven on to the Chinese coast is recorded only in Ming sources, but the account is highly detailed. They were under the command of Akashi Michitomo, who is described as *shitsuji* (steward) to Murayama Tōan. Around the middle of the fifth lunar month (late June to early July 1616) the two ships of Akashi Michitomo that had become separated from the rest of the fleet appeared off the coast of Fujian province and dropped anchor at Dongyong at the mouth of the Min River, which flows down from the city of Fuzhou. An eyewitness describes the ships as being large, with four horses tethered on their decks, copper and iron ballast in their holds and a large number of leather-covered boxes.[57] The arrival caused consternation, not least within the fort that guarded that stretch of the Chinese coast. Its garrison speculated whether the arrivals were *wakō* who would break open the castle gates and force their way in, and after a period of hesitation it was decided to send someone to make contact with the intruders. The man chosen was Dong Boqi, a senior military officer of the Ming, who voyaged out into the coastal waters while others kept watch on developments from nearby hills. Contact was made out in the bay towards Nangan Island (part of the Matsu Island group that is now controlled by Taiwan), and Dong Boqi was taken on board. Akashi Michitomo acted with great bravado in front of his guest, stating that they were not *wakō* but two ships from the fleet of no less a person than Murayama Tōan, the *daikan* of Nagasaki. By then it was night-time of the eighteenth day of the fifth lunar month (1 July). At noon of the following day the Japanese ships set sail for Nagasaki, taking Dong Boqi with them as hostage and envoy. After three days of confusion on land the Ming guard stood down and the inhabitants of Fujian waited to hear the fate of their brave representative.[58]

It was to be almost a year before Dong Boqi saw his homeland again. His arrival in Japan was the only remotely positive outcome to have arisen from Murayama Tōan's disastrous adventure, but it is one that the *bakufu* seem to have appreciated for its genuine worth, because the decision was made to return him to China along with envoys who would open trade negotiations. Murayama Tōan was chosen to organise the mission and in the absence of his son Juan, who had still not returned from the Taiwan venture, he selected Akashi Michitomo to lead it together with Masaki Yaji'emon and Shibata Katsuza'emon. A Chinese translator called Gao Zimei went with them as interpreter and the party was furnished with local produce to present as gifts. Their destination was Fujian province, perhaps because of its familiarity to the parties concerned, but the choice of a province distant from the centre of Ming power did not herald success. There had been no diplomatic contact with Ming China since 1549, so the *bakufu* were either unfamiliar with etiquette or believed that lower-ranking Chinese officials had more influence than they actually possessed.[59] As this was the first diplomatic mission to China for many decades and was being launched from Nagasaki, it is not surprising that its departure became known to the expatriate community there. Richard Cocks heard about it from 'the China Captain'[60] and notes in his diary for 13 April 1617:

> The China Capt. Came and told me he had received a letter from his brother Whaw, from Langasaque, how the Emperor of Japon had sent out a bark, well manned with above 100 men, for the coast of China, wherein went 30 gentlemen with a letter and present of worth for the Emperor of China, as 10 rich cattans[61] garnished with hilts and other necessaries of gold, with many pikes after same sort, and 200 taies in bars of silver[62]

The China captain, who was probably much better versed in the relations between China and Japan than the *bakufu*, was very pessimistic about the likely outcome, and Cocks finishes his diary entry by adding that it was believed, 'that they cannot tell what to judge of the matter, only they think the Emperor of China will accept of nothing which cometh from Japan, the hatred betwixt them is so great.'

The China captain was to be proved right. The Murayama ships arrived on the nineteenth day of the fourth lunar month (23 May 1617) and were immediately apprehended by Chinese troops under the command of Han Zhongyong, the deputy commander responsible for maritime defence. The records of his interrogation of Akashi Michitomo and his colleagues are comprehensive and add considerably to our meagre understanding of the motivation behind the Taiwan expedition of the previous year. Han Zhongyong put seven direct questions to them:

1. Why were Keelung and Danshui raided?[63]
2. Why were the harbours on the northern side of Taiwan targeted?
3. Why did you raid inland [China]?
4. Why was Dong Boqi taken?
5. Why have you now returned Dong Boqi?
6. Why was Ryūkyū invaded?
7. What is the significance behind your present arrival?[64]

Akashi did his best to answer all the questions as fully as he could, and Han Zhongyong eventually assured him that if in future any Japanese ships were blown on to the Chinese coast or called in for water they were free to do so provided they left immediately afterwards. Any attempt to move inland would be resisted. Concerning Taiwan, Akashi responded to the first question to say that from the time of Hideyoshi to the present days of the Tokugawa, more than ten trade ships had set out peacefully but unsuccessfully for Ming China. Any violence carried out against Taiwan must have been the work of pirates, and Akashi insisted brazenly that as soon as they returned to Japan he would ask the *bakufu* to investigate the allegations, and if it was proved that the raid was carried out by renegade Japanese merchants they would be executed on the Chinese coast in front of Han Zhongyong himself. If, however, they proved to be Chinese, they would be handed over and the Ming themselves could decide on a suitable punishment.[65] In a final statement about Taiwan Han Zhongyong makes the Chinese position abundantly clear. Should Japan make any further attempt to occupy Taiwan no trade contact would be allowed to continue; any aspirations to land Japanese ships on Taiwan were out of the question, and if this was done 'the merits and demerits of war would be recognised. The acquisition or loss of trade would be clearly recognisable'.[66]

Akashi and his colleagues eventually returned home apparently empty-handed, but their efforts were not entirely wasted, as was to be confirmed by a positive move made in 1621 from the Chinese side. Sadly, this was prompted by a renewal of *wakō* attacks on the coast of Zhejian province, but the example of the Akashi mission suggested the need to make meaningful contact with Japan over the pirate problem. A merchant called Shan Fengxiang sailed as envoy with two letters, one for the shogun and one for the *bugyō* of Nagasaki.[67] He was met in Kyūshū by Akashi Michitomo, who accompanied him as far as Kyoto. Shan Fengxiang's request to meet Hidetada in Edo was declined, so the first letter was handed over in the imperial capital. In the letter the point was made that the repatriation of Dong Boqi had brought great happiness to the Chinese people, and as a result the maritime controls against Japan had been relaxed. Unfortunately reports had been received of pirates taking advantage of the new situation to loot Chinese ships and murder officials and soldiers. The shogun was warned that these pirates might attempt to escape retribution in China by travelling back to Japan on merchant ships and try to slip unnoticed into Japan. All Chinese merchants should therefore be questioned, especially any 'gamblers and ruffians' who tended to become pirates. Any malefactors should be punished unmercifully.[68]

The contents of the letters were subjected to a high-level discussion that lasted three months. The Nagasaki *bugyō* Hasegawa Kenroku, who had held the post since 1615, decided among other criticisms that as identical letters had gone to the shogun and the Nagasaki *bugyō* the matter was disrespectful to Japan's ruler. Once again the language of the tributary system was being brought to bear upon what looked like a straightforward commercial deal: the resumption of direct trade in return for control of piracy.[69] Ultimately, in spite of all the efforts this positive approach from the Ming, the first for eighty years, was rejected.

Much discussion has taken place about why Tokugawa Hidetada and his advisors turned down this unique opportunity, but much had changed in Japan since the days of Ieyasu, and the new situation is best illustrated by what happened three years later. In 1624 Hayashi Razan drafted a reply for the new *daikan* of Nagasaki, Suetsugu Heizō, to a particular letter received from Fujian. There is no mention of tribute or trade. Instead the concentration is on the Tokugawa's current preoccupation with the suppression of Christianity.[70] Japan's ongoing obsession had once again trumped all other international diplomatic concerns, and on distant Taiwan that same year, the Dutch, who had long coveted a base of their own in China or on one of its outlying islands, slipped quietly into the political gap vacated by the inward-looking *bakufu*.

From an occupied Taiwan the Dutch could access traders in Fujian without having to deal directly with the Ming rulers, so in 1624, even though they had been defeated in Macao by the Portuguese, and then driven from the Pescadores Islands by Chinese threats, the Dutch returned to explore the harbour of Tayouan in the southern part of Taiwan, a place they had previously dismissed as unsuitable. The visitors found that Tayouan had been transformed from the quiet backwater they remembered by the arrival of an influx of industrious Fujianese who, together with the aborigines and some Japanese traders, were already developing a lucrative trading community. The Dutch made no attempt to address themselves to a non-existent centralised ruler or to demand tribute from a vassal. In their desire to trade Chinese silk for Japanese silver using Taiwan as a convenient intermediary the Dutch eschewed the language of the tributary system and used instead the language of gunpowder and the spade.[71] Forts were constructed, and when they realised that the production of rice, sugar and deer products could be enhanced and developed in their favour, the Dutch began to bring over thousands of Fujianese to work the land. In time existing Spanish outposts elsewhere in Taiwan were eliminated, producing, in the words of Andrade, 'a Chinese colony under Dutch rule'.[72]

The Japanese traders in Tayouan soon realised that the Dutch wished to exclude them from the island, so they refused to pay the trade duties that the newly dominant Dutch were demanding. The desperate Japanese even tried political theatre in their quest for independence.

In 1627, in a deeply ironic replay of Arima's conduct in 1611, Hamada Yahei, under instructions from Suetsugu Heizō in Nagasaki, rounded up a number of friendly aborigines and transported them to Japan where they were presented as ambassadors from the ruler of Taiwan. Through interpreters the members of this fake embassy asked for Japanese protection against Dutch aggression, in return for which Taiwan would be presented to the shogun. The *bakufu* did not know how to react and sent them home, where they were arrested by the Dutch. Four escaped, and the rest were freed when the Japanese on Taiwan kidnapped the incompetent Dutch governor Pieter Nuyts in another embarrassing international incident.[73]

Although nominally now the rulers of Taiwan, the Dutch were in a somewhat precarious position, and partly this was due to the poor location they had chosen for their principal base and fortress. Fort Zeelandia was built at one end of a chain of islands that protected Tayouan Bay. It was ideally located for handling cargo, but would be very difficult to defend against a serious attack from China or Japan. That was not a particularly important consideration when it was built, because its Dutch owners had reckoned that the only real threat to their existence would come from native rebellions. As a consequence, while trade flourished and grew indirectly with China through the independent-minded sea captains based in its greatest ports, a false sense of security developed within Fort Zeelandia. It would be shattered within a few years by the greatest upheaval China had seen for centuries, because in 1644 the once-mighty Ming dynasty collapsed. It sent shock waves through East Asia and led among other things to a renewed interest in what Japanese fighting men had to offer to a foreign employer.

Koxinga and Taiwan

By the mid-1640s the reputation of Japanese samurai warriors had spread far and wide, and no one took a keener interest in what they had to offer as mercenaries than the surviving family members and supporters of the Ming dynasty, whose last emperor hanged himself from a tree inside the Forbidden City on 24 April 1644. A combination of peasant unrest and Manchu invaders had destroyed centuries of Ming rule in a fierce rebellion, yet still some loyalists fought on, in spite of having been driven back as far as the coastal cities of southern China. These last redoubts were the very places that had long been the main bases for the *wakō*, thus forcing the Southern Ming, as the stubborn successor

149

dynasty was now known, to seek protection from the powerful illegal traders whose forebears had staunchly defied the Ming's bans on their activities.

The new process of accommodation with *wakō* may have been very unpalatable, but the man who was crowned as the Longwu Emperor in Fuzhou in August 1645 set an example of humility when he placed himself under the protection of the powerful Zheng Zhilong 鄭芝龍, known to the West as Nicholas Iquan, whose enormous influence had made him the virtual ruler of Fujian Province. Zheng Zhilong's family were given noble titles, and in an intensely symbolic gesture the childless Southern Ming emperor adopted Zheng's son Zheng Chenggong 鄭成功 as his own. The young man was granted the name Guoxingye 國姓爺 'Lord of the Imperial Surname', an expression that gave him the Western appellation of Koxinga.

Koxinga was half Japanese and had been born in Hirado to a Japanese mother who is believed to have been the daughter of a senior retainer of the Matsuura family. With such close ties to Japan – not to mention the traditionally strong Japanese component in the *wakō* bands – it was an obvious course of action for his father Zheng Zhilong to try and obtain military help from Japan to aid the Southern Ming against the Manchus. In 1645 Zheng Zhilong addressed himself to the shogun by sending a representative to Nagasaki. This was followed in 1646 by a specific request for men and equipment. Both appeals were turned down, with the Japanese authorities citing the ban on the export of Japanese armaments and the breakdown in relations between Japan and the Ming. A further attempt in October 1646 looked more promising. A personal representative of Zheng Zhilong went to Nagasaki as the official ambassador from the Lungwu Emperor and pleaded their case. The shogun's representatives asked for time to consider their response, but while they were waiting to make a decision news arrived that Zheng Zhilong had been defeated in battle with the Qing and had surrendered to them. All thoughts of military aid were abandoned and the relevant daimyo were informed of the decision.

Zheng Zhilong's son Zheng Chenggong, alias Koxinga, resolved to continue the fight following his father's capitulation, and further requests for Japanese aid followed. In 1647 a different Ming representative tried to make contact with Japan but was not even received by the Tokugawa. Faced by such intransigence from the shogun the Ming tried to appeal directly to a Japanese daimyo who had personal interests in the area. The Shimazu of Satsuma were the obvious candidates because they had annexed the Ryūkyūs in 1609 and had a vested interest in protecting the trade routes they now controlled on behalf of the shogun. When contacted they gave a sympathetic response and made an initial pledge to send 30,000 men to China, but disagreement among the Ming leaders eventually reduced the Satsuma contribution to a large quantity of copper coins, not samurai. The dynasty tried again in 1648, asking for tens of thousands of troops to resist the Manchu barbarians, and suggesting that war materials should be traded for Chinese medicines and silks. This was later reduced to an exchange of weapons and saltpetre for Chinese silver and other goods. The idea was then entertained of appealing to Japanese religious sensibilities by presenting a statue of Guanyin (Kannon) and a precious Buddhist sutra. The missions came to nothing in military terms, but the diplomatic efforts did result in the transport of Japanese grain, some weapons and metals.[74]

Why did the Japanese not help? First, even though they may not have cared much for the Qing dynasty, as the Manchu conquerors were now known, they had a very low opinion of the Southern Ming's military capacity and were reluctant to back an obvious loser. Secondly, even if the latter's cause was not hopeless in face of the Manchu onslaught, the Japanese were understandably reluctant to commit to one side or another in the ongoing war. Overseas military ventures might have upset the delicate balance of power within Japan that the Tokugawa were carefully creating, and it also evoked the ancient fears of invasion from abroad.[75] As a result, in spite of all the Chinese efforts no Japanese mercenaries were sent to fight for the Southern Ming against the Manchus. That at any rate was the official version, but there remains the intriguing possibility that some were supplied unofficially in a private capacity in the army of Zheng Zhilong's son Koxinga.

The Iron Men

Koxinga had become head of the Zheng family following his father's submission to the Qing and continued the struggle on behalf of the Southern Ming, even though their growing impotence led Koxinga to incline much more towards consolidating his own position rather than winning back their empire. He still fought bravely for the Ming cause, but Koxinga's crowning glory would be only indirectly related to the Ming/Qing dispute. This was his expedition to expel the Dutch from Taiwan in 1662, where a handful of eyewitness accounts of Koxinga's operations against Fort Zeelandia reveal the presence in Koxinga's army of a mysterious unit known as the Iron Men (*tie ren* 鐵人), who may well have been Japanese mercenaries.

The Iron Men were first deployed against the Manchus and are mentioned in connection with Koxinga's capture of Zhenjiang in August 1659. Koxinga had renewed his offensive against the Qing by seizing Guazhou on the northern shore of the Yangzi and then took on Zhenjiang, which lay opposite it on the southern bank. The capture of these places would allow control of the Grand Canal, cutting off supplies and communications to Beijing, so the fighting was fierce.[76] Yang Ying, Koxinga's close aide and a chronicler who was probably an eyewitness to the battle at Zhenjiang, describes how 'gunfire, cannon fire arrows and rocks' rained down but failed to stop the advance of the Iron Men, who marched forwards inexorably, supported by a hail of arrows from their archers.[77]

After the battle the dismembered bodies of horses and men lay everywhere, victims of the Iron Men's speciality of wielding long sharp-edged weapons in an almost detached manner. Their superhuman behaviour led to them being described as 'divine warriors', and the defeated Qing garrison commander, who had previously bragged about Manchu invincibility, lamented, 'I have come to China from Manchuria, and fought in battle seventeen times, but this is the first time I have been on the losing side'.[78]

Later in 1659 Koxinga tried to take Nanjing but was repulsed in spite of his Iron Men. Three years later, however, they would play a decisive role in Koxinga's greatest triumph: the capture of Taiwan from the Dutch colonists. Writing in 1666 an anonymous Spanish commentator on the Philippines related how the Dutch were at first contemptuous of the Chinese invaders of Taiwan, calling them 'men of the paypay' – that is, "of the fan", which all of that nation use, as if they were women'.[79] Their attitude soon changed, as is recorded by no less a person than the commander of Fort Zeelandia:

> On the following day [11 March], news was received that the Chinese were beginning to show their teeth; that they were discouraging those friendly to the Company in the Formosan villages by boasting loudly of Koxinga's war forces, stating that his soldiers were protected from head to foot with iron armour, which the Dutch muskets could not penetrate.[80]

This description of the Iron Men comes from the pen of Frederick Coyett, Taiwan's last Dutch governor, who had charge of Fort Zeelandia when Koxinga's invasion fleet arrived. The Dutch were ill prepared. Not only was his strategic position inherently weak, but Coyett also had only forty fighting men of any real experience, although there was enough food and gunpowder to last through a siege of six months if that should become necessary. During one of the initial attacks the Dutch discharged volley after volley of musket balls into the Chinese ranks, the front line of which was composed of the Iron Men. Undeterred, the main body of the Chinese continued their advance behind these formidable warriors:

> With bent heads and their bodies hidden behind the shields, they try to break through the opposing ranks with such fury and dauntless courage as if each one still had a spare body at home. They continually press onwards, notwithstanding many are shot down; not stopping to consider, but ever rushing forward like mad dogs, not even looking round to see whether they are followed by their comrades or not.[81]

The Dutch supplies of gunpowder were put to their best use when used to fire grapeshot and pieces of odd metal against a particularly fierce Chinese advance against the walls of the fort in an action reminiscent of the battle of the Cagayan River in 1574, leaving hundreds of mangled bodies strewn across the escarpment. Yet Coyett was never complacent about the situation, and when he was finally defeated his most telling comments about the action refer specifically to Koxinga's Iron Men:

> many wielded with both hands a formidable battle-sword fixed to a stick half the length of a man. Everyone was protected over the upper part of the body with a coat of iron scales, fitting below one another like the slates of a roof; the arms and legs being left bare. This afforded complete protection from rifle bullets and yet left ample freedom to move, as those coats only reached down to the knees and were very flexible at all the joints... Those with the sword-sticks – called soap knives by the Hollanders – render the same service as our lancers in preventing all breaking through of the enemy, and in this way establishing perfect order in the ranks ; but when the enemy has been thrown into disorder, the Sword-bearers follow this up with fearful massacre amongst the fugitives.[82]

Is this a description of mercenaries from Japan in action for the last time in their history? This tempting conclusion was first drawn by the Japanese historian Terao Yoshio and is based on inferences drawn from Coyett's remarkable account. One must perhaps allow for a certain national bias on the part of a Japanese military historian, but in Terao's eyes Coyett's observations provided very strong circumstantial evidence for the Iron Men's possession of Japanese armour and weapons at the very least. To Terao their formidable battle swords on a long shaft suggested the use of the Japanese *nagamaki*, a long sword of which the blade was the same length as its handle. It combined the strength and flexibility of a conventional Japanese sword with the reach of a pole arm, and was particularly effective when wielded on foot against cavalry.

Terao also believed that the description of their armour being not like traditional Chinese armour but made of overlapping iron scales that covered their entire bodies except for the arms and legs was further evidence of a Japanese origin. It was just like Japanese armour as it had developed by the seventeenth century, which typically consisted of a very solid *dō* (body armour) with lighter and more flexible armour protecting the limbs. The Iron Men's armour was also known to be bulletproof, which is also consistent with contemporary Japanese designs. Another interesting observation concerned the equally solid helmets and the fact that the wearers looked out through eye-slits.[83] This sounds like the use of a Japanese *mempo* (face mask).[84]

Terao also suggested a very plausible reason why so many samurai could easily have been available at the time, even though the Sengoku Period had long since passed into history. The Shimabara Rebellion of 1638 may have been the last major battle on Japanese soil until the nineteenth century, but occasional small-scale rebellions still shook the foundations of the Tokugawa state from time to time. The Iron Men could therefore have been fugitives from the Kanei Rebellion of 1651, an ill-fated insurrection also known as the Rōnin Rebellion, which was a plan to overthrow the Tokugawa government by force.[85] Its ringleaders were Yui Shōsetsu and Marubashi Chūya, who were employed as instructors in a sword-fighting school. Their ambitious plan was to choose a windy night and set off an explosion in a government magazine in Edo, thereby starting a conflagration that would spread rapidly through the tightly packed wooden buildings. Under the cover of the fire Edo Castle would be raided and high officials murdered as the start of a major uprising. The plot was betrayed when Chūya caught a fever and started babbling the details of their plans in his sleep. Chūya was arrested in Edo and crucified, while Yui Shōsetsu was apprehended in Sunpu and committed ritual suicide.[86] Others escaped, and it is not beyond the bounds of possibility that desperate *rōnin* could have made their way to southern China via the

Ryūkyūs. If so, Koxinga's Iron Men could be the last native Japanese Wild Geese to have fought overseas, and played their own part in a Chinese triumph when Coyett surrendered the island of Taiwan to Koxinga's army.

Notes

1. Tsai, Shih-Shan Henry, *Maritime Taiwan: Historical Encounters with the East and the West* New York: Sharpe, 2009, 5.
2. Wills, John E. Jr., 'The Seventeenth-Century Transformation: Taiwan Under the Dutch and the Cheng Regime' in Murray A. Rubinstein (ed.) *Taiwan: A New History* New York: Sharpe, 2007, 85.
3. Purnell, C.J., 'The Log Book of William Adams 1614-19 and related documents' *Transactions and Proceedings of the Japan Society* XIII:II (1914-15): 50.
4. 'bewe' probably indicates the Penghu Islands to the west of the main island of Taiwan, known then as the Pescadores.
5. Purnell 'The Log Book', 110.
6. Wills 'The Seventeenth Century Transformation', 86-7.
7. Shepherd, John Robert, *Statecraft and Political Economy on the Taiwan Frontier 1600-1800* Stanford University Press, 1993, 35.
8. Ibid, 38.
9. Toby, Ronald P. *State and diplomacy in early modern Japan: Asia in the development of the Tokugawa bakufu* Stanford University Press, 1991, 60-61 n 19
10. For the well-known story of the farcical situation whereby Hideyoshi's officials, who were only too aware of the importance of the tributary system, drew up a forged document stating that Hideyoshi would accept investiture as 'King of Japan' see Elisonas, Jurgis 'The Inseparable Trinity: Japan's Relations with China and Korea' in John Whitney Hall (ed.) *The Cambridge History of Japan Volume 4 Early Modern Japan* Cambridge University Press, 1991, 281-285.
11. This translation is from Kuno, Yoshi S., *Japanese expansion on the Asiatic Continent: a study in the history of Japan with special reference to her international relations with China, Korea and Russia Volume I* University of California Press, 1937, 311-312.
12. Boxer *The Christian Century*, 160-161.

13. Kerr, George H. *Okinawa: The History of an Island People (Revised Edition) with an after word by Mitsugu Sakihara* North Clarendon VT, Tuttle, 2000, 152.
14. Toby *State and diplomacy*, 63.
15. Kamiya, Nobuyuki 'Satsuma Ryūkyū shinnyū' [The Satsuma Invasion of Ryūkyū] in *Shin Ryūkyū shi*, [A New History of Ryūkyū] Vol. jō Naha, 1989, 33-72. For the political background see Toby *State and diplomacy*, 45-52.
16. All the extant documents relating to the 1609 expedition are usefully assembled in *Dai Nihon Shiryō* Tokyo: Tokyo Teikoku Daigaku, 1906, Pt. 12 Vol. 6, 132-139.
17. Harunobu's early career is well described in Jurgis Elisonas' chapter entitled 'Christianity and the daimyo' in John Whitney Hall (ed.) *The Cambridge History of Japan Volume 4: Early Modern Japan* Cambridge University Press, 1991,. 333-335 with his downfall and death on pp. 365-367.
18. *Dai Nihon Shiryō*, 132-139
19. *Dai Nihon Shiryō*, 132-133; Iwao Seiichi 'Nagasaki Daikan Murayama Tōan no Taiwan ensei to kenminshu' *Taihoku Teikoku Daigaku shigakka kenkyū nenpō* [Annual Bulletin of the Department of History, Taihoku Imperial University] I (1934), 17. See also Kuno *Japanese Expansion* Vol II, 293-294.
20. *Dai Nihon Shiryō*, 134.
21. *Dai Nihon Shiryō*, 134-137.
22. Iwao 'Nagasaki', 17.
23. *Dai Nihon Shiryō*, 138.
24. Hayashi Razan *Razan sensei bunshū* Kyoto: Kyoto Shisekikai, 1920, 130-32.
25. Toby *State and diplomacy*, 60
26. As memorably recounted in Boxer *The Christian Century*, 269-283.
27. Letter to Padre Luis Pinheiro, 23 February 1619, quoted in Alvarez-Taladriz, J.L., 'Fuentes Europeas sobre Murayama Toan (1562-1619) 1. – El pleito de Suetsugu Heizo Juan contra Murayama Toan Antonio (1617-1619) según el Padre Mattheus de Couros, Provincial de la Compañía de Jesús en Japón' *Tenri Daigaku gakuhō* 51 (1966), 95; Bernadino de Avila Girón 'Relación del Reino de Nippon' (edited by Doroteo Schilling OFM & Fidel de Lejarza) in *Archivo Ibero-Americano* Vol. 38 (1935), 122, n. 3.
28. Iwao 'Nagasaki', 388-389; Léon Pagés *Histoire de la Religion Chrétienne au Japan depuis 1598 jusqu'a 1651* Paris, Charles Douniol, 1869 Vol. I, 415 n. 2.

29. Boxer *The Christian Century*, 273.
30. Alvarez-Taladriz *Fuentes*, 95.
31. Cocks, Richard *Diary of Richard Cocks: Cape-merchant in the English Factory in Japan 1615-1622 with correspondence* edited by Edward Maunde Thompson London, Hakluyt Society, 1883, Vol. 1, 251. By the process of elimination the mysterious guest must have been Tōan's eldest son Andreas Murayama Tokuan, as Juan Murayama was then at sea and Francisco Murayama had perished during the siege of Osaka. Tōan's other sons were still young children. Andreas Murayama was to die a martyr's death two years later.
32. For a good account with full references of Tōan's religious life, his relationship with the Jesuits and his heroic stand against persecution see Elison *Deus Destroyed*,159-163.
33. A full account appears in Minako Debergh 'Deux Nouvelles Études sue l'Histoire du Christianite au Japan: 2 Les pratiques de purification et de penitence au Japan vues par les missionaries Jésuites aux XVIe et XVII siècles' *Journal Asiatique* 272 (1984), 195-200, based largely on the original eye-witness account by Bernadino de Avila Girón, who watched the events from his own front door in Nagasaki. See also Pagés *Histoire,* 275.
34. As noted by Hayashi Razan, Elison *Deus Destroyed*, 436 n. 52.
35. Pagés *Histoire,* 312.
36. The best account of the 1616 expedition is Iwao 'Nagasaki', 283-359. It is also covered in detail in the biography of Tōan by Kojima Yukie entitled *Nagasaki daikan Murayama Tōan: sono ai to junan* (Nagasaki: Seibo Bunko, 1998), 239-277. The primary sources are listed below.
37. Iwao 'Nagasaki', 25; Kojima *Nagasaki*, 242.
38. Aduarte, Diego OP *Historia de la Provincia del Sancto Rosario de la Orden de Predicadores en Philippinas, Japon, y China* Manila, 1640, Vol. II xxix p. 557; Iwao 'Nagasaki', 25.
39. Cocks *Diary*, 71.
40. Anthony Farrington *The English Factory in Japan 1613-1623* London: British Library, 1991, 380.
41. Iwao 'Nagasaki', 25
42. Cocks *Diary*, 131.
43. Farrington *The English Factory,* 380; Cocks *Diary*, 131
44. Cocks *Diary*, 26. There are several other references in the diary.
45. C.J.Purnell 'The Log Book', 10.
46. Cocks *Diary*, Entry for 7 July 1616, 149.
47. Kamiya 'Satsuma', 49.

48. W. Ph. Coolhaas (ed.) *Generale Missiven van Gouverneurs-generaal en Raden aan heren XVII der Verenigde Oostinische Compagnie* (M. Nijhof, The Hague, 1960) Vol. 1 p. 252; Iwao 'Nagasaki', 34.
49. Aduarte *Historia*, 557; Pagés *Histoire*, 415 n. 3; Kojima *Nagasaki*, 247; Iwao 'Nagasaki', 32-33.
50. Farrington *The English Factory*, 444.
51. Cocks *Diary*, 149.
52. Ibid.
53. Farrington *The English Factory*, 444.
54. *Farrington*, 456.
55. Cocks *Diary*, 277.
56. Aduarte *Historia*, 57; Iwao 'Nagasaki', 32-33; Kojima *Nagasaki*, 247.
57. Iwao 'Nagasaki' 30-31; Kojima *Nagasaki* 252.
58. The Chinese account of the Dong Boqi incident appears in Iwao 'Nagasaki', *pp.* 29-31; and the texts are usefully paraphrased into modern Japanese in Kojima *Nagasaki*, 251-255, which is the basis of my translations.
59. Kojima *Nagasaki*, 251.
60. This was Li Dan, who controlled much of the trade between Hirado and China.
61. *Katana* or Japanese swords
62. Cocks *Diary*, 249.
63. This question provides the only evidence we have for the locations where Tōan's ship put in to Taiwan. Danshui lies at the mouth of the estuary near modern Taipei. Nearby Keelung is now a major port. Both were strategic places where the Spanish and then the Dutch would establish forts within the next half century.
64. Iwao 'Nagasaki', 39-40; Kojima *Nagasaki*, 265-266.
65. Kojima, *Nagasaki*, 267-269.
66. Ibid.
67. Toby *Statecraft and diplomacy*, 61
68. Kondo Morishige, *Gaihan tsusho* [Japan's Foreign Correspondence] in *Kondo Seisai zenshu* Tokyo: Kokusho Kankoka, 1905, 57
69. Nagazumi Yoko, *Kinsei shoki no gaiko* [The Diplomacy of Early Pre-Modern Japan] Tokyo: Sobunsha, 1990, 117
70. Toby *State and diplomacy*, 64.
71. Shepherd *Statecraft*, 49-52.
72. Andrade, Tonio, 'The Rise and Fall of Dutch Taiwan, 1624-1662: Cooperative Colonization and the Statist Model of European Expansion' *Journal of World History* 17 (2006), 429-450.
73. Shepherd *Statecraft*, 52.

74. Struve, Lynn A. *Voices from the Ming-Qing Cataclysm: China in Tiger's Jaws* (Yale University Press, 1993), pp. 114-121.
75. Struve, Lynn A. *The Southern Ming, 1644-1662* (Yale University Press, 1984), pp. 117-120.
76. Hang, Xing *Conflict and Commerce in Maritime East Asia: The Zheng Family and the Shaping of the Modern World, c. 1920-1720* (New York: Columbia University Press, 2016), p. 122.
77. Yang, Ying; Cheng, Bisheng (ed.) *Xian wang shilu* (Fuzhou: Fujian renmin chubanshe, 1981), p. 201
78. Terao, Yoshio *Meimatsu no funkyo: Tei Seikō* (Tokyo: Tankobon, 1986), p. 121.
79. *Events in Manila 1662-63* (Unsigned, July 1666?) in Blair and Robertson 1903-09, vol. 36, p. 253.
80. Campbell, William *Formosa Under the Dutch: Described from Contemporary Records with Explanatory Notes and a Bibliography of the Island* (London, Kegan Paul, Trench and Trubner, 1903), p. 393
81. Quoted in Clements, Jonathan *Coxinga and the Fall of the Ming Dynasty* (Stroud, Sutton, 2004), p. 199
82. Campbell, William *Formosa Under the Dutch: Described from Contemporary Records with Explanatory Notes and a Bibliography of the Island* (London, Kegan Paul, Trench and Trubner, 1903). pp. 420-421.
83. Yang, Ying; Cheng, Bisheng (ed.) *Xian wang shilu* (Fuzhou: Fujian renmin chubanshe, 1981). p. 201.
84. Terao, Yoshio *Meimatsu no funkyo: Tei Seikō* (Tokyo: Tankobon, 1986), p. 110.
85. Terao, Yoshio *Meimatsu no funkyo: Tei Seikō* (Tokyo: Tankobon, 1986), p. 110.
86. Sansom, George *A History of Japan: 1615-1867* (Stanford: Stanford University Press, 1963), pp. 54-56.

Chapter 11

The Flight of the Wild Geese

As suggested by several of the accounts above, from 1623 onwards any reports of Japanese mercenary service by or against Europeans are to be found only as tiny snippets, and one of these minor engagements concerned Siamese involvement with a Spanish expedition against Macao. The great Portuguese colony comes back into the story in July 1623 when Dom Francisco Macarenhas was appointed to the newly created post of Captain-General of Macao. His new title seems to have gone to his head, and he haughtily informed his helpful Spanish ally Don Fernando de Silva that his services were no longer required. Indignantly, de Silva left Macao with two Spanish galleons in 1624 and passed the time on the return voyage by indulging in a little piracy along the way in the Gulf of Siam. This was the incident noted earlier when an attack on a Dutch vessel provoked retaliation from the Siamese king and his Japanese guards.

Retaliation followed in 1628 when the Spanish captured a Japanese red-seal ship sailing with Japanese permission and under Japanese protection. The shogun reacted with great anger, broke off relations with Manila and placed a trade embargo on the Portuguese trade with Nagasaki. The former meant but little to the Spanish; the latter was a very serious matter to the Portuguese, who felt, quite rightly, that they were not to blame for a Spanish act of piracy. The embargo was temporarily lifted in 1630, but the final closing of Japan to Catholic Europe was only a few years away.[1]

The other casualties of the new attitude were of course the Japanese mercenaries themselves, whom the shogun now regarded as renegades. As far as the Japanese government was concerned there was nothing to gain and much to lose by allowing their subjects to be used in military expeditions overseas. There was also the ongoing question of the perceived threat from Christianity. Foreign priests had been removed and native believers eliminated so thoroughly through exile, execution or apostasy that Christianity appeared to have been wiped out. It is now known that the church survived underground, but great emphasis was placed on reducing or controlling all foreign contacts, so from being soldiers of fortune sent or even travelling willingly from Japan the Japanese Wild Geese now became garrisons drawn only from exiles. Resigned to their fate, most of them provided loyal service until age and intermarriage reduced their numbers and their traditions as they merged into the indigenous communities.

One place where this process happened was Batavia. Even though the Dutch had officially washed their hands of Japanese mercenaries the Japanese inhabitants of Batavia redeemed themselves for the alleged treachery on Amboina by playing a heroic role in 1628 and again in 1629 when they helped defend Batavia against attacks by the Mataram kingdom of central Java. The garrison of 2,866 men included '210 Japanese and *mardykers* (freed Christian slaves)'. The Japanese were under the command of a 'Captain Flobij' whose name, according to Iwao, probably corresponds to Kurōbei.[2] The assailants suffered from a lack of supplies because the VOC had burned their military stores at Tégal and 200 vessels carrying rice were also destroyed.[3] This put great heart into the garrison, and only twelve Dutch and less than that number of Japanese and Chinese mercenaries died during the heroic and successful defence, with huge devastation being wrought among the besiegers.[4]

Coen's victory over Mataram guaranteed the safety of Batavia, but not long afterwards that great supporter of Japanese mercenaries died of an intestinal problem caused by tropical disease on 20 September 1629.[5] There are no records of Japanese providing military service in Batavia after 1633. In a census of 1632 108 Japanese were recorded as living in Batavia: forty-eight men, twenty-four women, eleven children and twenty-five slaves.[6] Some continued to serve in their company of its City Guard, which was a civic duty on all free inhabitants and was organised in companies according to the recruits' native origins.[7] When their service ended they were awarded a bonus which they used to start a new life as free citizens. As they became settled they began to get married, mostly to Asian women, especially from Bali. One enterprise in which some Japanese participated was money-lending, and some clubbed together to send ships overseas. Others participated in the slave trade, with one wealthy Japanese resident owning twenty-five slaves. With the encouragement of the VOC authorities the Dutch Reformed

Church evangelised among the non-Christian Japanese and quite a few children were baptised.[8]

Not only were these Japanese all exiles – both voluntary and involuntary – they could now no longer return to Japan because the shogun's edict of 1635 forbade on pain of death all residents abroad coming back to Japan. Instead more came to join them, including thirteen Japanese prisoners released from a captured Portuguese junk in 1637 who were given sanctuary at the request of the Japanese community. Two years later in 1639 the numbers of mixed-race Japanese in Batavia further increased as a result of the next Sakoku edict, when children of European descent and their mothers were banished from Nagasaki and Hirado. When the Dutch ship *Breda* left Hirado in October 1639 it had on board four Dutch families, seven children of Dutchmen, one daughter of an Englishman and two of an Italian, and six Japanese mothers. They arrived on 1 January 1640. This swelled the Japanese population of Batavia, although none would serve in any military capacity, and nothing at all would be heard of Japanese in Batavia after the early eighteenth century.[9]

On the Philippines Japanese mercenaries continued to be employed in local actions throughout the early seventeenth century and were used to quell a Chinese revolt in 1639. They also helped fight off a Dutch incursion in 1646, when the 'haughty heretic', as a Spanish commentator describes them, raided Manila.[10] 'The call to arms was immediately sounded in the port; the posts and vessels were manned by Spanish infantry, and the shore, from San Roque to what is called Estanquela, by Japanese and Indians, as assistants to the Spaniards'.[11] Two decades later another native rebellion broke out on 15 December 1660, and the army sent out to crush them included:

the Japanese of Dilao. They had four pieces of artillery, which carried four-libra balls.... On December 22 General Esteybar began the march by land; on the twenty-fourth General Don Felipe de Ugalde set out by sea... With the former went two hundred infantry, and other troops of all nationalities, Japanese and Merdicas;[12]

Koxinga would threaten the Spanish on the Philippines for a short period of time, although in practical terms China's great conqueror of Dutch Taiwan did little more than reawaken the old fears of an uprising by the Sangleys in conjunction with an invasion. On one occasion something approaching panic ensued, with Sangleys being attacked indiscriminately and churches demolished to clear outside areas for firing. The Spanish took appropriate military precautions, but for some reason known only to himself their commander refused to include Japanese in his forces, leaving them all 'mocked and humiliated, who had attributed to cowardice the forbearance dictated by his prudence'.[13] Fortunately for both the Spanish and the Sangleys, 'only a few days after his Lordship had placed his forces under the powerful protection of the holy archangel',[14] the great Koxinga died. Somehow the Spanish commentator on his death managed to pick up gross rumours of Koxinga's last moments:

> Cot-sen was walking one afternoon through the fort on Hermosa Island which he had gained from the Dutch. His mind began to be disturbed by visions, which he said appeared to him, of thousands of men who placed themselves before him, all headless and clamouring for vengeance on the cruelty and injustice which had been wreaked on them; accordingly, terrified at this vision (or else a lifelike presentation by his imagination) he took refuge in his house and flung himself on his bed, consumed by a fierce and burning fever. This caused him to die on the fifth day, fiercely scratching his face and biting his hands.[15]

The above reference to Japanese troops not being deployed against Koxinga is the last mention of them acting as mercenaries in the Philippines. There were still some Japanese living in Manila in 1728, although they were not there in any military capacity, because Juan Bautista de Uriarte notes that among the charitable provision made by the Santa Misericordia, 'the brotherhood distributes 25 or 30 pesos weekly to the Japanese *beatas* of San Miguel'.[16] The Wild Geese had given way to the blessed.

As for the rest of south-east Asia, the quotation relating to the King of Arakan with which this book began would appear to be the only recorded mention of the existence of Japanese mercenaries within Burma, and we look in vain for any record of their military involvement at the time of the Mughal invasions of Arakan in 1666. The king of Arakan may have threatened the invader that 'the dogs and wolves… would have a grand feast, served with wine from the blood of the Mughals and kebabs from the flesh of all those who are killed' with 'a shower of arrows and gun-shots and stones like rains', but Japanese are nowhere mentioned as the means by which it might be brought about.[17] By this time many Japanese people were also to be found in Dutch settlements in Borneo, the Celebes, Sumatra and in India,[18] although Pallicate (to the north of Madras) in 1633 is the only place where Iwao specifically identifies anyone as a soldier. This is a certain Manuel de Silva, who was apparently Japanese.[19]

Finally, the Japanese serving in the palace guard of the kings of Siam would see their last action in 1656. In August of that year King Prasat Thong died. His eldest son Prince Chai seized the throne, only to be deposed by his younger brother Prince Narai, who first placed his uncle Suthammaracha on the throne and then on 26 October deposed him and set himself up as King Narai. This was achieved with the aid of Japanese, Pattani Malays and perhaps even Persian Muslims.[20] The Royal Chronicles tell us that, 'Phraya Sena Phamuk and Phraya Chaiya, commanding forty Japanese, came to prostrate themselves and state their request to volunteer for royal service'.[21] In the subsequent unrest the Japanese took the side of the new king:

> the retainers and soldiers on the side of the Supreme-Holy Si Sutham Rachathirat and the retainers and soldiers on the side of the Supreme-Paramount-Reverence-and-Holy-Existing-Lord accordingly did battle with each other from the evening until dawn, and Japanese gathered together, came in to volunteer, and did go in to help with the fighting in that region under Raya Lila. Retainers and soldiers were cut and wounded on both sides.[22]

That was probably the last conflict in Siam in which Japanese soldiers participated. A Japanese detachment continued in some form, but its lowly commander and members only performed ceremonial duties such as cremations.[23] They continued to serve King Narai in this capacity,[24] and were seen by Guy Tachard during his second visit to Ayutthaya just before the deposition in May 1688 of the usurper Constantine Phaulkon, whose wife was Japanese.[25] Her mother and brothers were given over to the 'Japanese captain', a title that suggests a military rank but in fact identifies only the leader of the Japanese community.[26]

Neither the Japanese quarter nor its inhabitants survived the fateful Burmese attack on Ayutthaya in 1767. It is known that some foreign mercenaries were used by the Siamese in the city's defence and Harvey notes that, 'one of their outworks contained four hundred Chinamen',[27] but while the import of mercenaries from Japan would have been impossible at this stage there is no mention even of the once-renowned Japanese palace guards.[28] The Burmese account notes:

Having shut the gates tight and built fifty outlying bastions to defend the city, the Siamese placed big guns and cannon on numerous ships and boats and fired incessantly. They attacked the Myanmar army with countless millions of Indians, Panthay (Chinese Muslims), Chinese, Malays and Siamese. Despite these attacks, they suffered reverses several times and their strength was gradually diminished just as water dries up in a weir.[29]

King Taksin (r.1767–1782), who moved the Siamese capital from devastated Ayutthaya to Thonburi, is traditionally supposed to have made use of Chinese and Japanese mercenaries whose promised payment in gold is supposed to have caused severe financial difficulties for the struggling Siamese kingdom after they had expelled the Burmese, yet one looks in vain for any actual records of their service. A final tantalising piece of evidence that the Japanese guardsmen may have survived much later is presented by Cesare Polenghi, who quotes from a Thai document of 1836 that is concerned with arranging a visit of a US envoy. It refers to a troop of *asa yipun* (Japanese auxiliaries), showing that the tradition, if not the actual personnel of the king of Siam's favourite troops, lived on as a final reminder in the whole of south-east Asia of the days of the Japanese Wild Geese.[30]

Notes

1. Boxer, C.R. 'Portuguese and Spanish Rivalry in the Far East during the 17th Century' *Journal of the Royal Asiatic Society of Great Britain and Ireland* 2 (1946) pp. 158-159.
2. Iwao, Seiichi *Zoku Nan'yō Nihonmachi no Kenkyū: Nan'yō tōsho chiiki bunsan Nihonjin imin no seikatsu to katsudō* (Tokyo, 1987) pp. 57 & 63.
3. Pigeau, Theodore G. Th. and De Graaf, H.J. *Islamic States in Java 1500-1700: A Summary, Bibliography and Index.* (The Hague, 1976), pp. 42-43.
4. Vlekke, Bernard H.M. *Nusantara: A History of the East Indian Archipelago* (Cambridge Mass., 1945), p.128.
5. Vlekke, Bernard H.M. *Nusantara: A History of the East Indian Archipelago* (Cambridge Mass., 1945), p.128.

6. Murakami, N 'The Japanese at Batavia in the XVIIth Century' *Monumenta Nipponica* 2 (1939), p. 358.

7. Vlekke, Bernard H.M. *Nusantara: A History of the East Indian Archipelago* (Cambridge Mass., 1945), p.133.

8. Iwao, Seiichi *Zoku Nan'yō Nihonmachi no Kenkyū: Nan'yō tōsho chiiki bunsan Nihonjin imin no seikatsu to katsudō* (Tokyo, 1987) pp. 3-4.

9. Murakami, N 'The Japanese at Batavia in the XVIIth Century' *Monumenta Nipponica* 2 (1939), p. 358; Iwao, Seiichi *Zoku Nan'yō Nihonmachi no Kenkyū: Nan'yō tōsho chiiki bunsan Nihonjin imin no seikatsu to katsudō* (Tokyo, 1987) p. 6.

10. *Affairs in Filipinas, 1644-47*. Fray Joseph Fayol (of the Order of Mercy); Manila, 1647 in Blair and Robertson 1903-09, vol. 35 p. 253.

11. *Affairs in Filipinas, 1644-47*. Fray Joseph Fayol (of the Order of Mercy); Manila, 1647 in Blair and Robertson 1903-09, vol. 35 p. 256.

12. *Insurrections by Filipinos in the seventeenth century.* [Accounts by various early writers covering the period I621 -83.]. in Blair and Robertson 1903-09, vol. 38, p. 167.

13. *Events in Manila 1662-63* (Unsigned, July 1666?) in Blair and Robertson 1903-09, vol. 36, pp. 246 & 253.

14. *Events in Manila 1662-63* (Unsigned, July 1666?) in Blair and Robertson 1903-09, vol. 36, p. 247.

15. *Events in Manila 1662-63* (Unsigned, July 1666?) in Blair and Robertson 1903-09, vol. 36, pp. 248-249.

16. *The Santa Misericordia of Manila.* Juan Bautista de Uriarte, (Manila, 1728) in Blair and Robertson 1903-09, vol. 47 p. 65.

17. Chowdhury, Mohammed Ali *Bengal-Arakan Relations (1430-1666 A.D.)* (Kolkata, 2004), pp. 117-118.

18. Iwao, Seiichi *Zoku Nan'yō Nihonmachi no Kenkyū: Nan'yō tōsho chiiki bunsan Nihonjin imin no seikatsu to katsudō* (Tokyo, 1987) pp. 274-279.

19. Iwao, Seiichi *Zoku Nan'yō Nihonmachi no Kenkyū: Nan'yō tōsho chiiki bunsan Nihonjin imin no seikatsu to katsudō* (Tokyo, 1987) p. 278.

20. Wyatt, David K. *Thailand: A Short History* (Yale, 1982), p. 107; Satow, Ernest M. 'Notes on the Intercourse between Japan and Siam in the Seventeenth Century' *Transactions of the Asiatic Society of Japan* 13 (1885) p. 208; Smith, George Vinal *The Dutch in Seventeenth-Century Thailand* (Northern Illinois University, 1977) p. 35.

21. Cushman, Richard D (trans.) *The Royal Chronicles of Ayutthaya: A Synoptic Translation* (Bangkok, 2000) p. 229.

22. Cushman, Richard D (trans.) *The Royal Chronicles of Ayutthaya: A Synoptic Translation* (Bangkok, 2000) p. 230.

23. Quaritch-Wales, H. *Ancient Siamese Government Administration* (London, 1934), p. 150.
24. Jumsai, M.L. Manich *The Story of King Narai and his ambassador to France in 1686, Kosaparn* (Paris, 1986) p. 20.
25. Smithies, Michael *Mission made impossible: the second French Embassy to Siam, 1687* (Chiang Mai, 2002), p. 230; Blair, Emma Helen and Robertson, James Alexander (eds.) *The Philippine Islands, 1493-1803 Volume 1* (Cleveland, 1903-9), Part 42 p. 215.
26. Le Blanc, Marcel *The History of Siam, 1688* (translated and edited by Michael Smithies) (Chiang Mai, 2003), p. 98; Iwao, Seiichi *Zoku Nan'yō Nihonmachi no Kenkyū: Nan'yō tōsho chiiki bunsan Nihonjin imin no seikatsu to katsudō* (Tokyo, 1987) p. 3.
27. Harvey, G.E. *A History of Burma: From the Earliest Times to 10 March 1824, the Beginning of the English* Conquest (London, 1925), p. 252.
28. Terwiel, Barend Jan 'Who destroyed Ayutthaya?' *Indian Journal of Tai Studies* IX (2009), pp. 105-110.
29. Myint, Soe Thuzar; Chutintararond and Baker, Chris (Eds.) *The Portrayal of the Battle of Ayutthaya in Myanmar Literature* Bangkok, Chulalongkom University Institute of Asian Studies, 2011), p. 75.
30. Polenghi, Cesare *Samurai of Ayutthaya: Yamada Nagamasa, Japanese Warrior and Merchant in Early Seventeenth-Century Siam* (Bangkok, 2009), pp. 63-64.

Bibliography

Agoncillo, Teodoro A. *History of the Filipino People* (Quezon City, 1960).

Alvarez-Taladriz, J.L., 'Fuentes Europeas sobre Murayama Toan (1562-1619) 1. – El pleito de Suetsugu Heizo Juan contra Murayama Toan Antonio (1617-1619) según el Padre Mattheus de Couros, Provincial de la Compañía de Jesús en Japón' *Tenri Daigaku gakuhō* 51 (1966), 93-114.

Andrade, Tonio, 'The Rise and Fall of Dutch Taiwan, 1624-1662: Cooperative Colonization and the Statist Model of European Expansion' *Journal of World History* 17 (2006), 429-451.

Avila Girón Bernadino de 'Relación del Reino de Nippon' (edited by Doroteo Schilling OFM & Fidel de Lejarza) in *Archivo Ibero-Americano* Vol. 38 (1935), 103-130.

Baker, Chris; Pombejra, Dhieravat na; Van der Krann, Alfons; Wyatt, David K., *Van Vliet's Siam* (Chiang Mai, Silkworm Books, 2005).

Bernard, Henri and Tientsin, S.J. 'Les Débuts des Relations Diplomatiques Entre le Japon at les Espagnols des Iles Philippines' (1571-1594) *Monumenta Nipponica* 1,1 (1938) pp. 99-137.

Bernardes de Carvalho, Rita. 'Bitter enemies or Machiavellian friends? Exploring the Dutch-Portuguese relationship in Seventeenth-Century Siam' *Anais de História de Além-Mar* Vol. X (2009), pp. 363-387.

Blair, Emma Helen and Robertson, James Alexander (eds.) *The Philippine Islands, 1493-1803*.(Cleveland: Oxford Univ. Press on behalf of the American Historical Association, 1903–09).

Borao, José Eugenio 'The massacre of 1603: Chinese perception of the Spaniards in the Philippines' *Itinerario*, vol. 23, No. 1, 1998, pp. 22-39.

Borri, Christoforo *Cochin-China* (originally published in 1631 as *Relatione della nuova missione delli pp. della Compagnia di Giesu al regno della Cocincina*) (Rome, 1970).

Borschberg, Peter *The Singapore and Melaka Straits: Violence, Security and Diplomacy in the 17th Century.* (Singapore, NUS Press, 2010).

Boxer, C.R. 'The siege of fort Zeelandia and the capture of Formosa from the Dutch 1661-1662' *Transactions and Proceedings of the Japan Society of London* Vol 24 (1926), pp. 16-47.

Boxer, C.R. *The affair of the Madre de Deus: a chapter in the history of the Portuguese in Japan* (London, 1929).

Boxer, C.R. 'Swansong of the Portuguese in Japan, 1635-9' *Transactions of the Japan Society of London* XXVII (1930) pp. 4-11.

Boxer, C.R. 'Portuguese and Spanish Rivalry in the Far East during the 17th Century' *Journal of the Royal Asiatic Society of Great Britain and Ireland* 2 (1946) pp. 150-164.

Boxer, C.R. *Jan Compagnie in Japan, 1600-1850 an essay on the cultural, artistic and scientific influence exercised by the Hollanders in Japan from the seventeenth to the nineteenth centuries.* (The Hague, 1950).

Boxer, C.R. *The Christian Century in Japan: 1549-1650* (Berkeley, 1951).

Boxer, C.R. 'Asian potentates and European artillery in the 16th-18th centuries: A footnote to Gibson-Hill' *Journal of the Malayan Branch of the Royal Asiatic Society* XXXVIII (1966) pp. 156-172.

Boxer, C.R. *Fidalgos in the Far East 1550-1770* (Hong Kong: Oxford University Press, 1968).

Boxer, C.R. 'Portuguese and Spanish Projects for the Conquest of southeast Asia 1580-1600' *Journal of Asian History* III (1969) pp. 118-136.

Boxer, C.R. 'The 24th June 1622 – A Portuguese feat of Arms' in *Estudos Para A História de Macau: Séculos XVI a XVIII (Obra Completa I)* (Lisbon, 1991) pp. 43-56.

Bremner, M.J. (trans.) 'Report of Governor Balthasar Bort on Malacca 1678, with an introduction and notes by C.O. Blagden' *Journal of the Malayan Branch of the Royal Asiatic Society* 5 (1927) pp. 1-37.

Briggs, L.P. 'Spanish Intervention in Cambodia 1593-1603' *T'oung Pao* 39 (1950), pp. 132-160.

Campbell, William *Formosa Under the Dutch: Described from Contemporary Records with Explanatory Notes and a Bibliography of the Island* (London, Kegan Paul, Trench and Trubner, 1903).

Cano, Glòria. 'Blair and Robertson's 'The Philippine Islands, 1493-1898': Scholarship or Imperialist Propaganda?' *Philippine Studies*, vol. 56, no. 1, 2008, pp. 3–46.

Caron, François and Schouten, Joost *A True Description of the Mighty Kingdoms of Japan and Siam.* Reprinted from the English edition of 1663 with Introduction, Notes and Appendices by C.R. Boxer (London, 1935).

Caron, François and Schouten, Joost *A True Description of the Mighty Kingdoms of Japan and Siam*. A Facsimile of the 1671 London edition in a contemporary translation from the Dutch by Roger Manley. Introduction and notes by John Villiers. (Bangkok, 1986).

Chandler, David *A History of Cambodia* (Boulder, Colorado, 1983).

Charney, Michael *south-east Asian Warfare, 1300-1900* (Leiden, 2004).

Chen, Chingho A *Historical Notes on Hội An (Faifo)* (Carbondale, Illinois, 1974).

Cheng, Wei-chung *War, trade and piracy in the China Seas (1622-1683)* (Dissertation, University of Leiden 2012).

Chowdhury, Mohammed Ali *Bengal-Arakan Relations (1430-1666 A.D.)* (Kolkata, 2004).

Clements, Jonathan *Coxinga and the Fall of the Ming Dynasty* (Stroud, Sutton, 2004).

Clements, Jonathan *A Brief History of China* (Tokyo, Tuttle, 2019)

Clulow, Adam 'Pirating in the Shogun's Waters: The Dutch East India Company and the San António Incident' *Bulletin of Portuguese/Japanese Studies* 13 (2006) pp. 65-80.

Clulow, Adam 'Unjust, Cruel and Barbarous Proceedings: Japanese Mercenaries and the Amboyna Incident of 1623' *Itinerario* XXXI (2007) pp. 15-34.

Clulow, Adam 'From Global Entrepôt to Early Modern Domain: Hirado, 1609–1641' *Monumenta Nipponica* 65 (2010) pp. 1-35.

Clulow, Adam 'Like Lambs in Japan and Devils outside Their Land: Diplomacy, Violence and Japanese Merchants in south-east Asia' *Journal of World History* 24, 2 (2013), pp. 335-358.

Clulow, Adam. "Commemorating Failure: The Four Hundredth Anniversary of England's Trading Outpost in Japan." *Monumenta Nipponica*, vol. 68, no. 2, 2013, pp. 207–231.

Clulow, Adam. *The Company and the Shogun: the Dutch encounter with Tokugawa Japan* (New York: Columbia University Press, 2014).

Clulow, Adam. '"Great help from Japan"' The Dutch East India Company's experiment with Japanese soldiers' in Clulow, Adam & Mostert, Tristan. *The Dutch and English East India Companies: Diplomacy, Trade and violence in Early Modern Asia* (Amsterdam: Amsterdam University Press, 2018), p. 179-210.

Clulow, Adam. *Amboina, 1623: Fear and Conspiracy on the Edge of Empire* (New York: Columbia University Press, 2019).

Cocks, Richard. *Diary of Richard Cocks; Cape Merchant in the English Factory in Japan 1615-1622 with correspondence* Volume II (London, 1883).

Colenbrander, H.T. and Coolhaas, W.T. (Eds.) *Jan Pieterzoon Coen: Bescheiden Omtrent Zijn Bedriff in Indië*, (The Hague, Martinus Nijhoff, 1919-1954).

Coolhaas W. Ph. (ed.) *Generale Missiven van Gouverneurs-generaal en Raden aan heren XVII der Verenigde Oostinische Compagnie* Vol. 1. M. Nijhof, The Hague, 1960.

Cooper, Michael *They Came to Japan: An Anthology of European Reports on Japan, 1543-1640* (London: Thames and Hudson, 1965).

Cooper, Michael 'The Mechanics of the Macao-Nagasaki Silk Trade' *Monumenta Nipponica* Vol. 27, 4, pp. 423-433.

Cooper, Michael *Rodrigues the Interpreter: An Early Jesuit in Japan and China* (New York, 1974).

Corpuz, O.D. *The Roots of the Filipino Nation* Volume I (Quezon City, 1989).

Crossley, John H. 'The Early History of the Boxer Codex' *Journal of the Royal Asiatic Society Series 3*, 24, 1 (2014) pp. 115-124.

Cushman, Richard D (trans.) *The Royal Chronicles of Ayutthaya: A Synoptic Translation* (Bangkok, 2000).

Dai Nihon Shiryō Volume 12 Part 10 pp. 199-209.

Debergh Minako 'Deux Nouvelles Études sue l'Histoire du Christianite au Japan: 2 Les pratiques de purification et de penitence au Japan vues par les missionaries Jésuites aux XVIe et XVII siècles' *Journal Asiatique* 272 (1984), 167-217.

De Witt, Dennis *History of the Dutch in Malaysia : in commemoration of Malaysia's 50 years as an independent nation and over four centuries of friendship and diplomatic ties between Malaysia and the Netherlands* (Petaling Jaya, Selangor, 2008).

Dodenhoff, George H. 'A Historical Perspective of Mercenaries' *Naval War College Review* 21, 7 (1969), pp. 91-109.

Elison, George *Deus Destroyed: The Image of Christianity in Early Modern Japan*. (Harvard, 1988).

Elisonas, Jurgis 'Christianity and the daimyo' In Hall, John Whitney and McLain, James L. (eds.) *The Cambridge History of Japan. Vol. 4 Early modern Japan* Cambridge University Press, 1991. pp. 301-372.

Elisonas, Jurgis 'The Inseparable Trinity: Japan's Relations with China and Korea' in John Whitney Hall (ed.) *The Cambridge History of Japan Volume 4 Early Modern Japan* Cambridge University Press, 1991.

Farrington Anthony *The English Factory in Japan 1613-1623* London: British Library, 1991.

Flynn, Dennis O. 'Comparing the Tokugawa Shogunate with Hapsburg Spain: two silver-based empires in a global setting,' in James D. Tracy (ed.), *The Political Economy of Merchant Empires: State Power and World Trade, 1350-1750*, pp. 332-359. (Cambridge, 1991), pp. 332-359.

Fogel, Joshua A (ed.) *Sagacious Monks and Bloodthirsty Warriors: Chinese Views of Japan in the Ming-Qing period* (New York 2002).

Foster, William *Letters Received by the East India Company from its Servants in the East* (London, 1896-1902) 6 Vols.

Fujita, Tatsuo 'Piracy Prohibition Edicts and the Establishment of Maritime Control System in Japan. c. 1585-1640' in Ota, Atsushi (Ed.) *In the Name of the Battle against Piracy: Ideas and Practices in State Monopoly of Maritime Violence in Europe and Asia in the Period of Transition* (Leiden:Brill, 2018), pp. 171-198.

Geerts, Dr 'The Arima Rebellion and the conduct of Koeckebaker' *Transations of the Asiatic Society of Japan* XII pp. 51-116.

Gracián y Morales, Baltasar *El criticón Part II* Clásicos castellanos 166 (Madrid: Espace-Calpe 1971).

Hale, J.R. *War and Society in Renaissance Europe 1450-1620* (London: Fontana 1985).

Hall, John Whitney (ed.) *Japan Before Tokugawa: Political Consolidation and Economic Growth, 1500 to 1650* (Princeton, 1981).

Hang, Xing. 'Contradictory Contingencies: The Seventeenth-Century Zheng Family and Contested Cross-Strait Legacies.' *American Journal of Chinese Studies*, vol. 23, 2016, pp. 173–182.

Hang, Xing *Conflict and Commerce in Maritime East Asia: The Zheng Family and the Shaping of the Modern World, c. 1920-1720* (New York: Columbia University Press, 2016).

Harvey, G.E. *A History of Burma: From the Earliest Times to 10 March 1824, the Beginning of the English* Conquest (London, 1925).

Hayashi Razan *Razan sensei bunshū* [The Collected Works of Hayashi Razan *Sensei*] Kyoto: Kyoto Shisekikai, 1920.

Hayashi, Senkichi (ed.) *Shimabara Hantō-shi Volume II* (Nagasaki, 1954).

Igawa, Kenji 'At the Crossroads: Limahon and wakō in Sixteenth Century Philippines' in Anthony, Robert J. (Ed.) *Elusive Pirates, Pervasive Smugglers: Violence and Clandestine Trade in the Greater China Seas* (Hong Kong, Hong Kong University Press, 2010), pp. 73-84.

Iwamoto, Yoshiteru 'Yamada Nagamasa and his relations with Siam' *Journal of the Siam Society* 95 (2007) pp. 73-84.

Iwao Seiichi 'Nagasaki Daikan Murayama Tōan no Taiwan ensei to kenminshu' [The Taiwan Expedition and Ming Embassy of the Nagasaki *Daikan* Murayama Tōan] *Taihoku Teikoku Daigaku shigakka kenkyū nenpō* [Annual Bulletin of the Department of History, Taihoku Imperial University] I (1934), 283-359.

Iwao, Seiichi 'Matsukura Shigemasa no Ruzonto ensei keikaku' *Shigaku Zasshi* 45, 9, (1934) pp. 81-109. Iwao, Seiichi *Nan'yō Nihonmachi no Kenkyū* (Tokyo, 1940).

Iwao, Seiichi *Zoku Nan'yō Nihonmachi no Kenkyū: Nan'yō tōsho chiiki bunsan Nihonjin imin no seikatsu to katsudō* (Tokyo, 1987).

Iwao, Seiichi 'Reopening of the diplomatic and commercial relations between Japan and Siam during the Tokugawa period' *Acta Asiatica* V.4 (July 1963), pp. 1–31.

Jourdain, John, *Journal of John Jourdain, 1608-17: His Experiences in Arabia, India and the Malay Archipelago* (Cambridge: Printed for the Hakluyt Society, 1905), p. 210.

Jumsai, M.L. Manich *The Story of King Narai and his ambassador to France in 1686, Kosaparn* (Paris, 1986).

Jumsai, M.L. Manich *History of Thailand and Cambodia (From the days of Angkor to the present)* (Bangkok, 1987).

Kamiya, Nobuyuki 'Satsuma Ryūkyū shinnyū' [The Satsuma Invasion of Ryūkyū] in *Shin Ryūkyū shi,* [A New History of Ryūkyū] Vol. jō Naha, 1989.

Kerr, George H. *Okinawa: The History of an Island People (Revised Edition) with an after word by Mitsugu Sakihara* North Clarendon VT, 2000.

Kersten, Carool (translated and annotated) *Strange Events in the Kingdoms of Cambodia and Laos (1635-1644)* (Bangkok, 2003).

Klekar, Cynthia. "'Prisoners in Silken Bonds': Obligation, Trade, and Diplomacy in English Voyages to Japan and China." *Journal for Early Modern Cultural Studies*, vol. 6, no. 1, 2006, pp. 84–105.

Kojima Yukie *Nagasaki daikan Murayama Tōan: sono ai to junan* [The Nagasaki *Daikan* Murayama Tōan: His Passion and Suffering] Nagasaki: Seibo Bunko, 1998.

Kondo Morishige, *Gaihan tsusho* [Japan's Foreign Correspondence] in *Kondo Seisai zenshu* Tokyo: Kokusho Kankoka, 1905.

Koop, Albert J. and Inada, Hogitarō *Japanese names and how to read them: a manual for art-collectors and students* (London: Routledge, 1923).

Kuno, Yoshi S., *Japanese expansion on the Asiatic Continent: a study in the history of Japan with special reference to her international relations with China, Korea and Russia Volume I* University of California Press, 1937.

Laver, Michael *Japan's economy by proxy in the seventeenth century: China, the Netherlands and the Bakufu* (London, 2008).

Laures, Johannes, SJ 'An Ancient Document on the Early Intercourse between Japan and the Philippines' *Culture Social* XXXIX (1941), pp. 1-15.

Le Blanc, Marcel *The History of Siam, 1688* (translated and edited by Michael Smithies) (Chiang Mai, 2003).

Leupe, P.A., and Mac Hacobian. 'The Siege and Capture of Malacca from the Portuguese in 1640-1641.' *Journal of the Malayan Branch of the Royal Asiatic Society*, vol. 14, no. 1 (124), 1936, pp. i-178.

Li, Tana *Nguyễn Cochinchina: Southern Vietnam in the Seventeenth and Eighteenth Centuries* (New York, Cornell University, 1998).

Loth, Vincent C. 'Armed Incidents and Unpaid Bills: Anglo-Dutch Rivalry in the Banda Islands in the Seventeenth Century' *Modern Asian Studies* 29 (1995), pp. 705-740.

Lucenza, Alfonso de; Schütte, Joseph Franz (Trans. & Ed.) *Erinnerungen aus der Christenheit von Omura.* (Rome, 1972).

Macchiavelli, Niccolò *The Prince* (Translated with an introduction by George Bull) (London: Penguin Books, 1961)

Manrique, Sebastien *Travels of Fray Sebastien Manrique Vol. 1: Arakan* The Hakluyt Society, 2nd Series No. LIX (1926).

Marshall, P.J. 'Western Arms in Maritime Asia in the Early Phases of Expansion' *Modern Asian Studies* 14. 1 (1989), pp. 13-28.

Martínez de Zúñiga, Joaquín *Historia de las islas Philipinas* (Sampaloc, 1803).

Matsuda, Kiichi *Hideyoshi no Nanban gaikō: San Feripe Gō Jiken* (Tokyo, 1972).

Matsuda, Kiichi and Kawasaki, Momota (Trans.) *Kanyaku Furoisu Nihon shi Vol. 6:* (Tokyo: Chuokoron-Shinsha, 2000).

Matsuda, Kiichi and Kawasaki, Momota (Trans.) *Kanyaku Furoisu Nihon shi Vol. 9:* (Tokyo: Chuokoron-Shinsha, 2000).

McCarthy, Charles J. 'On The Koxinga Threat of 1662' *Philippine Studies* Vol. 18, 1 (1970), pp. 187-196.

Mendoza, Juan González de *The history of the great and mighty kingdom of China and the situation thereof* Vol. 2 Translated by Parke, Robert (1588), edited by Staunton, Sir George Thomas (London, Hakluyt Society 1853-54).

Milton, Giles. *Nathaniel's Nutmeg: how one man's courage changed the course of history* (London, Hodder and Stoughton 1999).

Miyamoto, Kazuo *Vikings of the Far East* (New York, Vantage Press, 1975).

Mockler, Anthony *Mercenaries* (London: Macdonald 1970)

Moran, J.F. *The Japanese and the Jesuits: Alessandro Valignano in sixteenth-century Japan* (London, 1993).

Morga, Antonio de *History of the Philippine Islands from the discovery by Magellan in 1521 to the beginning of the XVII Century; with descriptions of Japan, China and adjacent countries* Volumes I and II translated and edited by Blair, E.H. and Robertson, J.A. (Cleveland, 1907, reprint New York, 1970).

Morris, Ivan *The Nobility of Failure: Tragic Heroes in the History of Japan* (London, 1975).

Mostert, Tristan 'Scramble for the spices: Makassar's role in European and Asian Competition in the Eastern Archipelago up to 1616' in Clulow, Adam & Mostert, Tristan. *The Dutch and English East India Companies: Diplomacy, Trade and violence in Early Modern Asia* (Amsterdam: Amsterdam University Press, 2018), p. 25-54.

Mulder, W.Z. *Hollanders in Hirado: 1597-1641* (Haarlem, Fibula-Van Dishoeck, 1985).

Munro-Hay, Stuart *Nakhon Sri Thammarat: The Archeology, History and Legends of a Southern Thai* Town (Bangkok, 2001).

Murakami, N. 'The Japanese at Batavia in the XVIIth Century' *Monumenta Nipponica* 2 (1939), pp. 355-373.

Murdoch, James *A History of Japan Volume 2* (London, 1903).

Murphy, James H. 'The Wild Geese' *The Irish Review* 16, (1994), pp. 23–28.

Murteria, André 'Dutch attacks against the Goa-Macao-Japan route, 1603-1618' in Wei, C.X. George *Macao - The Formation of a Global City* (Oxford: Routledge, 2014), pp. 95-106.

Myint, Soe Thuzar; Chutintararond and Baker, Chris (Eds.) *The Portrayal of the Battle of Ayutthaya in Myanmar Literature* Bangkok, Chulalongkom University Institute of Asian Studies, 2011).

Nagasaki Prefecture *Nagasaki-ken shi* (Nagasaki, 1973).

Nagazumi Yōko, *Kinsei shoki no gaiko* [The Diplomacy of Early Pre-Modern Japan] Tokyo: Sobunsha, 1990.

Nagazumi, Yōko 'Ayutthaya and Japan: Embassies and Trade in the Seventeenth Century' in Breazeale, Kennon (ed.) *From Japan to Arabia* (Bangkok, 1999) pp. 89-102.

Pagés Léon *Histoire de la Religion Chrétienne au Japan depuis 1598 jusqu'a 1651* Paris, Charles Douniol, 1869 Vol. I.

Paske-Smith, T.R. 'Japanese Trade and Residence in the Philippines' *Transactions of the Asiatic Society of Japan* XLII (2) (1914), pp. 683-710.

Péri, Nöel, 'Essai sur les relations du Japon et de l'Indochine aux XVIe et XVIIe siècles' *Bulletin de l'Ecole française d'Extrême-Orient* 23 (1923), pp. 1-104.

Pigeau, Theodore G. Th. & De Graaf, H.J. *Islamic States in Java 1500-1700: A Summary, Bibliography and Index* (The Hague, 1976).

Pinto, Paulo Jorge de Souza; Roy, Roopanjali (Trans.) *The Portuguese and the Straits of Melaka, 1575-1619: Power, Trade and Diplomacy* (Singapore: NUS Press, 2012).

Pinto, Paulo Jorge de Souza 'Share and Strife: The Strait of Melaka and the Portuguese (16th and 17th centuries)' *Orientierungen Themenheft* (2013), pp. 64-85.

Polenghi, Cesare *Samurai of Ayutthaya: Yamada Nagamasa, Japanese Warrior and Merchant in Early Seventeenth-Century Siam* (Bangkok, 2009).

Purnell, C.J., 'The Log Book of William Adams 1614-19 and related documents' *Transactions and Proceedings of the Japan Society* XIII:II (1914-15), 156-302.

Quaritch-Wales, H. *Ancient Siamese Government Administration* (London, 1934).

Ramerini, Marco *Le Fortezze Spagnole nell'Isola di Tidore, 1521-1663* (Roma, 2008) http://www.colonialvoyage.com/it/asia/indonesia/molucche/tidore/index_4.html (accessed 19 November, 2011)

Reid, Anthony *South-east Asia in the Age of Commerce 1450-1680: Volume Two, Expansion and Crisis* (New Haven, 1993).

Ribiero, Madalena. 'The Japanese Diaspora in the Seventeenth Century, according to Jesuit Sources' *Bulletion of Portuguese/Japanese Studies* 3 (2001) pp. 53-83.

Sadler, A.L., *The Maker of Modern Japan: The Life of Tokugawa Ieyasu* London, Allen & Unwin, 1937.

Sainsbury W. Noel (ed.) *Calendar of State Papers Colonial, East Indies, China and Japan*, Volume 4: 1622-1624, August 1622 in British History Online, http://www.british-history.ac.uk/report.aspx?compid=69749&strquery= (accessed 10 November 2011).

Sanabrais, Sofia '"The Spaniards of Asia": the Japanese presence in colonial Mexico' *Bulletin of Portuguese-Japanese Studies* 18, 2009 pp. 223-251.

San Agustin, Gaspar de; Mañeru, Luis Antonio (Trans.) *Conquistas de las Islas Filipinas: Conquest of the Philippine Islands 1565-1615* (Manila: San Agustin Museum, 1998).

San Antonio, Gabriel Quiroga de *A Brief and Truthful Relation of Events in the Kingdom of Cambodia* (originally published as *Breve y Verdadera Relacion de los Successos del Reyno de Camboxa* in 1604) (Bangkok, 1998).

Sansom, George *A History of Japan: 1615-1867* (Stanford: Stanford University Press, 1963)

Satow, Ernest M. 'Notes on the Intercourse between Japan and Siam in the Seventeenth Century' *Transactions of the Asiatic Society of Japan* 13 (1885) pp. 139-210.

Schwade, Arcadio. 'Matsukura Shigemasa no Ruzonto ensei keikaku' *Kirishitan Kenkyū* 9 (1964), pp. 337-350.

Shapinsky, Peter D. *Lords of the Sea: Pirates, Violence and Commerce in Late Medieval Japan* (Ann Arbor: University of Michigan, 2014).

Shepherd, John Robert, *Statecraft and Political Economy on the Taiwan Frontier 1600-1800* Stanford University Press, 1993.

Shimada, Ryūto 'Siamese Products in the Japanese Market during the Seventeenth and Eighteenth Centuries' in Nagazumi, Yōko (Ed.) *Large and Broad: The Dutch Impact on Early Modern Asia. Essays in Honor of Leonard Blussé* (Tokyo: Toyo Bunko, 2010), pp. 151-165.

Shimizu, Junzo 'The Inscriptions by some Japanese Found at Angkor Wat' in Matsumoto, Noburo (ed.) *Indo-Chinese Studies. Synthesis Research of the Culture of Rice-Cultivation Races in south-east Asia* (Tokyo, 1965), p. 265.

Smith, George Vinal *The Dutch in Seventeenth-Century Thailand* (Northern Illinois University, 1977).

Smithies, Michael *Mission made impossible: the second French Embassy to Siam, 1687* (Chiang Mai, 2002).

Struve, Lynn A. *The Southern Ming, 1644-1662* (Yale University Press, 1984).

Struve, Lynn A. *Voices from the Ming-Qing Cataclysm: China in Tiger's Jaws* (Yale University Press, 1993).

Subrahmanyam, Sanjay. *The Political Economy of Commerce: Southern India, 1500-1650.* (New York: Oxford University Press, 2011).

Syukri, Ibrahim *History of the Malay Kingdom of Patani: Serajah Kerajaan Malaya Patani* (Chiang Mai, 2005).

Tachard, Guy *Second voyage du Père Tachard at des Jésuites envoyés par le Roi au royaume de Siam* (Amsterdam, 1689).

Takegoshi, Yosaburo *The Story of the Wakō: Japanese Pioneers in the Southern Regions* (translated by Hideo Watanabe) (Tokyo, 1940).

Tanaka, Takeo 'Japan's Relations with Overseas Countries' in Hall, John Whitney and Toyoda, Takeshi (eds.) *Japan in the Muromachi Age* (Berkeley, 1977).

Tarling, Nicholas (ed.) *The Cambridge History of south-east Asia Vol 1 from Early Times to 1800* (Cambridge, 1992).

Teixeira, Manuel *The Portuguese Missions in Malacca and Singapore (1511-1958) Volume I – Malacca* (Macao, 1986).

Terao, Yoshio *Meimatsu no funkyo: Tei Seikō* (Tokyo: Tankobon, 1986).

Terwiel, Barend Jan 'Who destroyed Ayutthaya?' *Indian Journal of Tai Studies* IX (2009), pp. 105-110.

Terwiel, Barend Jan 'What Happened at Nong Sarai? Comparing Indigenous and European Sources for Late 16th Century Siam' *Journal of the Siam Society* 101 (2013), pp. 19-34.

Thomson, Janice *Mercenaries, Pirates, and Sovereigns: State Building and Extraterritorial Violence in Early Modern Europe* (Princeton University Press, 1996).

Toby, Ronald P. *State and Diplomacy in Early Modern Japan: Asia in the Development of the Tokugawa Bakufu* (Princeton, 1984).

Toby, Ronald P. 'The "Indianness" of Iberia and Changing Japanese Iconographies of Other' in Schwartz, Stuart B. (ed.) *Implicit Understandings: Observing, Reporting and Reflecting on the Encounters between Europeans and Other Peoples in the Early Modern Era* (Cambridge: Cambridge University Press, 1995), pp. 323-351.

Tremml-Werner, Birgit *Spain, China, and Japan in Manila, 1571-1644: Local Comparisons and Global Connections* (Amsterdam: Amsterdam University Press, 2015).

Tremml-Werner, Birgit 'Friend or Foe? Intercultural Diplomacy between Momoyama Japan and the Spanish Philippines in the 1590s' in Andrade, Tonio (Ed.) *Sea Rovers, Silver, and Samurai: Maritime East Asia in Global History, 1550-1700* (Honolulu: University of Hawai'i Press, 2016), pp. 65-85.

Tsai, Shih-Shan Henry, *Maritime Taiwan: Historical Encounters with the East and the West* New York: Sharpe, 2009.

Tsuchiya, Kenji and Siegel, James 'Invincible Kitsch or as Tourists in the Age of Des Alwi' *Indonesia* 50, 25th Anniversary Edition (Oct., 1990), pp. 61-76.

Tully, John *A Short history of Cambodia: From Empire to* Survival (London, 2005).

Turnbull, Stephen *Japanese Fortified Temples and Monasteries Ad 710-1602* (Oxford, Osprey Publishing 2005)

Turnbull, Stephen. *The Samurai Capture a King, Okinawa 1609* (Oxford, 2009).

Turnbull, Stephen. 'Onward, Christian Samurai! The Japanese Expeditions to Taiwan in 1609 and 1616' *Japanese Studies* Vol. 30 No. 1 (2010) pp. 3-21.

Turnbull, Stephen 'The ghosts of Amakusa: localised opposition to centralised control in Higo Province, 1589-90.' *Japan Forum* 25 (2) 2013, pp. 191-211.

Turnbull, Stephen 'Wars and Rumours of Wars: Japanese Plans to invade the Philippines, 1593-1637' *Naval War College Review* Vol. 69, no, 4, (2016) pp. 107-120.

Valignano, Alessandro; Alvarez-Taladriz, José Luis (Ed.) *Sumario de las comas de Japon (1583). Adiciones del sumario de Japon (1592)* Monumenta Nipponica Monographs 9. (Tokyo: Sophia University Press, 1954).

Van der Kraan, Alfons 'The Dutch in Siam: Jeremias van Vliet and the 1636 Incident at Ayutthaya' *Journal of the University of New England Asia Centre* (2000) pp. 1-14.

Van der Kraan, Alfons *Murder and Mayhem in Seventeenth-Century Cambodia: Anthony van Diemen vs. King Ramadhipati I* (Chiang Mai, 2009).

Van Ittersum, Martine Julia. 'Debating Natural Law in the Banda Islands: A Case Study in Anglo-Dutch Imperial Competition in the East Indies, 1609-1621' *History of European Ideas* 42, 4 (2016), pp. 450-501.

Van Linschoten, John Huighen; Philip, William (trans.) *His Discours of Voyages Into Ye Easte [and] West Indies: Deuided Into Four Bookes* (London: John Wolfe, 1598).

Various Authors *Nihon Jōhaku Taikei Vol 17* (Tokyo: Shinjimbutsu, 1980)

Vlekke, Bernard H.M. *Nusantara: A History of the East Indian Archipelago* (Cambridge Mass., 1945).

Vu Minh, Gang 'The Japanese Presence in Hoi An' in *Ancient town of Hoi An : International Symposium held in Danang on 22-23 March 1990* (Danang, 1990) pp. 135-141.

Wang Yong 'Realistic and Fantastic Images of "Dwarf Pirates": The Evolution of Ming Dynasty Perceptions of the Japanese' in Fogel, Joshua A (ed.) *Sagacious Monks and Bloodthirsty Warriors: Chinese Views of Japan in the Ming-Qing period* (New York 2002) pp. 17-41.

Wickberg, Edgar *The Chinese in Philippine Life, 1850-1898* (Manila, 2000).

Wills, John E. Jr, 'Review: Maritime Asia, 1500-1800: The Interactive Emergence of European Domination' *American Historical Review* 98 (1993), 83-105.

Wills, John E. Jr., 'The Seventeenth-Century Transformation: Taiwan Under the Dutch and the Cheng Regime' in Murray A. Rubinstein (ed.) *Taiwan: A New History* New York: Sharpe, 2007, 84-106.

Wilson, Peter H. 'The German 'Soldier Trade' of the Seventeenth and Eighteenth Centuries: A Reassessment' *The International History Review* 18, 4 (1996), pp. 757-792.

Winstedt, R.O. *A History of Malaya* (London, 1935).

Wolters, O.W. 'Ayudhyā and the Rearward Part of the World' *The Journal of the Royal Asiatic Society of Great Britain and Ireland* No. 3/4 (Oct., 1968), pp. 166-178.

William D. Wray, 'The Seventeenth-century Japanese Diaspora: Questions of Boundary and Policy,' in Ina Baghdiantz McCabe (co-ed.), *Diaspora Entrepreneurial Networks: Four Centuries of History*, (Oxford, Berg, 2005).

Wyatt, David K. *Thailand: A Short History* (Yale, 1982).

Yamamoto, Hirofumi *Kanei Jidai* (Nihon Rekishi Sōsho Vol. 39) (Tokyo, 1989).

Yamashita, Noboru 'The Jesuit Mission in Hirado and the Vanished Christians of Takushima - A Historical and Anthropological Research' (Nagasaki University Academic Output Site, 2015), pp. 37-56: http://hdl.handle.net/10069/35761 (Accessed 29 January 2019).

Yang, Ying; Cheng, Bisheng (ed.) *Xian wang shilu* (Fuzhou: Fujian renmin chubanshe, 1981).

Zaide, Gregorio F. *Philippine Political and Cultural History Vol. 1* (Manila, 1957).

Index

181